AF594388

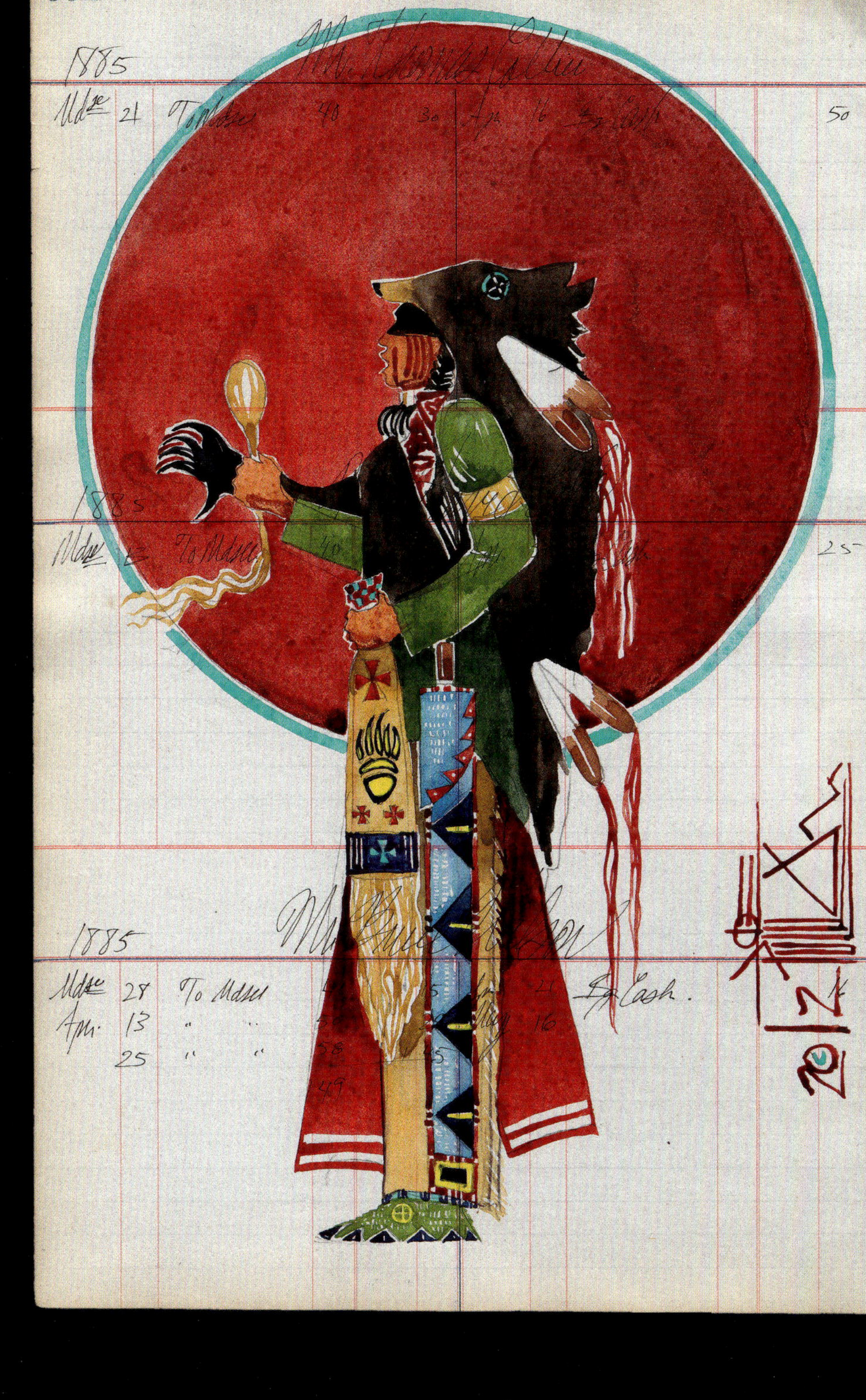

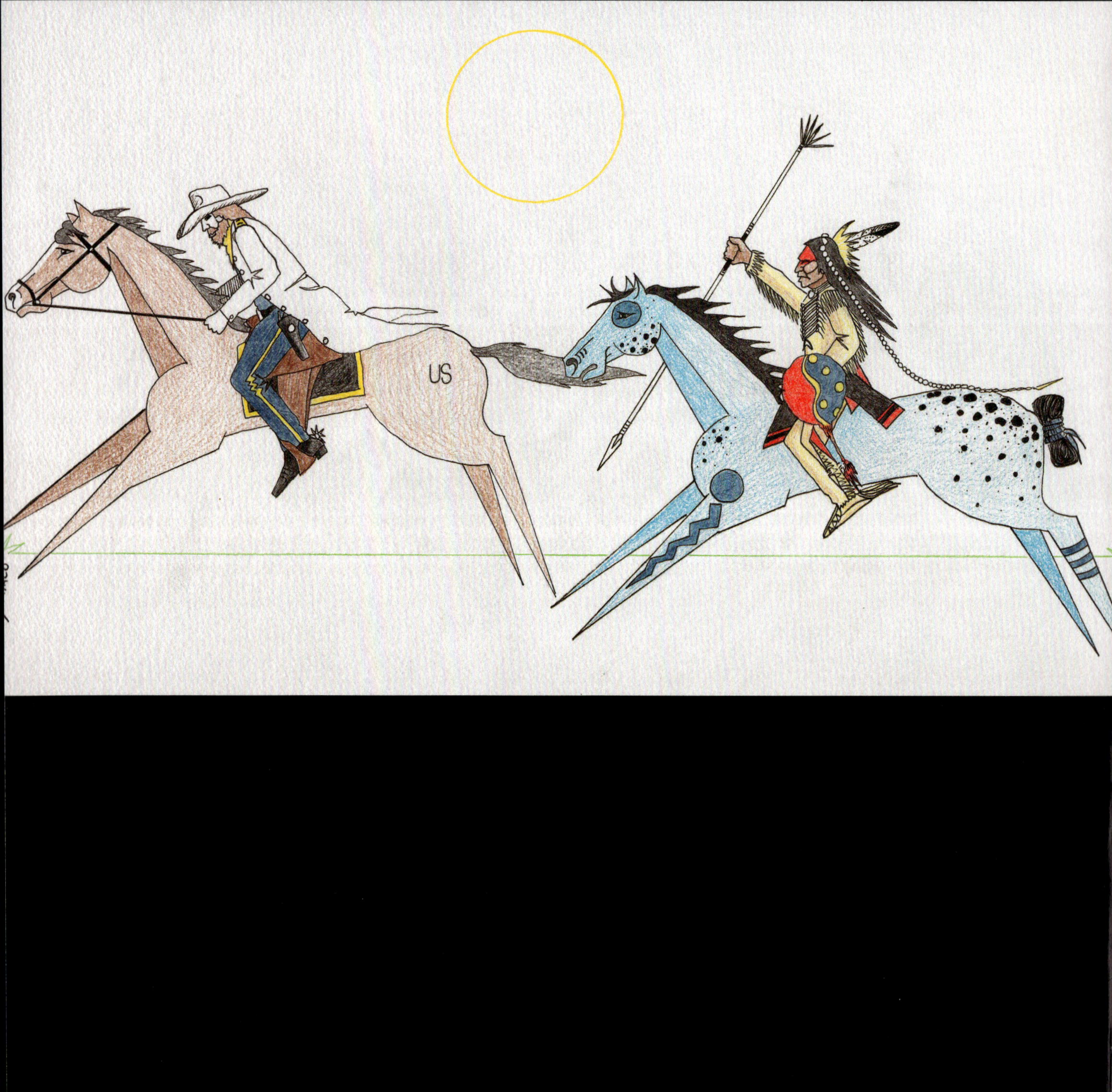
US

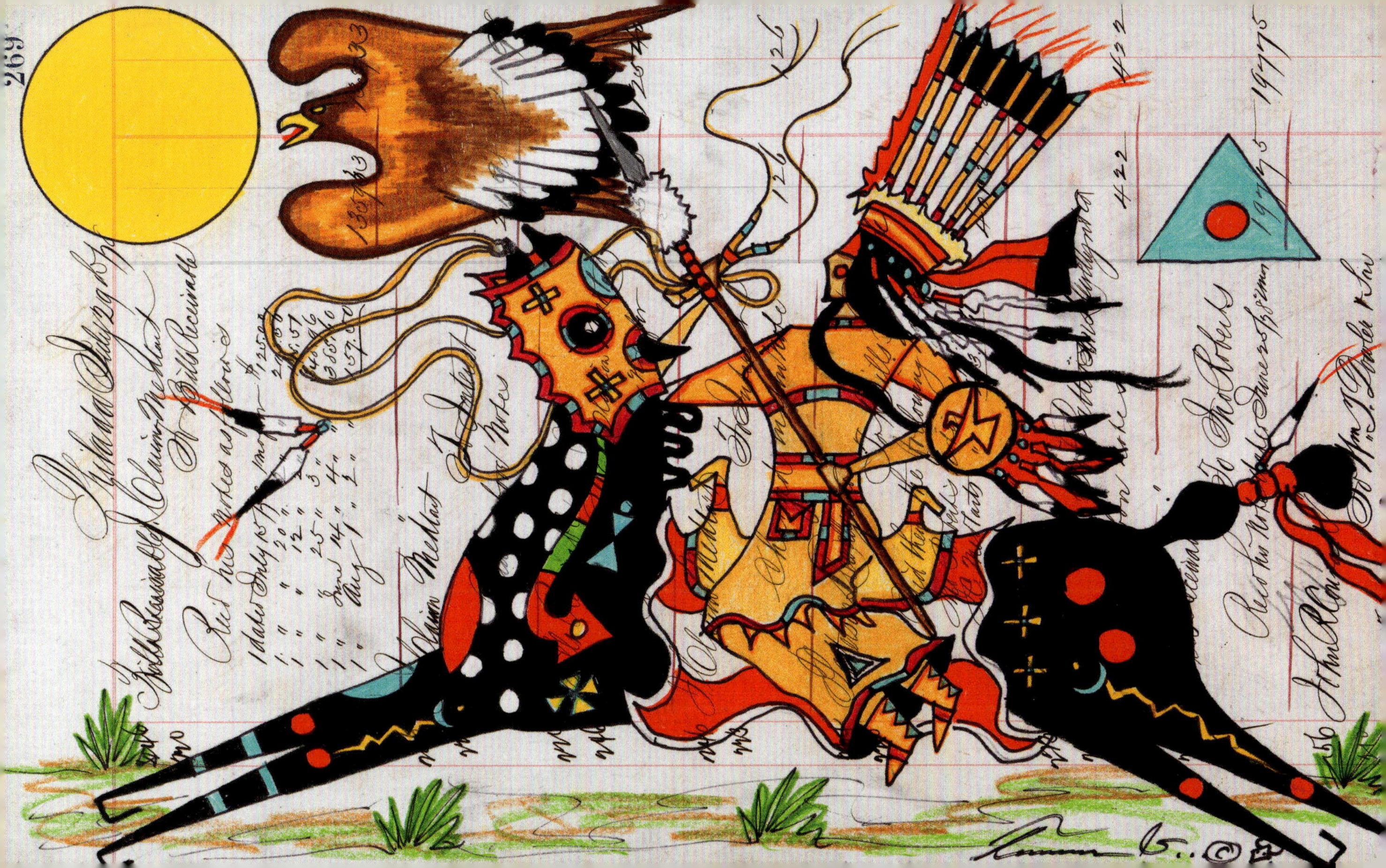

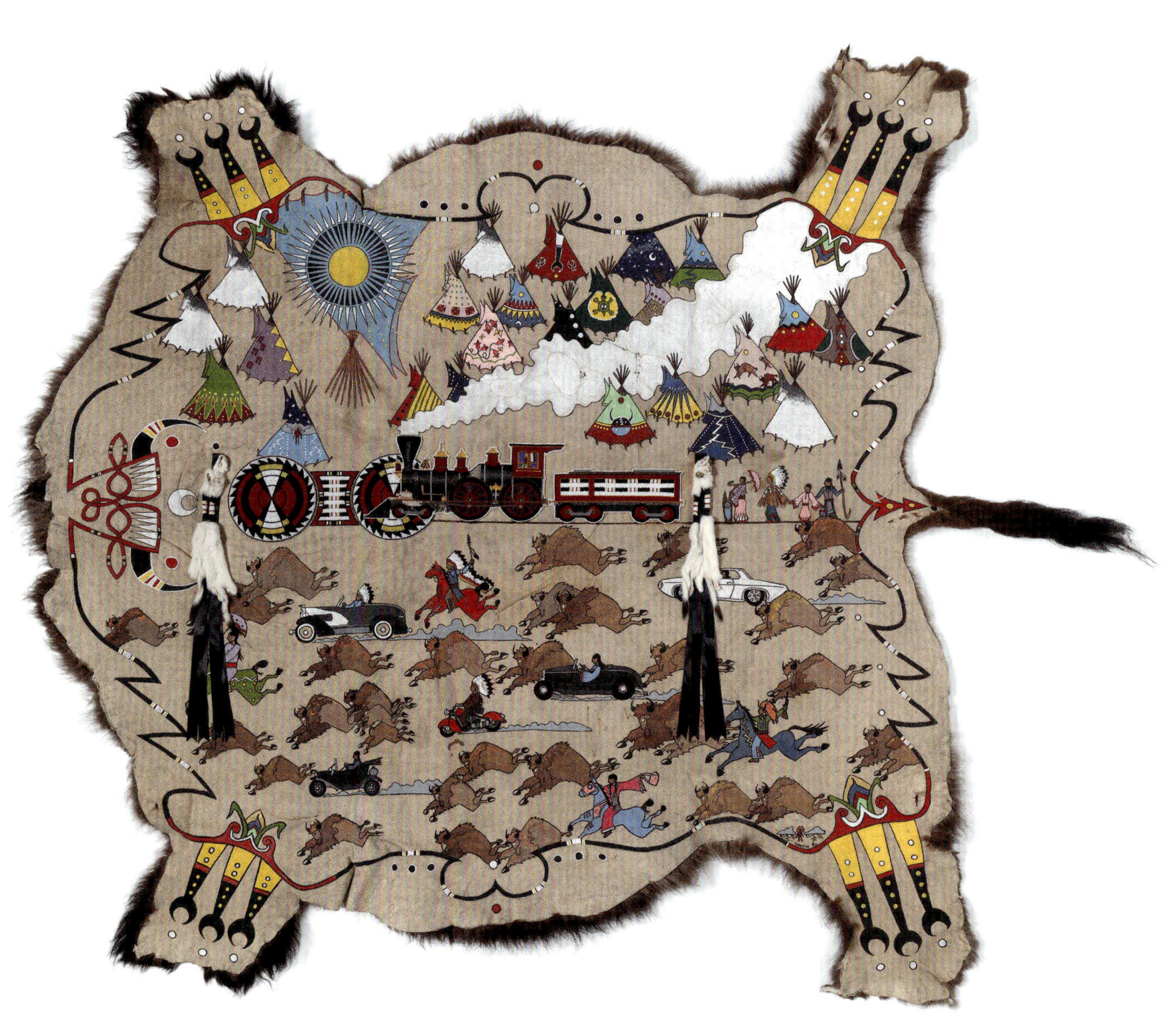

UNBOUND

NARRATIVE ART OF THE PLAINS

General Editor, Emil Her Many Horses

Published by the National Museum of the American Indian,
Smithsonian Institution, in association with D Giles Limited

First published in 2024 by GILES
An imprint of D Giles Limited
66 High Street
Lewes BN7 1XG
gilesltd.com

The Smithsonian's National Museum of the American Indian

Vision
Equity and social justice for the Native peoples of the Western Hemisphere through education, inspiration, and empowerment.

Mission
In partnership with Native peoples and their allies, the National Museum of the American Indian fosters a richer shared human experience through a more informed understanding of Native peoples.

For more information about the Smithsonian's National Museum of the American Indian, visit www.AmericanIndian.si.edu.

Director: Cynthia Chavez Lamar (San Felipe Pueblo/Hopi/Tewa/Navajo)
Associate Director for Museum Research, Scholarship and Public Engagement: David W. Penney
General Editor: Emil Her Many Horses (Oglala Lakota)
Publications Manager: Tanya Thrasher (Cherokee Nation)
Project Editor: Sally Barrows
Designer: Julie Allred, BW&A Books, Inc.
Rights and Permissions: Wendy Hurlock Baker, Julie B. Macander

Published in conjunction with the exhibition *Unbound: Narrative Art of the Plains,* opening at the Smithsonian's National Museum of the American Indian in Washington, DC, in May 2024.

D Giles Limited
Production Director: Louise Ramsay
Editorial Director: Allison McCormick
Proofreader: Sarah Kane

Generous support for the *Unbound: Narrative Art of the Plains* project is provided by the Terra Foundation for American Art and the Wyeth Foundation for American Art.

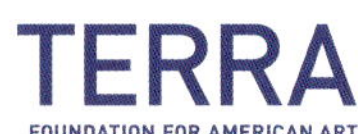

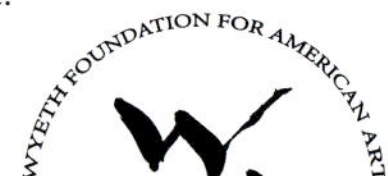

First Edition
10 9 8 7 6 5 4 3 2 1
Printed and bound in Canada
ISBN: 978-1-913875-48-0

Library of Congress Cataloging-in-Publication Data
Names: Emil Her Many Horses, editor. | National Museum of the American Indian (U.S.)
Title: Unbound : narrative art of the Plains / General Editor, Emil Her Many Horses.
Description: Washington : National Museum of the American Indian, Smithsonian Institution, in association with D Giles Limited, [2023] | Includes bibliographical references and index. | Summary: "This book traces the evolution of narrative art among Native nations of North America's Great Plains region, from historical hides, muslins, and ledger books to more than 50 contemporary works commissioned by the National Museum of the American Indian (NMAI). Illustrating everything from war deeds and ceremonial events to pop culture, the selected artworks are as diverse as the individuals who created them. Plains narrative art took shape through various media such as painted hide tipis, robes, and shirts. In the late 19th century, as trade broadened, artists created scenes of battles and ceremonies on muslin and paper. Some artists filled the pages of ledger books with narrative drawings to record their past and preserve their cultures. Native artists began reviving "ledger art" in the 1970s, creating a vibrant form that takes on contemporary topics, uses a variety of media, and is widely collected. Edited by NMAI curator Emil Her Many Horses (Oglala Lakota), Unbound features historical masterworks by 14 artists and unveils new works from 11 contemporary artists. The book also includes scholarly and personal essays by Her Many Horses, David W. Penney, Michael Paul Jordan, and Lauren Good Day"—Provided by publisher.
Identifiers: LCCN 2023026375 | ISBN 9781913875480 (hardcover)
Subjects: LCSH: Indian art—Great Plains—Pictorial works. | Narrative art—Great Plains—Pictorial works. | Indian ledger drawings—Great Plains—Pictorial works. | Indians of North America—Great Plains—Pictorial works. | LCGFT: Illustrated works.
Classification: LCC E98.A7 U525 2024 | DDC 970.00497—dc23 / eng/20230815
LC record available at https://lccn.loc.gov/2023026375

front cover: Darryl Growing Thunder (Dakota/Nakoda, b. 1967). *Chicken Dancer,* 2012. Antique ledger paper, colored pencil, gold marker, graphite, ink; 40.5 × 27.5 cm. 26/8959
page i: Joel Pulliam (Oglala Lakota, b. 1968). *His Bear Medicine,* 2012. Antique ledger paper, watercolor, graphite, ink; 31.8 × 20 cm. 26/8955
page ii: Ronald L. Burgess (Comanche, b. 1950). *Tha Tsi Koa,* 2012. Paper, graphite, colored pencil, ink; 38.5 × 56.5 cm. 26/8933
page iii: Terrance Guardipee (Blackfeet, b. 1968). *Running Eagle–Blackfeet Warrior Woman,* 2012. Antique ledger paper, colored pencil, graphite, ink; 21.2 × 34.7 cm. 26/8906
page iv: Dallin Maybee (Northern Arapaho/Seneca, b. 1974). *Conductors of Our Own Destiny,* 2013. Commercial tanned bison hide, cut-glass beads, glass seed beads, gold beads, steel beads, copper beads, ermines, satin ribbon, Swarovski crystals, acrylic paint, ink, brass bells; 204.3 × 245.5 × 7 cm. 26/9328
page vii: Painting of a buffalo hunt, 2013. Made by Sherman Chaddlesone (Kiowa, 1947–2013). Paper, graphite, ink, watercolor; 56.5 × 76 cm. 26/9180
page viii: Lauren Good Day (Arikara/Hidatsa/Blackfeet/Plains Cree, b. 1987). *Making of Relatives,* 2012. Antique ledger paper, colored pencil, graphite, ink, felt-tipped marker; 45.1 × 28.8 cm. 26/9023
back cover: Drawing, ca. 1885. Made by Rain In The Face (Hunkpapa Lakota, ca. 1835–1905). North Dakota or South Dakota. Paper, graphite, colored pencil; 11.4 × 17.7 cm. 20/1628

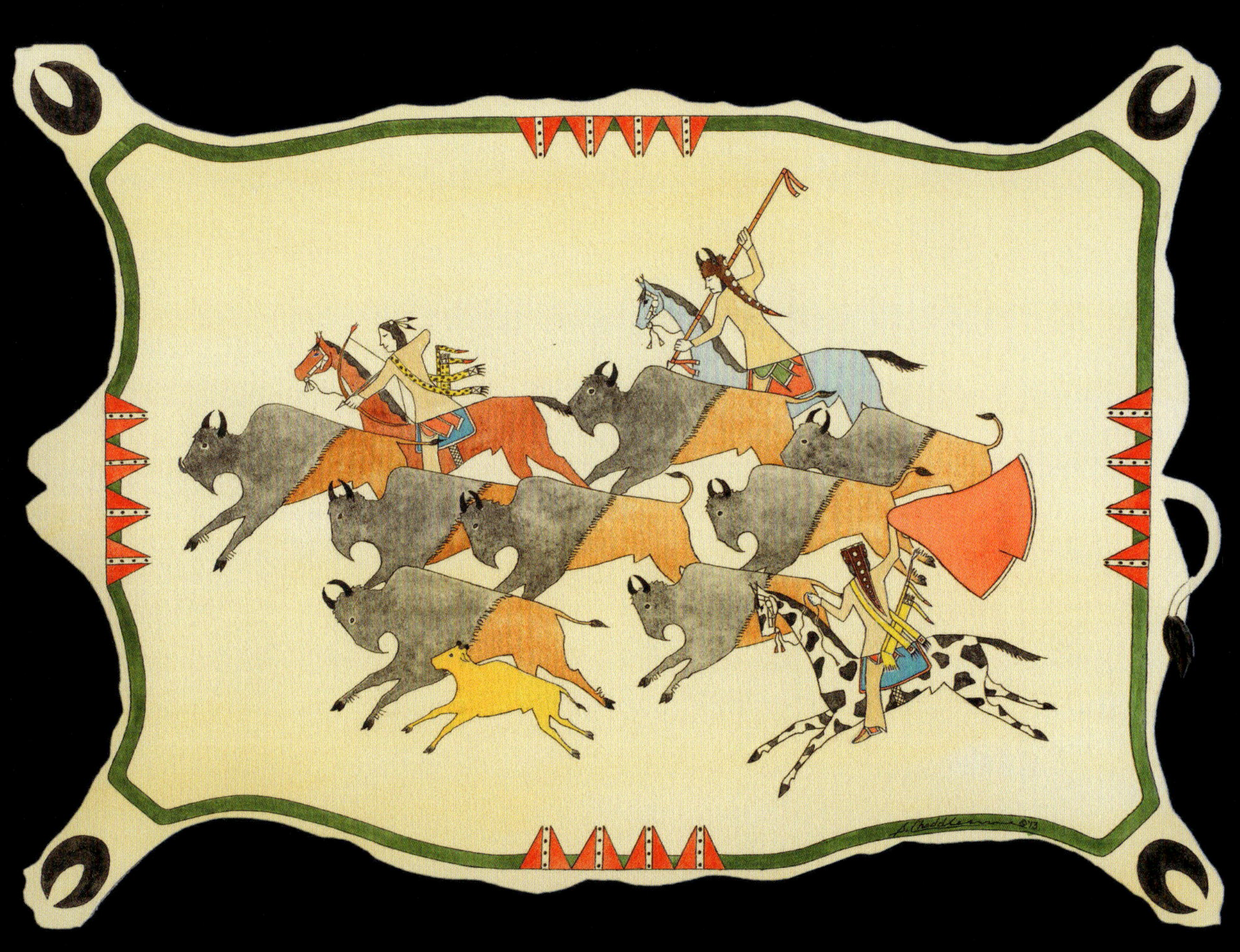

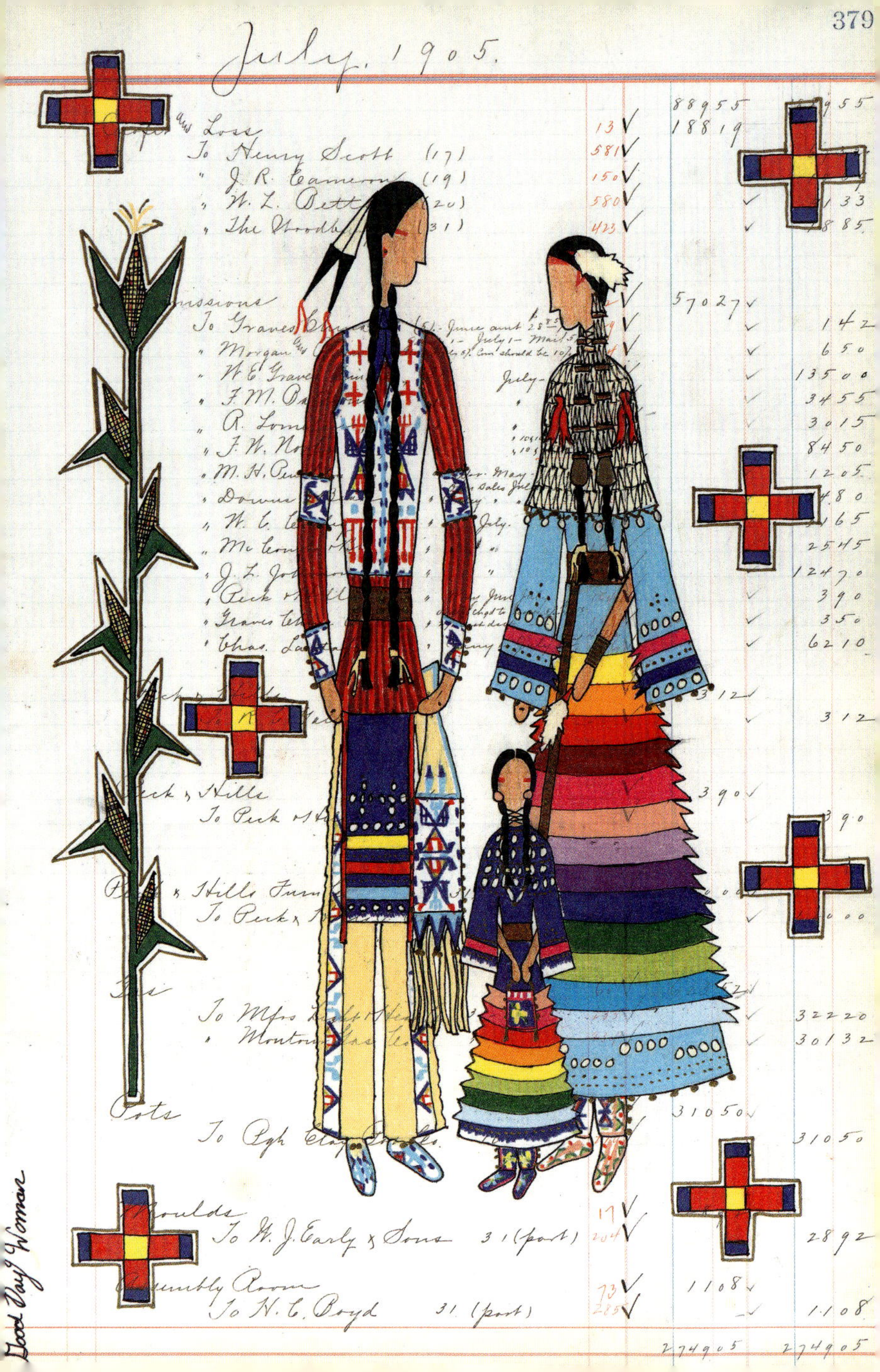

July. 1905.

Loss

To Henry Scott (17) 13 88955
" J. R. Cameron (19) 581 18819
" W. L. Bett (20) 150
" The Woodb (31) 423 580 133 885

missions 57027

To Graves June acct 142
" Morgan July 1 — Mail 650
" W. E. Grave July 13500
" F. M. B 3455
" R. Lom 3015
" F. W. No 8450
" M. H. Pe May 1205
" Downs Sales Jul 480
" W. C. July 165
" McCom 2545
" J. L. Joh 12470
" Peck & H 390
" Graves 350
" Chas. La 6210

312

Peck & Hills 312

Peck & Hills
To Peck & H 390 390

Peck & Hills Furn
To Peck & H

To Mfrs 32220
" Montour 30132

Pots
To Pgh Clay 31050 31050

Moulds
To W. J. Early & Sons 31 (part) 17 204 2892

Assembly Room
To H. C. Boyd 31 (part) 73 285 1108 1108

274905 274905

Good Day Woman

CONTENTS

FOREWORD

Since the earliest encounters between Indigenous and European peoples in North America, inaccurate but powerful narratives about the continent's Native peoples have been embedded in American culture. Until the late twentieth century, most museums that focused on Indigenous cultures further entrenched the damaging assumptions and distorted histories. One of the founding principles of the National Museum of the American Indian (NMAI), however, is that Native people are the most powerful interpreters of their stories and experiences. In all that we present and do at NMAI, we work to amplify Indigenous perspectives.

In many Native communities, culture keepers and elders have connected past and future generations through oral storytelling and pictographic narrative art. In the cultures of North America's Great Plains region, artists traditionally recorded notable events on hide calendars known as winter counts. Warriors depicted their battle achievements on hide shirts and robes. Later, as bison populations dwindled, Plains artists turned to paper and cloth as the media for recording the events that shaped their personal and communal lives.

Encountering narrative art during the reservation era, Anglo-European collectors, including George Gustav Heye, the founder of NMAI's predecessor museum, acquired the hide, paper, and cloth pieces. But collectors such as Heye often had little understanding of the stories or cultural values the artists had expressed. In the late twentieth century, however, curators and tribal historians began to look at narrative drawings and paintings more closely. During the same mid-twentieth-century period, new generations of Plains artists were attracted to the narrative style, adapting it as their ancestors had to express the resilience, continuity, and power of their cultures.

As he describes in the following pages, NMAI curator Emil Her Many Horses (Oglala Lakota), himself an artist, encountered Plains narrative artists at art markets and fairs throughout the United States. He proposed that NMAI put together an

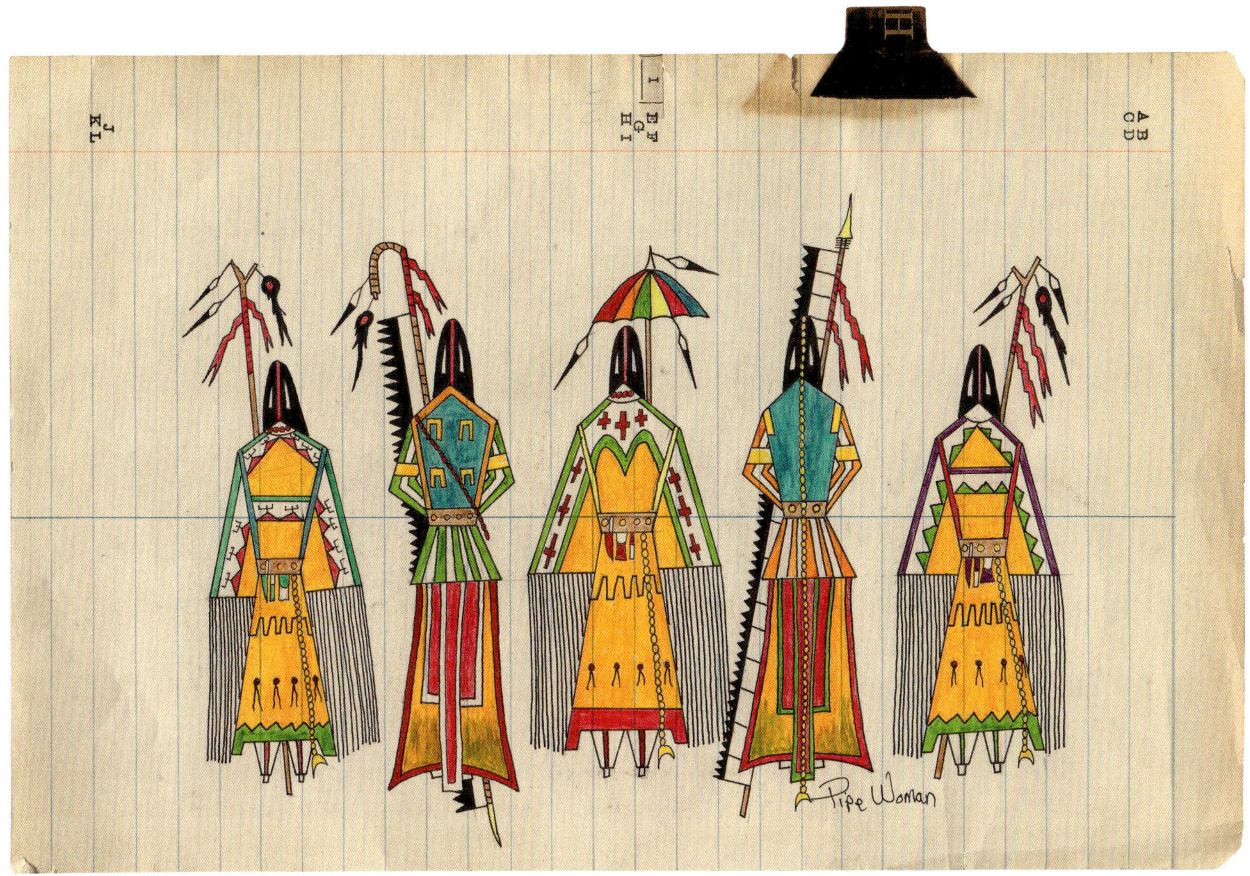

Drawing of a Victory Dance, 2012. Made by Norman Frank Sheridan Sr. (Southern Cheyenne/Arapaho, 1950–2014). Antique ledger paper, graphite, colored pencil, felt-tipped marker, ink, leather; 27 × 38 cm. 26/8946

exhibition of contemporary artists' work, juxtaposing their diverse interpretations of the form with the nineteenth-century pieces already in the museum's collection. Originally on view in our New York museum in 2016 and reopening in Washington, DC, in 2024, the exhibition and this book celebrate the adaptability and endurance of a truly Indigenous American art form and the artists who continue to shape it. Fulfilling the museum's mission of creating a nuanced, shared understanding of Native cultures, the project—which includes excerpts from interviews with the contemporary artists—synthesizes Native art, storytelling, and history. It features compelling works from past and present to demonstrate how Indigenous artists can through their works not only communicate cultural strength but also embody it.

Cynthia Chavez Lamar (San Felipe Pueblo/Hopi/Tewa/Navajo)
Director, National Museum of the American Indian

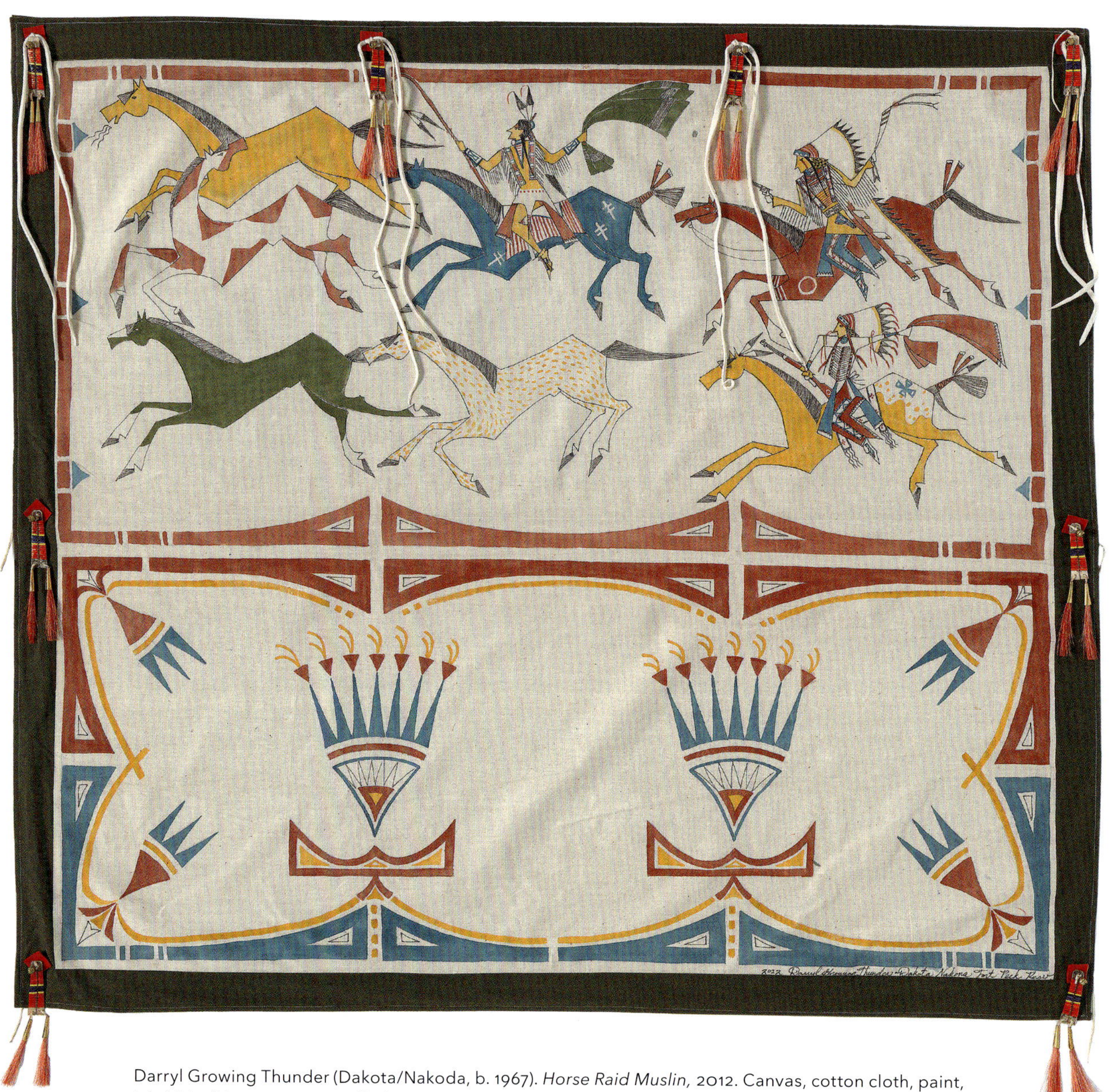

Darryl Growing Thunder (Dakota/Nakoda, b. 1967). *Horse Raid Muslin,* 2012. Canvas, cotton cloth, paint, ink, hide, felt, porcupine quills, horsehair, brass cones, brass bells, dye; 107.3 × 99 × 2.5 cm. 26/8991

INTRODUCTION

UNBOUND

Narrative Art of the Plains

Warrior-artists from the Native nations of North America's plains have long practiced a pictorial style of illustration. Some depicted visionary experiences, while others recorded communal events in calendar sequences known as winter counts. To memorialize their personal accomplishments, many Plains warriors painted hide tipis, robes, and shirts with scenes of their exploits in battle and horse raiding. The paintings identify battle participants, detail weaponry, and specify who killed, captured, or wounded the enemy. For the artists, these pictorial narratives were public reminders and validation of heroic deeds.

Freedom was vastly curtailed during the reservation era (1870–1920). The U.S. government enacted policies that forced Plains peoples to give up their traditions and attempted to erase their Native identities. Narrative drawing and painting became a way of addressing cultural upheaval. Their lives changing dramatically, artists used pictorial storytelling to record the past and preserve their cultures. With its representational figures, strong solid colors, events shown in sequence, and stylized symbols, narrative art continued to express what was important to the artists and their communities.

As the buffalo were decimated, artists increasingly worked on canvas and muslin cloth rather than hide. Paper also became widely available. Warrior-artists created more intricate chronicles of their own and others' exploits with factory-made pens, pencils, brushes, ink, crayons, and watercolor. So many Native artists drew in books meant for accounting that their style became known as ledger art, even after

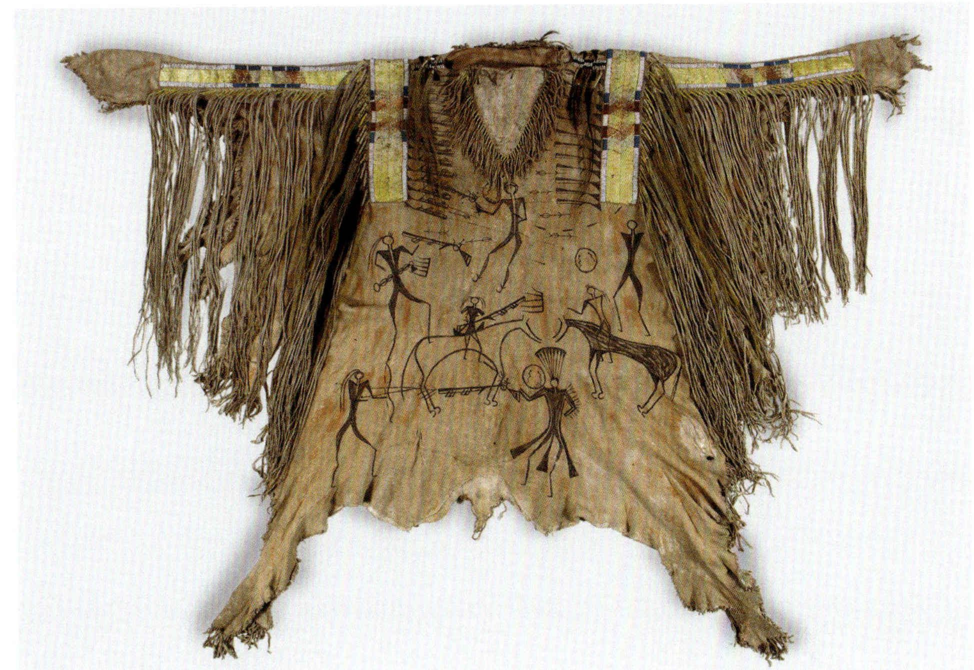

Man's shirt (back), ca. 1840. Upper Missouri region. Deerhide, horsehair, porcupine quills, human hair, glass pony beads, paint, pigment, sinew; 116 × 165 × 5 cm. 17/6345

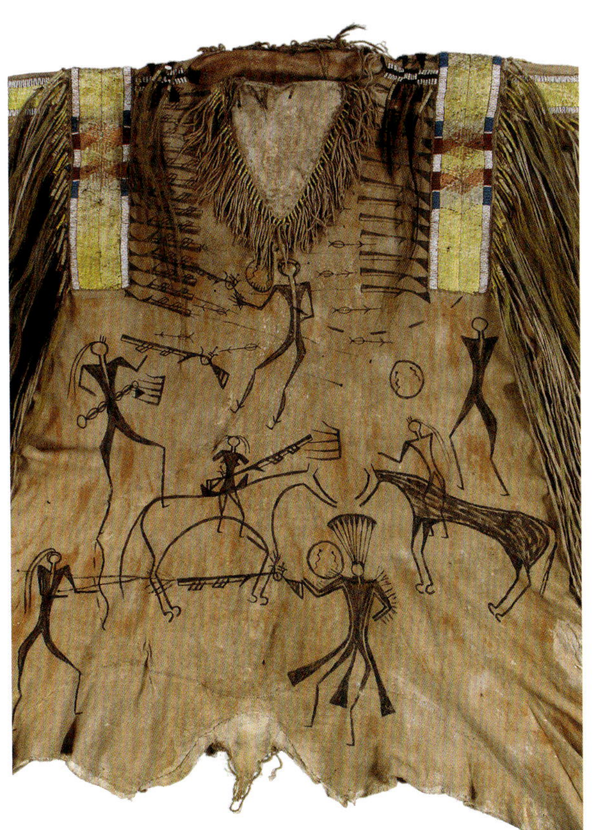

Three battle scenes on this shirt are organized horizontally from top to bottom. Each tells of a victory by the warrior drawn on the right. The victor is the same individual, who is indicated by a shield bearing two dots, each with a zigzag.

1. He moves from right to left, first overtaking a standing enemy holding a rifle, then using the captured rifle against a second, long-haired enemy who holds a tomahawk. A hand symbol shows that the victor took his enemy's tomahawk.
2. The hand symbol indicates that the warrior mounted on the darker horse has captured a rifle from his enemy.
3. The war bonnet and military frock coat show that the victor is respected in his community.

they began using drawing books and other kinds of paper. Today, the terms *ledger art* and *narrative art* are nearly interchangeable. The title of this book refers to the wide variety of media used to create the narrative records.

In the 1870s and 1880s, the focus of Plains narrative drawings began to change. Many of the drawings had been created for Native viewers, but non-Native collectors and tourists increasingly were interested in them. Accordingly, artists less frequently illustrated battles against white adversaries. Instead, they depicted scenes of buffalo hunts, courtship, and family.

Some of the best-known examples of ledger-style drawing were made by Southern Plains fighters who were arrested at the end of the Red River War in 1875 and imprisoned at Fort Marion in St. Augustine, Florida. Men from the Cheyenne, Arapaho, and Kiowa nations used pictorial storytelling to not only evoke their former lives on the Plains but also document their new environment and navigate their changed circumstances. In his essay for this book, associate professor of ethnology Michael P. Jordan shows how their work inspired contemporary Kiowa artist Sherman Chaddlesone, whose drawings of Kiowa ceremonies pay tribute to warrior traditions.

Whether they feature scenes of battle, ceremony, or daily life, narrative paintings and drawings resonate as interpretations of personal and cultural histories. In his essay, David W. Penney, NMAI's associate director for research and scholarship, traces the collection history of a large muslin painting created by the Hunkpapa Lakota holy man Siyosapa. He describes the ways in which the painting, perhaps intended for sale to white collectors, powerfully expresses the artist's personal and communal experiences. He also describes how ethnographers and curators were for decades unable to recognize its significance.

Around the turn of the twentieth century, many ledger artists entered boarding schools and were introduced to Western-oriented styles. As a result, the production of narrative art declined. The 1960s, however, saw a resurgence of Native-led art. The establishment in 1962 of the Institute of American Indian Arts in Santa Fe encouraged new expressions informed and inspired by cultural traditions. Ledger art flourished and began to be widely collected.

Today both men and women draw on their cultural traditions, individual histories, and artistic sensibilities as they continue to shape the Plains narrative style. As their predecessors did, many contemporary narrative artists use the form to tell personal, family, and community stories. Artist Lauren Good Day (Arikara/Hidatsa/Blackfeet/Plains Cree) adopts the traditionally male narrative art form to explore the strength of her family ties and her Northern Plains heritage. She celebrates the making of art and regalia as an act of cultural strength, and through her work forges links to her ancestors and descendants.

To carry out its mission of fostering a rich and informed understanding of Native peoples, the National Museum of the American Indian has long focused on acquiring significant works of modern and contemporary Native art in diverse media. In 2011, I proposed that the museum expand on its collection of nineteenth-century Plains narrative paintings by commissioning new works from contemporary ledger artists. The artists were selected from Native nations that traditionally practiced pictorial storytelling. With no limits on theme or approach, each artist created works that embody his or her distinctive voice. While some reproduced historical images, others were inspired by contemporary events such as ceremonial dances, military society gatherings, and powwows. Some documented family stories, incorporated humor, or depicted social situations.

The exhibition *Unbound: Narrative Art of the Plains* brings together the drawings and paintings of fourteen nineteenth-century pictorial storytellers with works by eleven contemporary artists. Organized chronologically, it seeks to highlight the enduring artistry, liveliness, and communicative power of the Plains narrative style.

Like the exhibition, this book celebrates an art form that preceded and has extended far beyond the ledger books of the reservation period. Contemporary Plains artists have honored and continue to expand on the works of their ancestors. They have reinterpreted and strengthened a narrative practice that has always expressed the resilience of Plains cultures.

Emil Her Many Horses (Oglala Lakota)
Curator, National Museum of the American Indian

WARRIOR ART

Male warrior-artists from the Native nations of the North American plains traditionally painted tipis, robes, and shirts with scenes of battle exploits such as taking horses, killing enemies, or rescuing wounded comrades. In the late nineteenth century, as buffalo hide became scarce, they increasingly worked on cloth or paper, often using new tools such as pens, pencils, ink, crayons, and watercolor.

With the new media, the artists depicted more intricate chronicles of their accomplishments and communities. Their drawings were a means of cultural revival during a time of upheaval.

Narrative imagery employs a stylized shorthand, with outlined profiles and flat color. For example, black coats and flat-topped hats often indicate white people. Hair and clothing styles distinguish tribal identities, while name glyphs and personal effects identify individuals.

These paintings detail the exploits of the Shoshone chief Washakie in the war between his nation and the Ute. Revered for statesmanship and respected in battle, Chief Washakie united his people into a significant political and military force. A skilled orator and charismatic figure, he negotiated land and education settlements for the Shoshone.

In 1868 Washakie signed a treaty that established a three-million-acre reservation in Wyoming's Wind River country. The reservation is still the home of the Shoshone. Washakie remained an active and respected leader until his death in 1900 at age 102. He was accorded a full military funeral. ◊

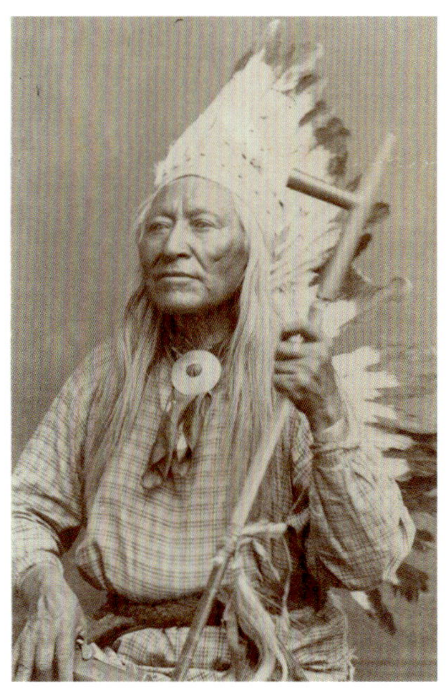

Chief Washakie, 1884–85. Photo by Baker and Johnson. P06829

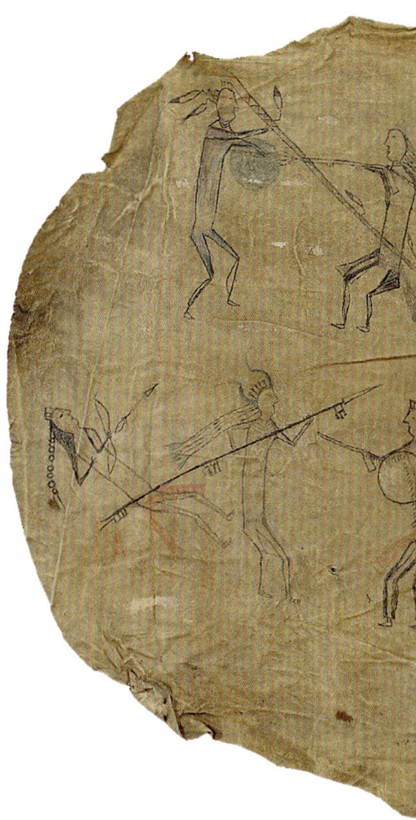

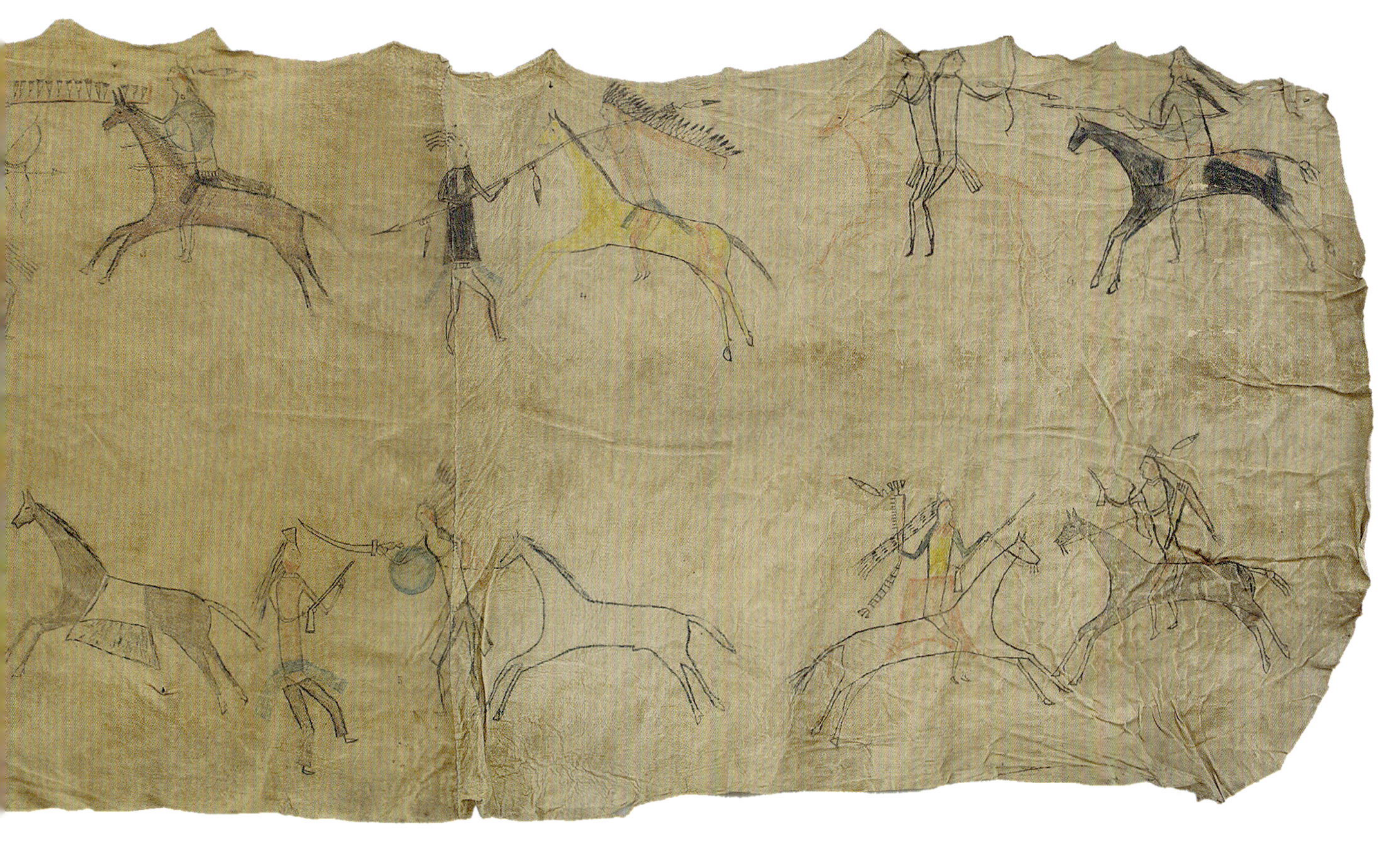

Shoshone hide, ca. 1890. Wyoming. Deerhide, paint, thread; 62 × 147 cm. 16/4845

Canté-wani'ća, or No Heart, was a well-known Yanktonai medicine man. He took part in the Sun Dance ceremony at age twenty and had a hundred scars on each arm. The lower half of this painted muslin depicts what appears to be a battle or mock-battle. The upper left corner shows a Victory Dance and the upper right a Sun Dance scene. ◊

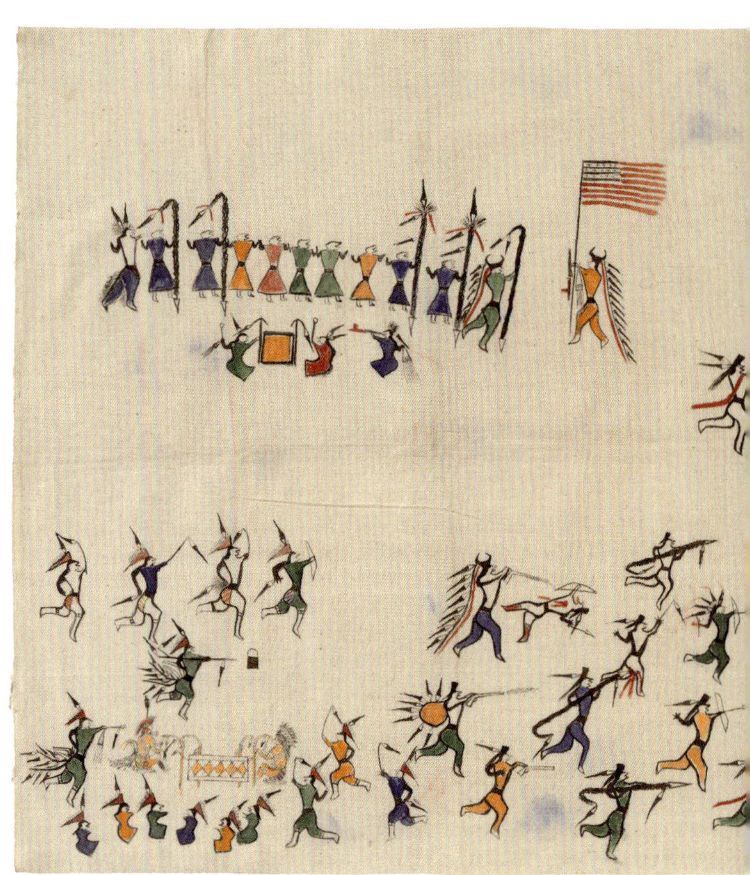

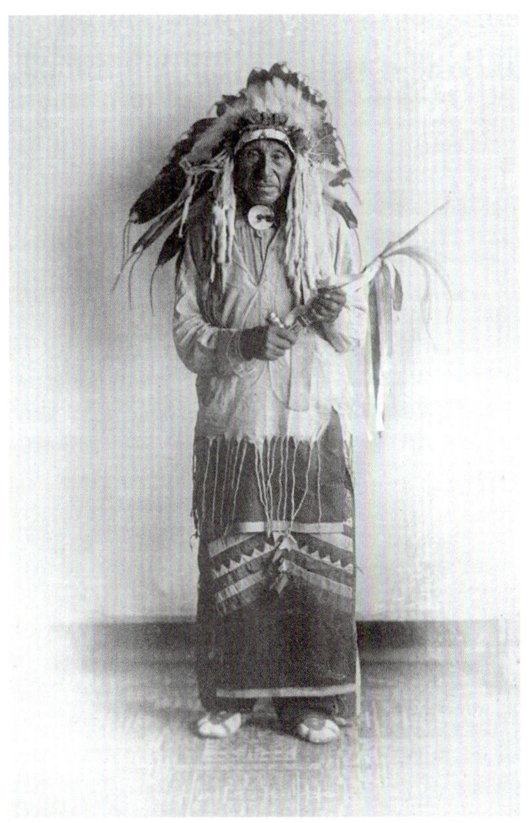

Canté-wani'ća, or No Heart, 1912. Photo by Frances Densmore. National Anthropological Archives, Smithsonian Institution 03523

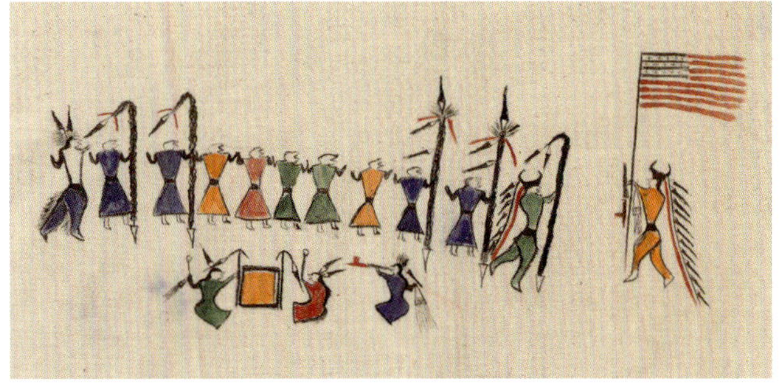

Muslin (detail), ca. 1910. Painted by No Heart (Yanktonai Nakota, ca. 1842–1934). North Dakota or South Dakota. Muslin, paint; 91 × 178 cm. 12/2167

A Victory Dance.

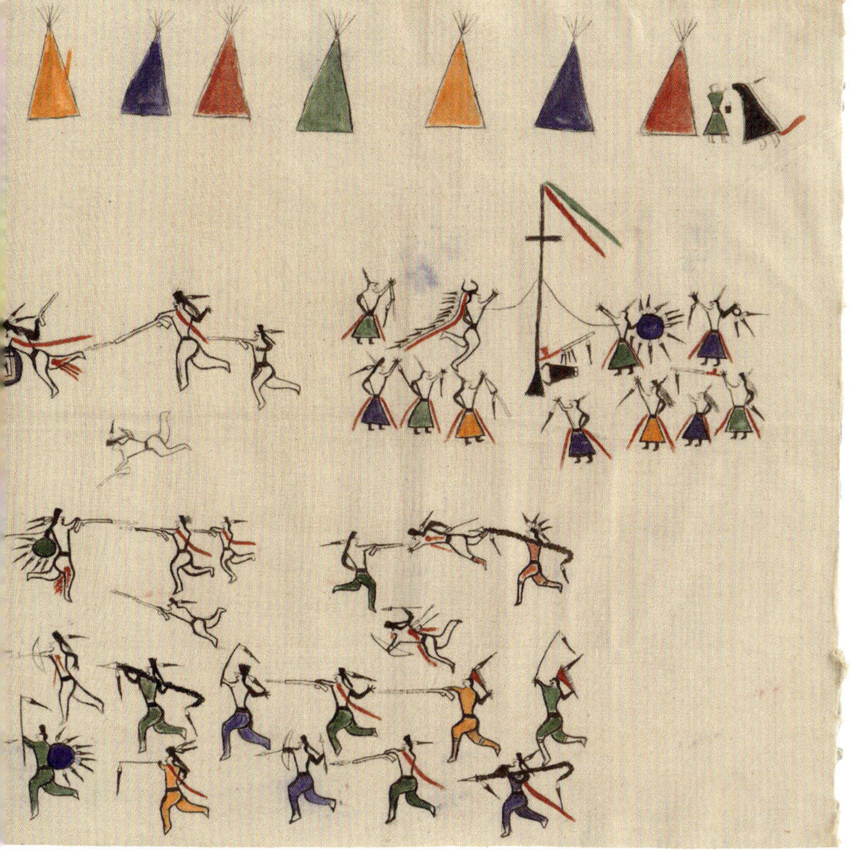

Muslin, ca. 1910. Painted by No Heart (Yanktonai Nakota, ca. 1842–1934). North Dakota or South Dakota. Muslin, paint; 91 × 178 cm. 12/2167

Muslin (detail), ca. 1910. Painted by No Heart (Yanktonai Nakota, ca. 1842–1934). North Dakota or South Dakota. Muslin, paint; 91 × 178 cm. 12/2167

A battle, or mock-battle.

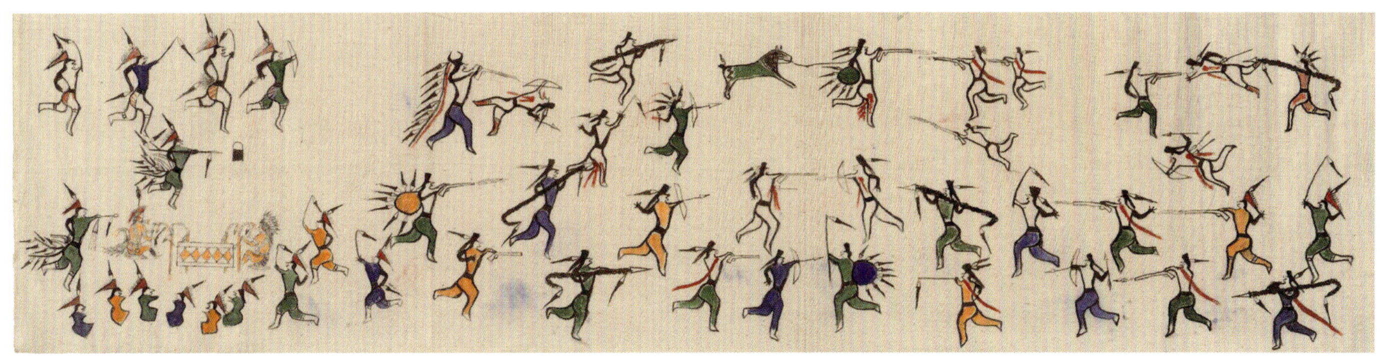

Of the ten battle scenes Spotted Tail (Apsáalooke [Crow]) painted on this robe, five celebrate the war deeds of an Apsáalooke warrior named White Swan. Recognizable at the upper right by his red cape, White Swan uses a lance to take down an enemy armed with a rifle and pistol. This daring feat counted as an important coup, or accomplishment.

At the lower right corner of the robe White Swan carries a red and blue flag, the standard he bore in his official capacity as Lieutenant Colonel George A. Custer's scout. The red on the horse and on White Swan's leg indicates that both are wounded. Despite these handicaps, White Swan counts coup on his enemy by striking him with his coup stick and then killing him. ◊

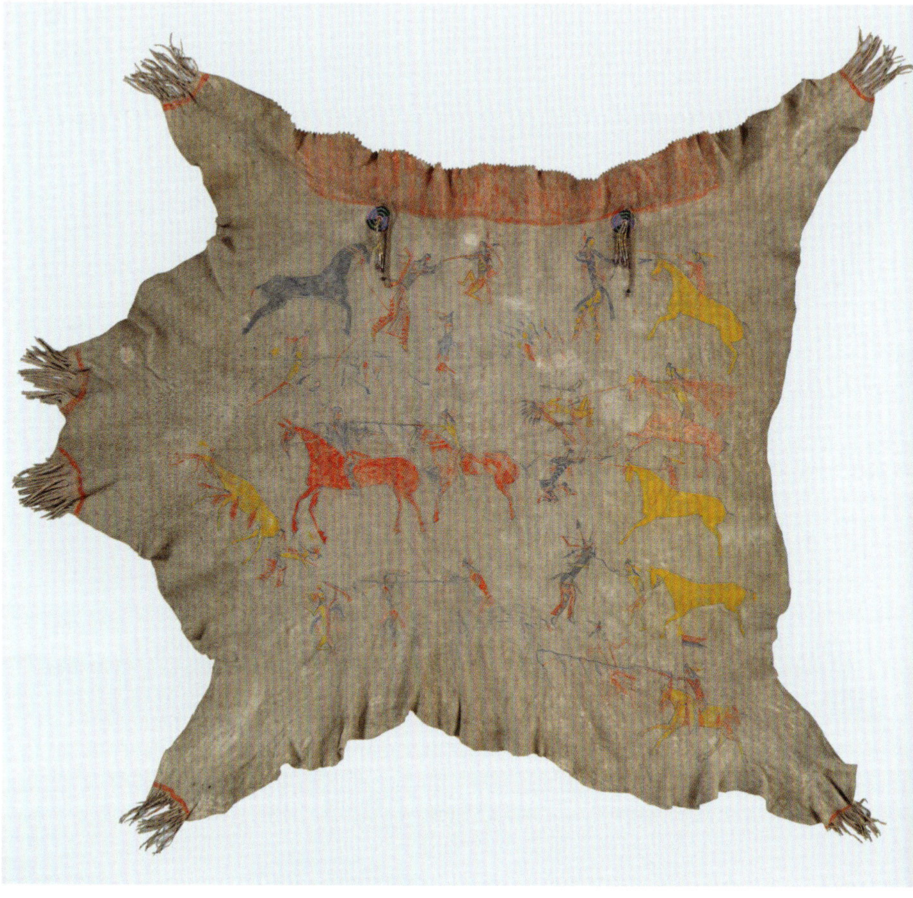

Robe, ca. 1880. Painted by Spotted Tail (Apsáalooke [Crow]). Montana. Elkhide, paint, glass beads; 210 × 205 cm. 14/3602

Robe (detail), ca. 1880. Painted by Spotted Tail (Apsáalooke [Crow]). Montana. Elkhide, paint, glass beads; 210 × 205 cm. 14/3602

White Swan, wearing a red cape, uses a lance to take down an enemy.

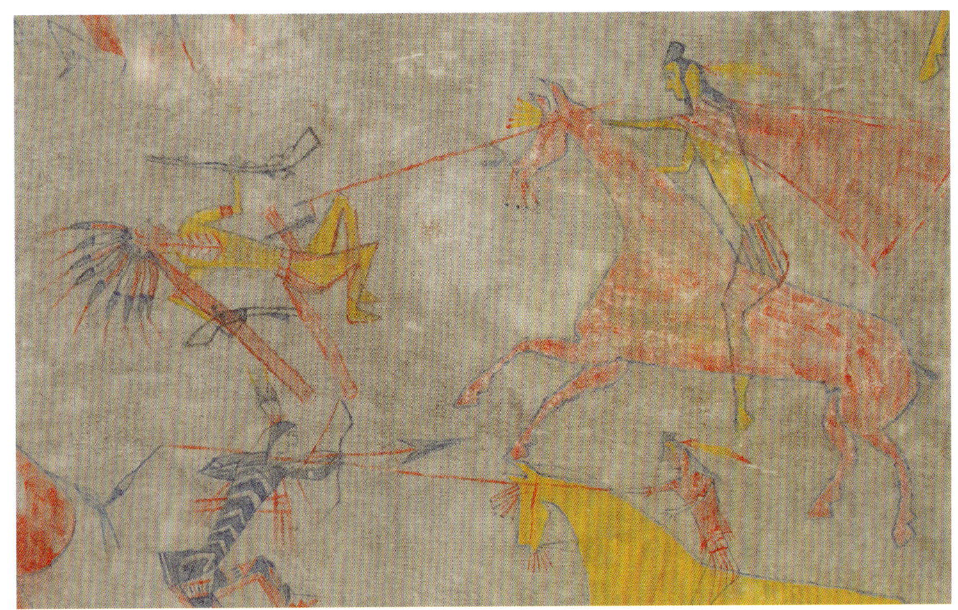

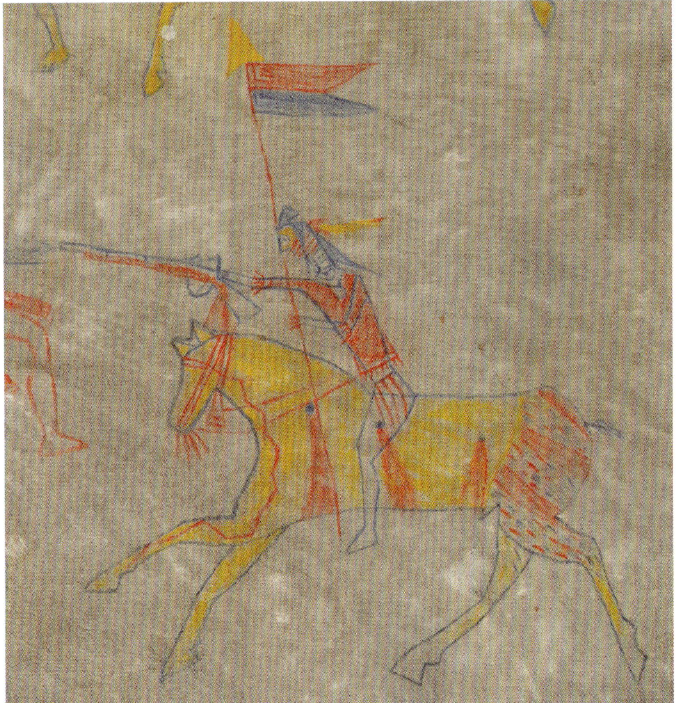

Robe (detail), ca. 1880. Painted by Spotted Tail (Apsáalooke [Crow]). Montana. Elkhide, paint, glass beads; 210 × 205 cm. 14/3602

White Swan carries a red and blue flag.

In a series of scenes that begins in the upper right corner, Ćehu'pa, or Jaw (Hunkpapa Lakota), tells the story of a successful raid in which he captured seventy Apsáalooke, or Crow, horses. Ćehu'pa can be identified by the wolf skin hanging first outside his tipi and then on his back. In the upper row he leads his war party and looks at the enemy camp through a telescope.

In the lower set of illustrations, he unties the horses while the unsuspecting Apsáalooke warriors sleep inside their tipis. The Apsáalooke are painted as upper torsos and heads, each with a distinctive hairstyle. The hoof prints and horse figures show Ćehu'pa returning to his camp victorious. In referring to this exploit Ćehu'pa said, "I did not waken nor kill any of the Crows; I just took their horses. No Sioux ever took more horses in one night." ◊

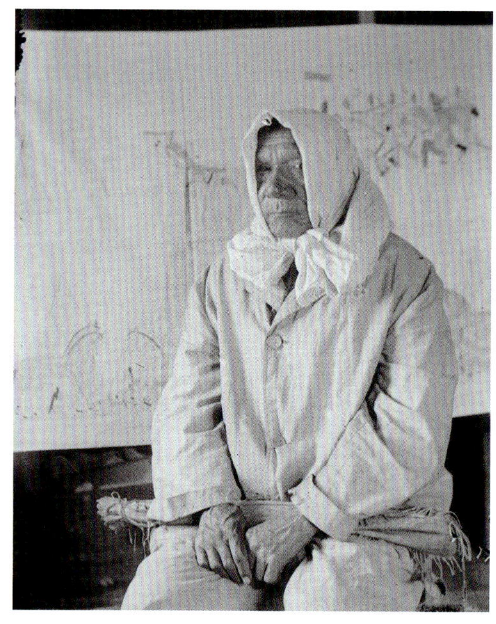

Ćehu'pa, or Jaw, 1913. Photo by Frances Densmore. National Anthropological Archives, Smithsonian Institution 03358

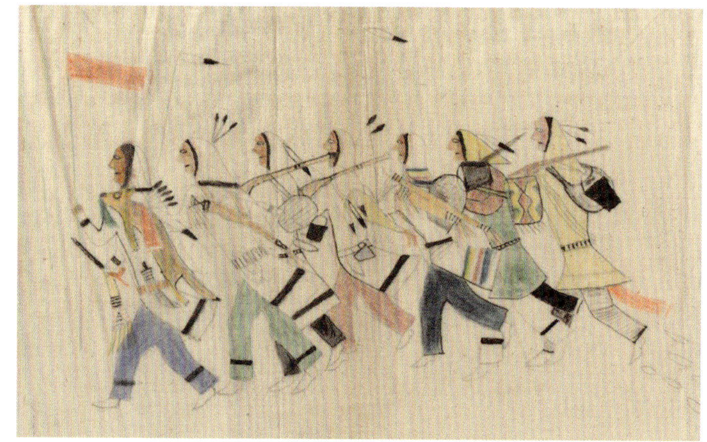

Muslin (detail), ca. 1913. Painted by Ćehu'pa, or Jaw (Hunkpapa Lakota, 1850–ca. 1925). North Dakota or South Dakota. Muslin, ink, paint, graphite; 91 × 192 cm. 6/7932

Ćehu'pa leads a war party.

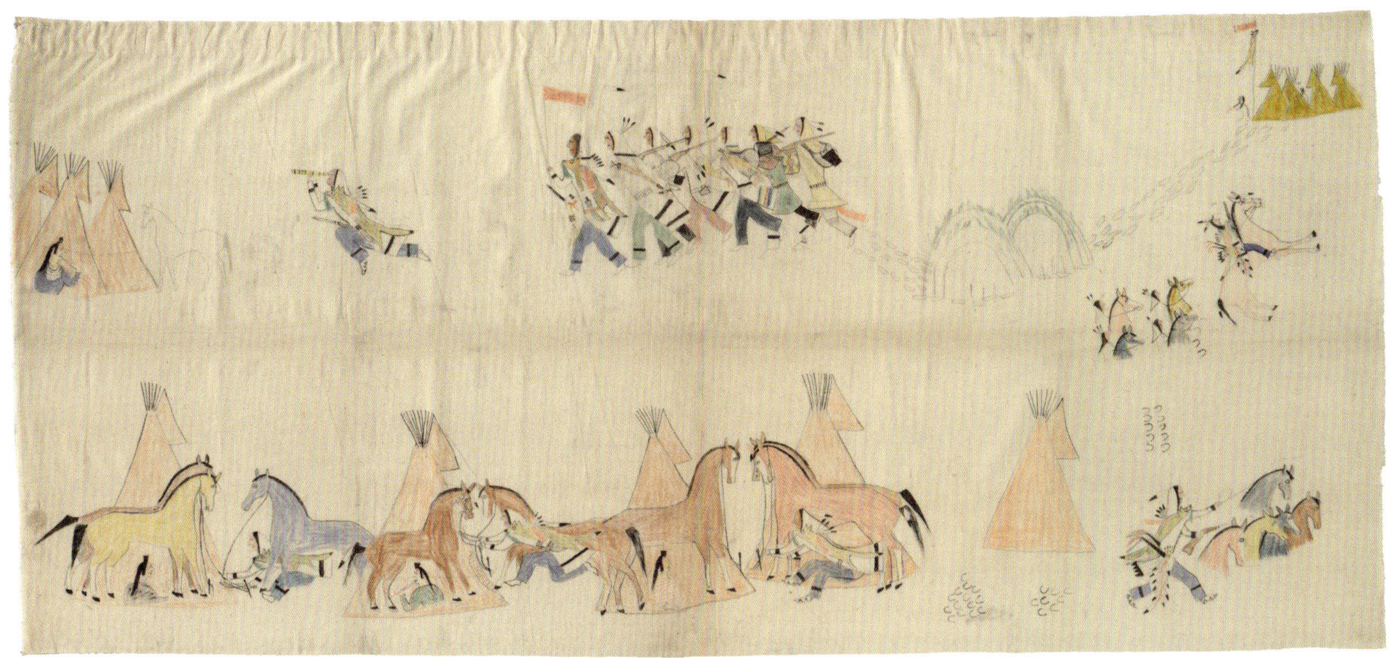

Muslin, ca. 1913. Painted by Ćehu'pa, or Jaw (Hunkpapa Lakota, 1850–ca. 1925). North Dakota or South Dakota. Muslin, ink, paint, graphite; 91 × 192 cm. 6/7932

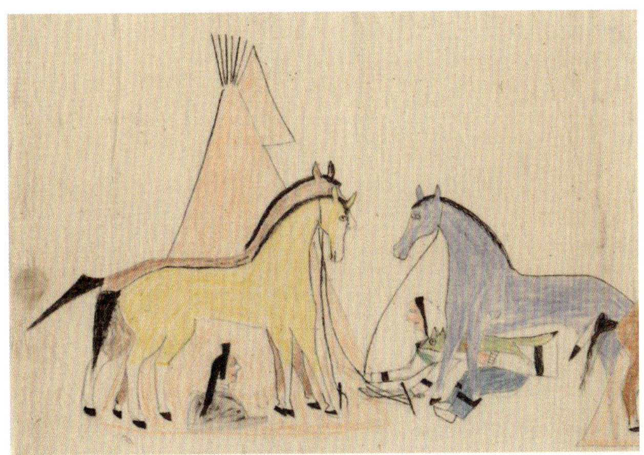

Muslin (detail), ca. 1913. Painted by Ćehu'pa, or Jaw (Hunkpapa Lakota, 1850–ca. 1925). North Dakota or South Dakota. Muslin, ink, paint, graphite; 91 × 192 cm. 6/7932

Ćehu'pa unties horses next to tents in which Apsáalooke (Crow) warriors sleep.

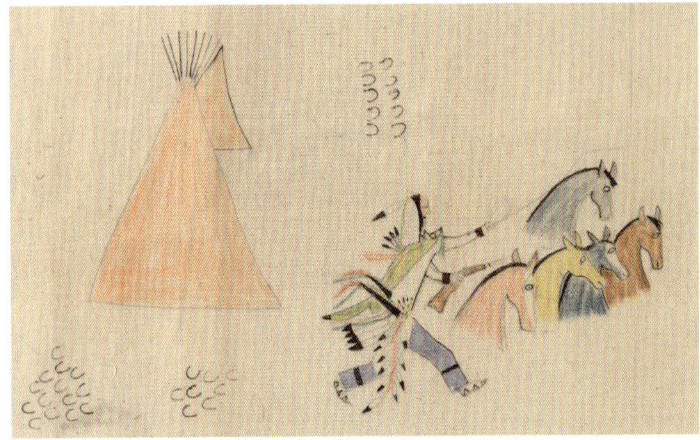

Muslin (detail), ca. 1913. Painted by Ćehu'pa, or Jaw (Hunkpapa Lakota, 1850–ca. 1925). North Dakota or South Dakota. Muslin, ink, paint, graphite; 91 × 192 cm. 6/7932

Ćehu'pa returns to camp with captured horses.

In this drawing, the dancer on the right carries a staff meant to honor a horse that was a comrade in battle. The artist, Rain In The Face, was a Hunkpapa Lakota leader who was among the most sensationalized Plains Indians of the 1800s. He allied with other Lakota leaders, such as Red Cloud and Sitting Bull, and fought the U.S. Army throughout the 1860s and 1870s. Known equally well by journalists and cavalry officers, he sought to gain back control of land along the Bozeman Trail in Wyoming, and to protect the Black Hills in South Dakota. In 1876 Rain In The Face was one of the leading warriors in the defeat of Lieutenant Colonel George A. Custer and the Seventh Cavalry at the Battle of Little Bighorn. ◊

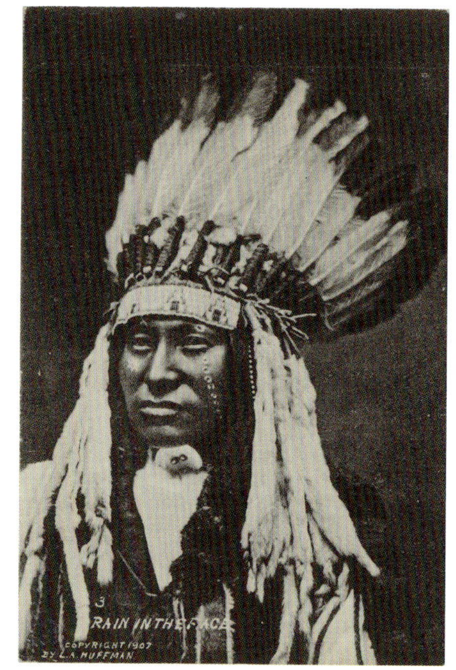

Rain In The Face, ca. 1907. Photo by Laton Alton Huffman. P16692

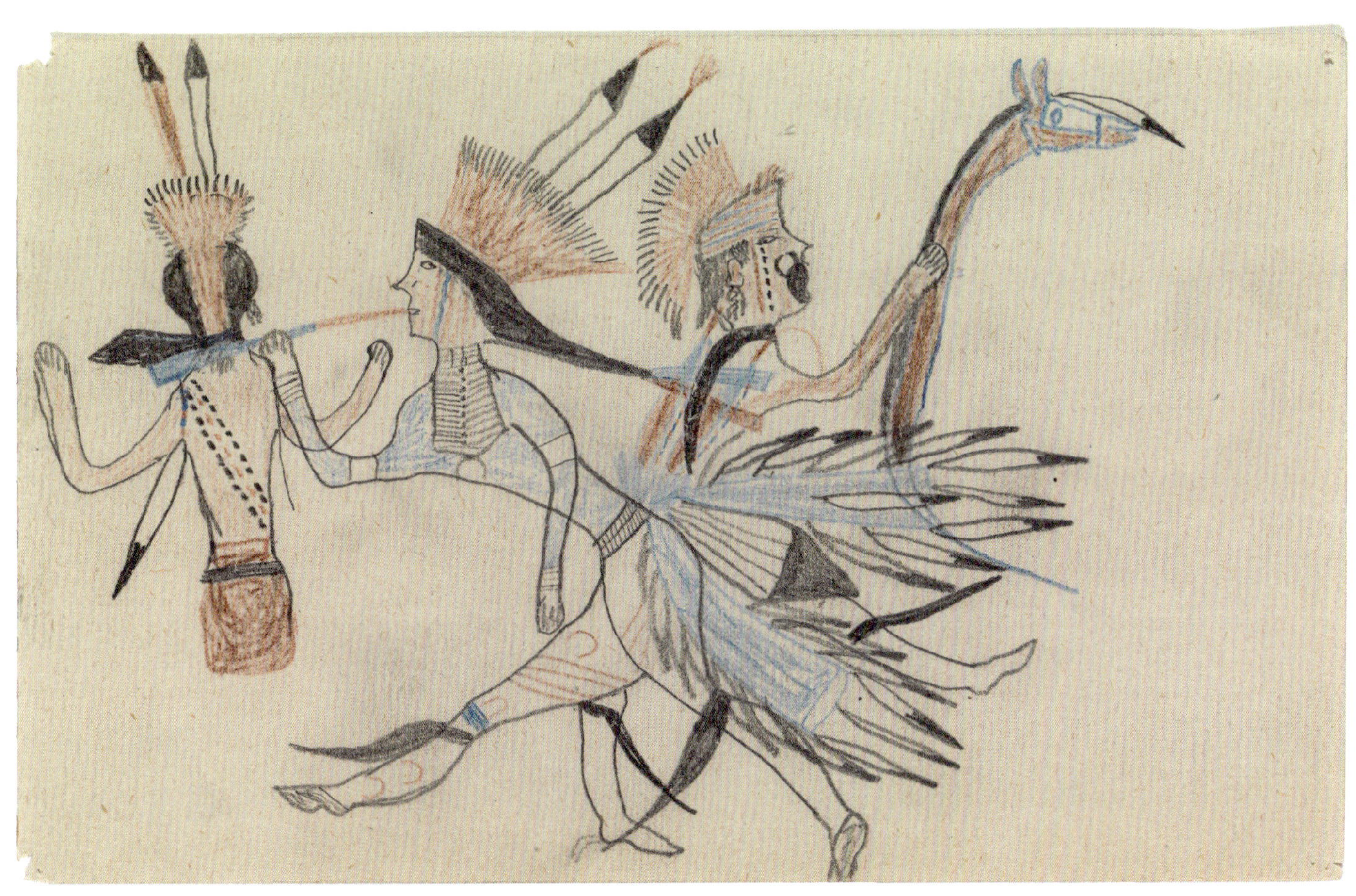

Drawing, ca. 1885. Made by Rain In The Face (Hunkpapa Lakota, ca. 1835–1905). North Dakota or South Dakota. Paper, graphite, colored pencil; 11.4 × 17.7 cm. 20/1628

This drawing illustrates an expedition that the Lakota warrior Tatank'-ehan'ni, or Old Buffalo, led against the Apsáalooke, or Crow, when he was twenty-eight years old. Tatank'-ehan'ni's band of the Lakota had been living in the "queen's land" (Canada) but traveled into the United States on a buffalo hunt. One night, the Apsáalooke stole the Lakota horses, so Tatank'-ehan'ni and twelve others set out to retaliate. The fully drawn figure in red represents Tatank'-ehan'ni surrounded by Apsáalooke warriors, who are shown only as heads. The scene in the upper right corner with a figure in black depicts a fasting ceremony, probably conducted before the battle. ◊

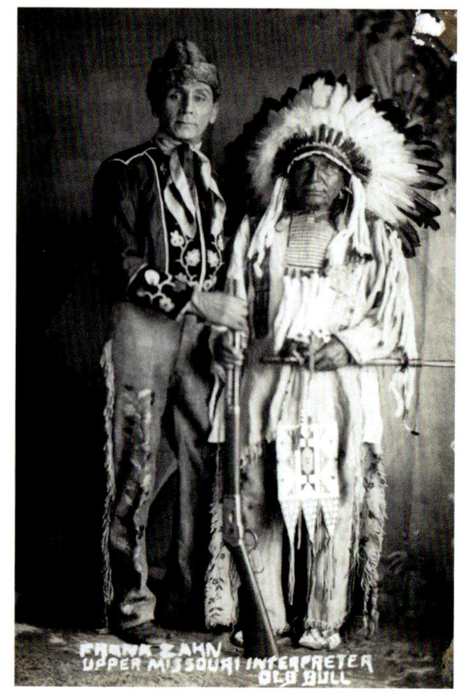

Tatank'-ehan'ni, or Old Buffalo, or Old Bull (right), with interpreter Frank Zahn, ca. 1935. Photographer unknown. Western History Collections, University of Oklahoma Libraries, W. S. Campbell 2058A

Muslin (detail), ca. 1913. Painted by Tatank'-ehan'ni, or Old Buffalo (Lakota, ca. 1851–ca. 1935). North Dakota or South Dakota. Muslin, graphite, colored pencil; 89.5 × 134.2 cm. 6/7935

A fasting ceremony.

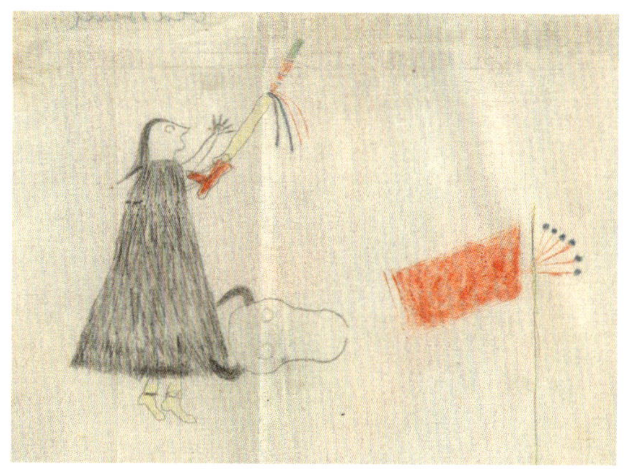

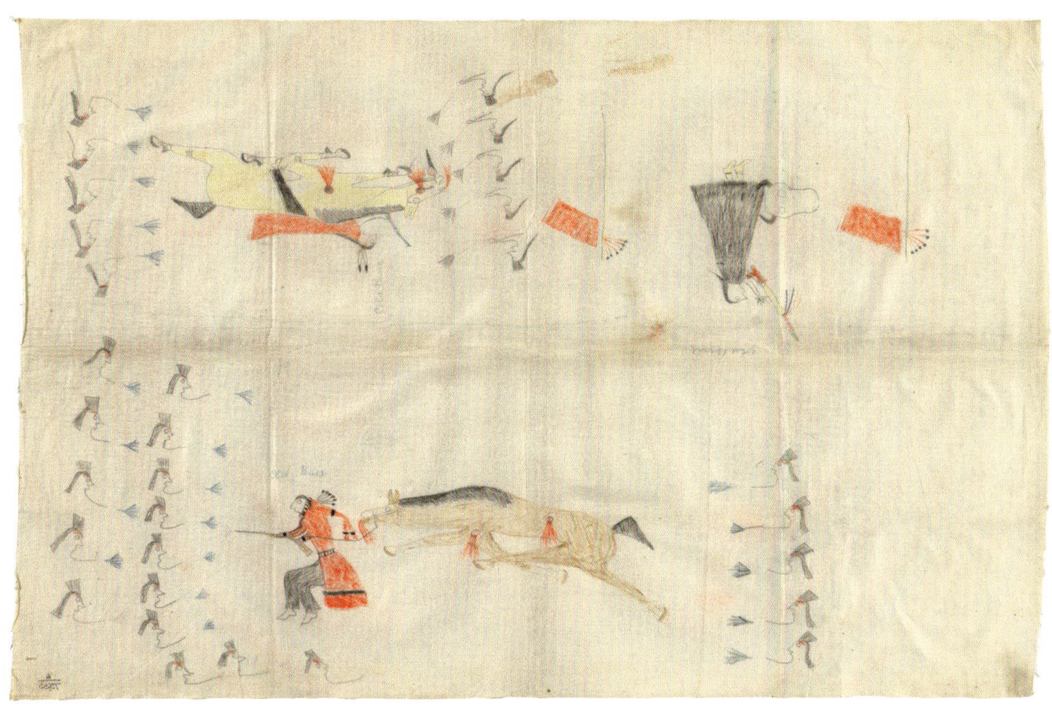

Muslin, ca. 1913. Painted by Tatank'-ehan'ni, or Old Buffalo (Lakota, ca. 1851–ca. 1935). North Dakota or South Dakota. Muslin, graphite, colored pencil; 89.5 × 134.2 cm. 6/7935

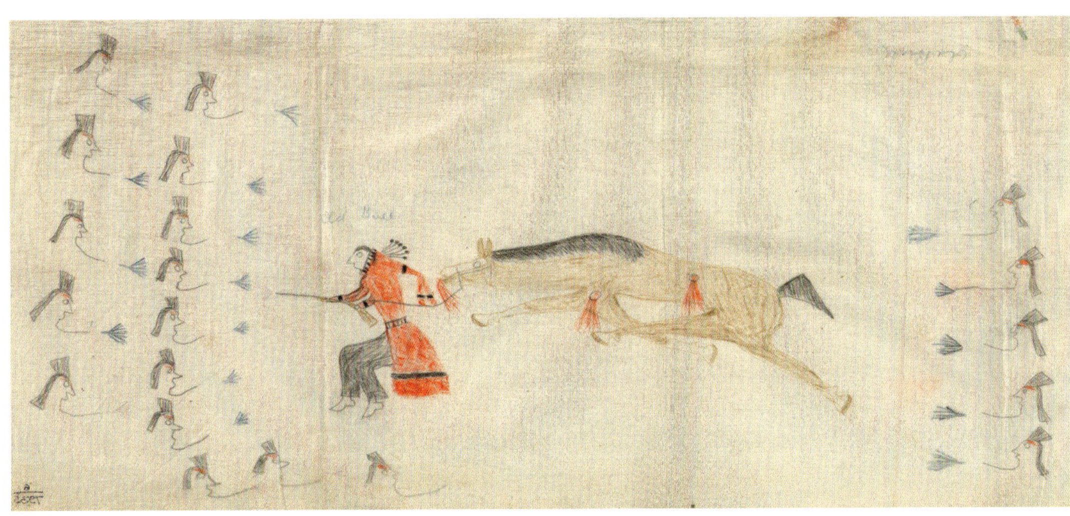

Muslin (detail), ca. 1913. Painted by Tatank'-ehan'ni, or Old Buffalo (Lakota, ca. 1851–ca. 1935). North Dakota or South Dakota. Muslin, graphite, colored pencil; 89.5 × 134.2 cm. 6/7935

Tatank'-ehan'ni is surrounded by Apsáalooke, or Crow, warriors.

MESSAGE IN A MUSLIN

Siyosapa's Sun Dance Painting at the National Museum of the American Indian

David W. Penney

The National Museum of the American Indian (NMAI) is fortunate to possess two paintings by Siyosapa, or Black Chicken (ca. 1845–ca. 1902), a charismatic Hunkpapa Lakota *wicasa wakan*, or holy man, who lived the latter part of his life enrolled as a Yanktonai in the Poplar River community at the Fort Peck Reservation in Montana. The paintings are two of several he produced and sold to officials, military officers, and others at the Fort Peck Agency. Siyosapa painted his compositions on lengths of muslin, a loosely woven cotton cloth that was distributed as part of government-issued annuity goods through reservation agencies. Muslin painted with images often found use as an insulating inner wall for a summer tipi. With the advent of reservation-era cabins, muslin paintings were installed as wall coverings.[1] This shift prompted a broad expansion of muslin painting as an expressive medium, with representations of historical events and cultural practices in innovative compositions.

Siyosapa arranged the images on the larger NMAI muslin in three groupings. Uppermost and probably most significant is a representation of the Sun Dance, the most powerful of Lakota sacred rites. Men performed the Sun Dance in fulfillment of vows: to heal ailing family members; to promote the health and well-being of the people; to prevail over enemies; or to capture enemy horses or perform other notable acts. Siyosapa shows the dancers gathered within a circle representing the Sun Dance lodge, a structure erected especially for the occasion. Short Bull, an

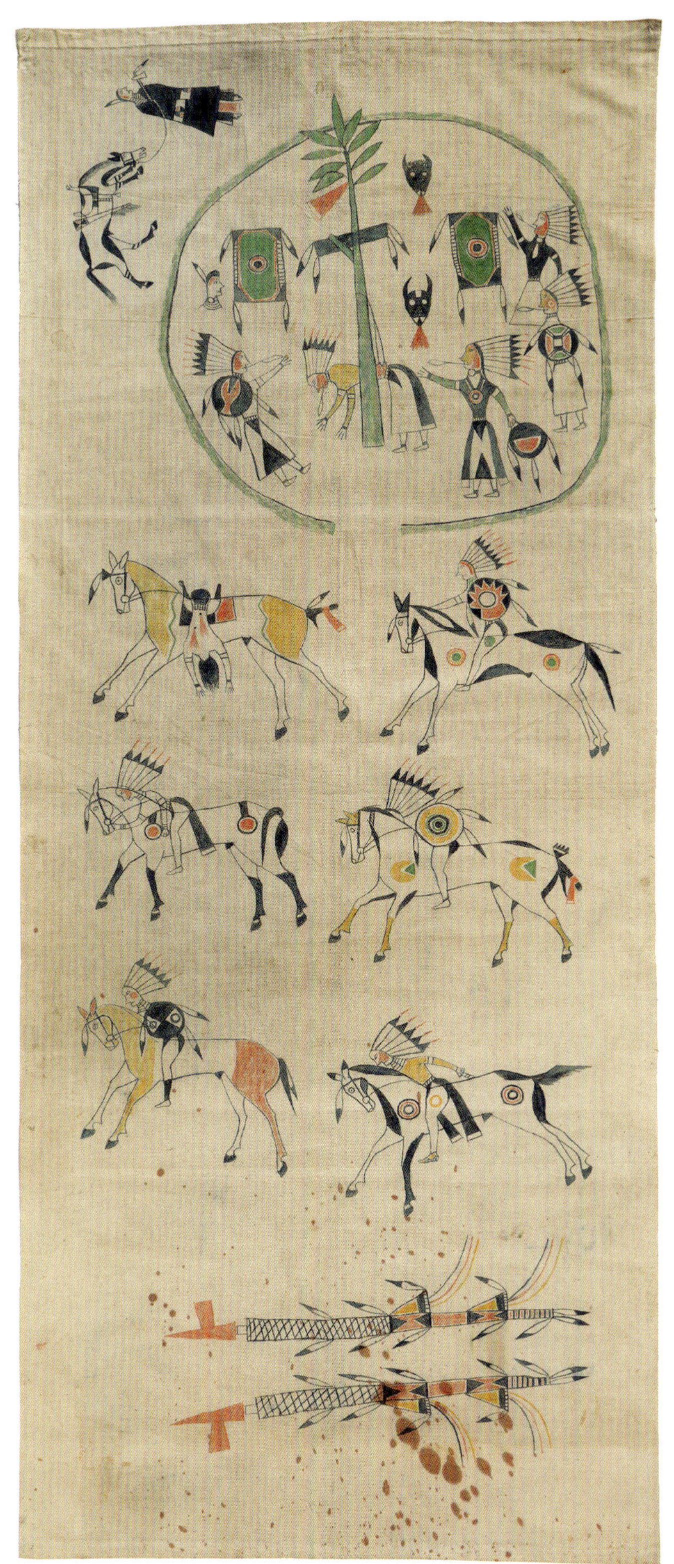

Muslin, ca. 1890. Painted by Siyosapa (Yanktonai Nakota, ca. 1845–ca. 1902). Montana. Muslin, ink, paint; 216.4 × 89.5 cm. 2/3304

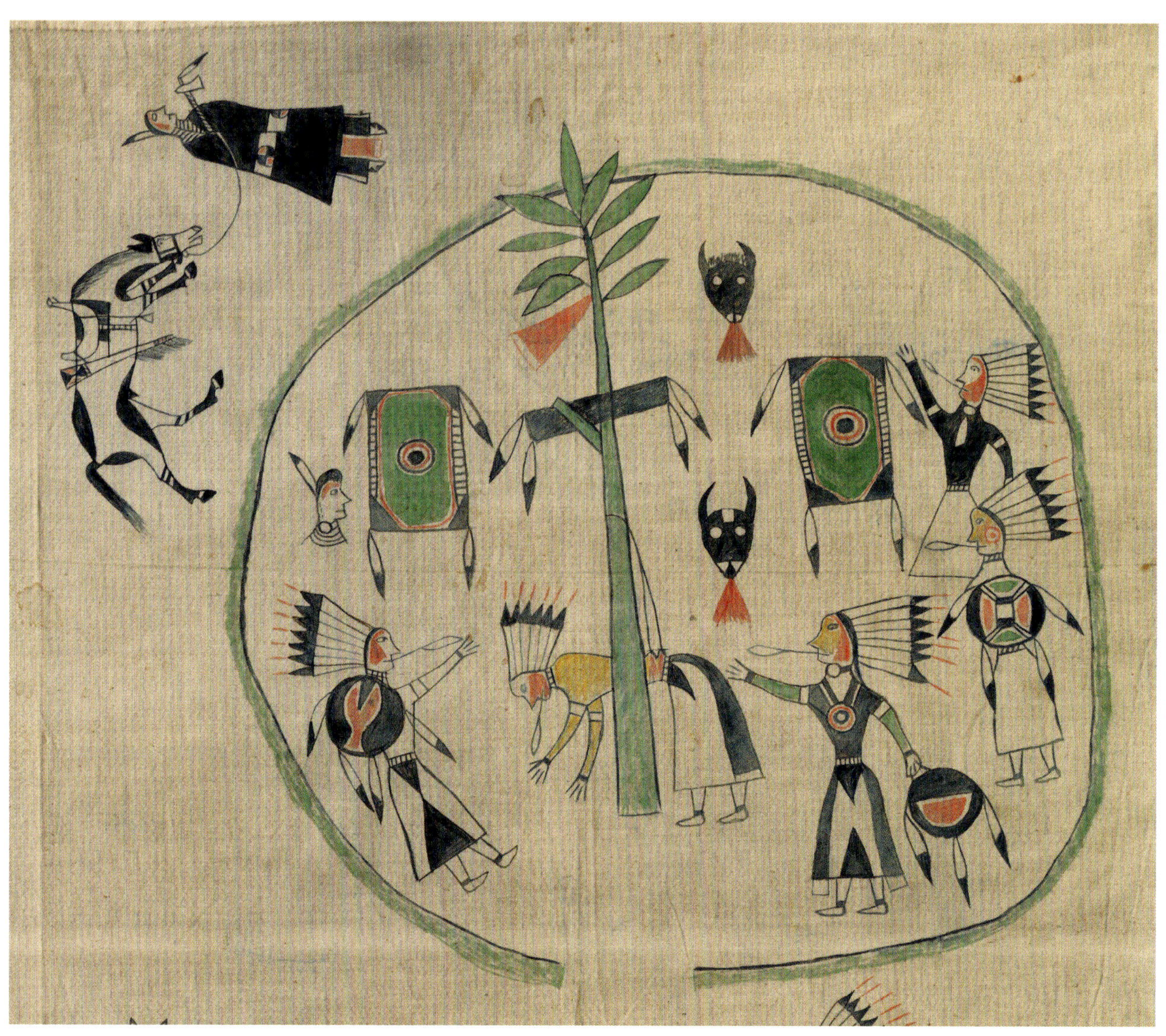

Muslin (detail), ca. 1890. Painted by Siyosapa (Yanktonai Nakota, ca. 1845–ca. 1902). Montana. Muslin, ink, paint; 216.4 × 89.5 cm. 2/3304

Oglala Lakota wicasa wakan, described the space to ethnographer James R. Walker as "a circular bower covered with green leaves with its entrance toward the sun at midday."[2] In the center is the sacred pole, a cottonwood tree ceremonially cut down and stripped of branches, leaving a fork at the top and the uppermost leaves. "The leaves must not be taken from the top, for these leaves are like the scalp of mankind and they control the spirit-life of the tree," Bad Heart Bull, another Oglala holy man, told Walker.[3] A Sun Dance bundle, sacred items wrapped in a rawhide container, is placed in the fork of the pole with a red banner (the color of the sun) tied above.[4]

Siyosapa's painting shows four standing dancers wearing feather headdresses and Sun Dance kilts, eagle-bone whistles in their mouths, three of them holding shields and raising one arm to the sacred pole. These dancers evidently vowed the most basic form of dancing: enduring a grueling fast and dancing from sunrise to sunset with their faces upraised toward the sun.[5] A fifth dancer hangs suspended from the pole by lanyards attached to awls piercing the muscles of his lower back. This is the highest level and most severe form of Lakota sun dancing.[6]

There is good indication that Siyosapa's rendering of the Sun Dance is self-referential, illustrating his own vow and sacrifice on the way to becoming a wicasa wakan. Lakota holy men told Walker, "If one wishes to become a shaman of the highest order, he should dance the Sun Dance suspended from the pole so that his feet will not touch the ground."[7] Royal Hassrick was told, similarly, "Dreamers wishing to undergo the Sun Dance in the fourth degree [suspension off the ground] could be eligible for shamanship."[8] After reviewing the record of such statements, scholar David C. Posthumus recently summarized, "Although it was not absolutely necessary to dance the Sun Dance to become a shaman, those who did dance the fourth and most trying grade, suspended from the *čhaŋwákȟaŋ* (sacred tree), were held in higher public esteem and hence acquired more prestige than those who did not."[9] All of Siyosapa's Sun Dance pictures, and there are several, feature this ritual act as the focus of the ceremony.

Siyosapa's status at Fort Peck as a respected but intimidating stone dreamer and holy man is well established. Mary Rippey Heistand, who accompanied her husband, Lieutenant Henry O. S. Heistand, when he was posted to Camp Poplar River at the Fort Peck Agency from 1880 to 1884, wrote about Siyosapa in her column for *Army and Navy Life* magazine, claiming, "He enjoyed among his people a great reputation for skill in all the magic and black art both for healing and other purposes."[10] Stewart Culin, an ethnographer then working for the University of Pennsylvania Museum, visited Siyosapa at his home in 1900 and interviewed him about his sacred stones. Stone dreamers possessed the ability to heal the sick; predict future events; and locate missing objects, herds of animals, or the enemy. Regarding Siyosapa's sacred stones, Culin reported, "The large one he called 'Beats the Drum.' When horses are stolen, the doctor made a tipi in his house under which he placed his drum with this stone. After a time, the rock would beat the drum and reveal the thief and the location of the horses. When a person was very sick and his death anticipated, he painted the two smaller stones. These he called the 'Large and Small Doctor.'"[11]

"To dream of a sacred stone was regarded by the Teton Sioux as a sign of great import," explained Smithsonian ethnomusicologist Francis Densmore, "indicating that the dreamer, by fulfilling the requirements of his dream, would become possessed of supernatural power, in the exercise of which he would use the sacred stones."[12] As such, to prepare for his status as a stone dreamer and wicasa wakan, Siyosapa would have likely vowed advanced grades of the Sun Dance, as referenced in his paintings.

Siyosapa's Sun Dance composition includes other elements that may refer to his own experiences and powers rather than to the Sun Dance generally, since they do not correspond to historical statements or illustrations of Sun Dance practice. Yet these details appear consistently in his Sun Dance paintings. Two large, green rectangles with circles in the centers and feathers at the four corners flank the sacred pole. These seem to represent square hand drums of a type known to have been made by Siyosapa. He also painted two black buffalo heads, one stacked above the other, to one side of the sacred pole, the small red fans beneath their snouts representing their sacred breath. In other Sun Dance compositions, Siyosapa positioned the buffalo heads above the square drums so that the animals breathe directly on

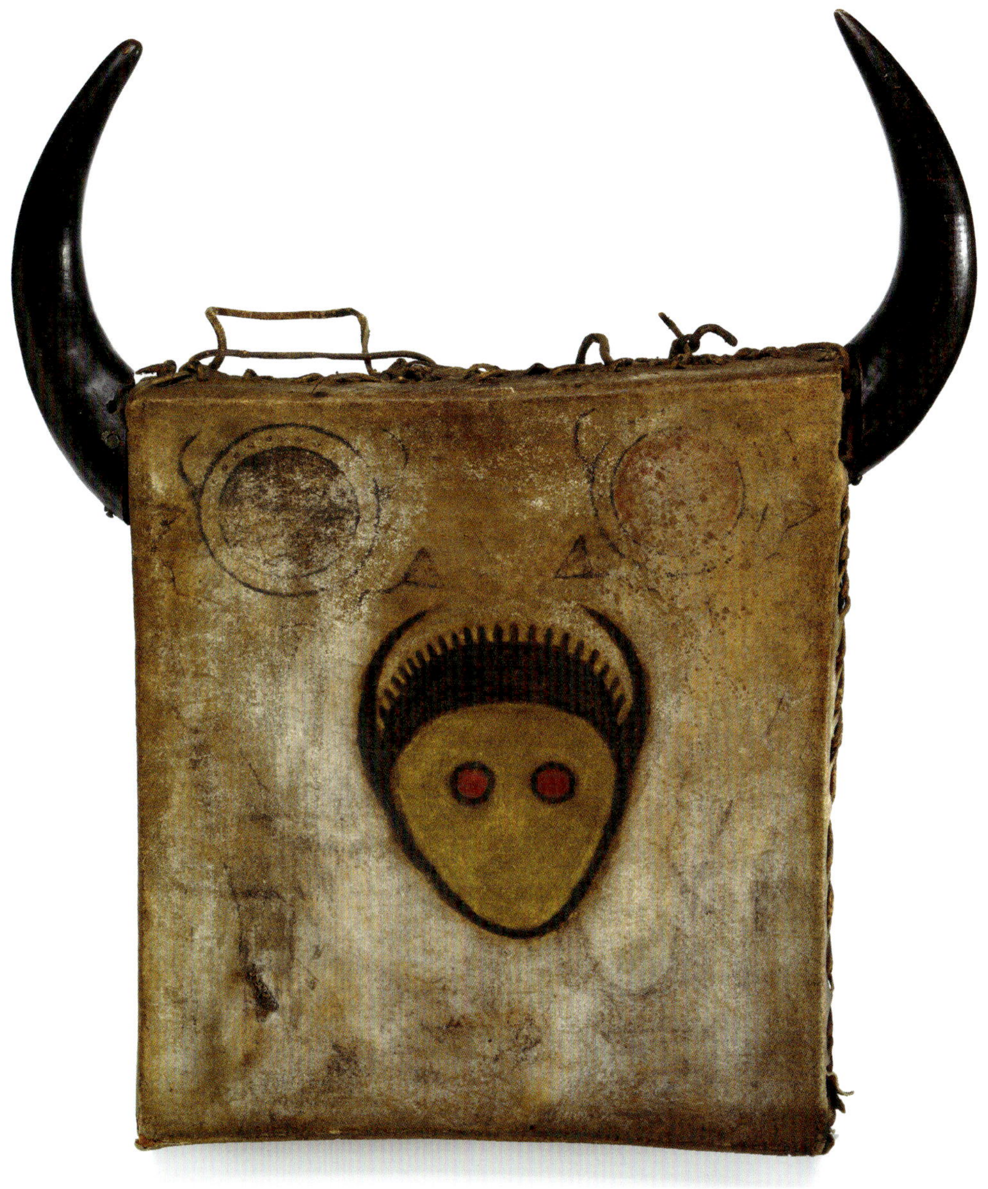

Drum, 1860–70. Painted by Siyosapa (Yanktonai Nakota, ca. 1845–ca. 1902). Montana. Wood, rawhide, buffalo horn, paint, hide thong; 59 × 49 × 7 cm. 23/2202

them. Painted hand drums were essential to Siyosapa's practice as a stone dreamer and healer. The Oglala holy man George Sword told Walker, "A shaman should have a drum and two rattles; these should be made by ceremony."[13] Siyosapa made several drums, now housed in museum collections, each of them painted with either a buffalo or a thunder being. The consistent appearance of paired drums sanctified by buffalo breath in his Sun Dance paintings may correspond to a vow or vision linked to his Sun Dance experience, endowing him with the rights and powers to create and consecrate hand drums for ceremony.[14]

The lower two-thirds of the painting at NMAI feature different kinds of images, although their significance likely relates in some way to the Sun Dance. Directly below the Sun Dance circle, Siyosapa painted six riders on horseback, arranged two-by-two. Five wear feather headdresses. Three carry shields. The first, in the upper left, lies across his saddle with two bleeding wounds in his back. Warriors on horseback are another recurrent feature of Siyosapa's paintings, some including many more riders. One of the riders always suffers wounds. One of the earliest known Siyosapa paintings, collected in 1880, features a group of mounted Apsáalooke (Crow) warriors, recognizable by their distinctive hairstyles, and Lakota warriors with headdresses. One of the Apsáalooke fighters is wounded.

When depicting battles, Plains artists often re-created a particular event: a coup or a heroic act by a known protagonist. This does not seem to be the case here. The mounted fighters are generalized. Even their shields are painted with generic circles or sunbursts instead of vision-inspired designs linked to an individual. No one is shown inflicting wounds on the bleeding man. Success over one's enemies was a customary Sun Dance vow, and Siyosapa's Sun Dance experiences, which would have taken place early in his life, before he joined the Yanktonai at Fort Peck in 1872, probably occurred during the 1850s or 1860s, when the Hunkpapa often fought with the Apsáalooke. Are the six warriors a representation of Siyosapa's Sun Dance vow or vision promising success in battle? Other paintings by Siyosapa vary the number of combatants depending upon the painting's format and scale, but the message is always the same: Lakota success over Apsáalooke enemies.

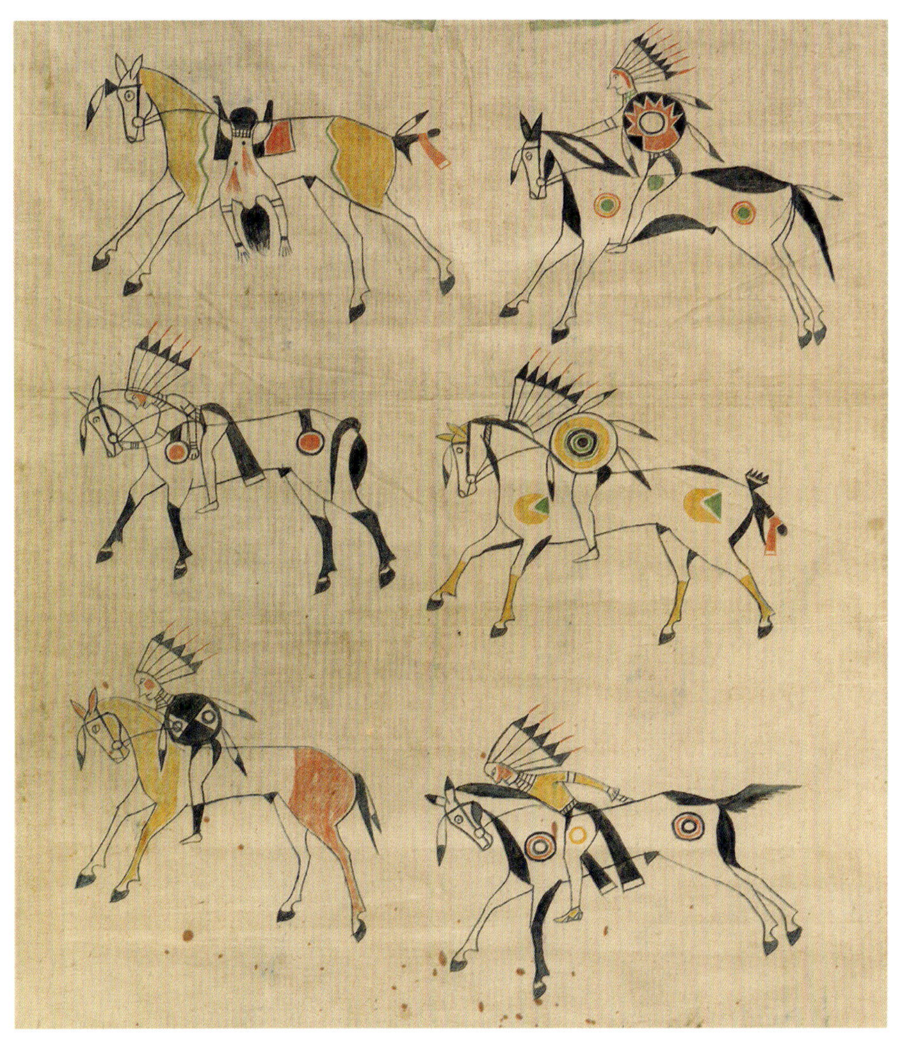

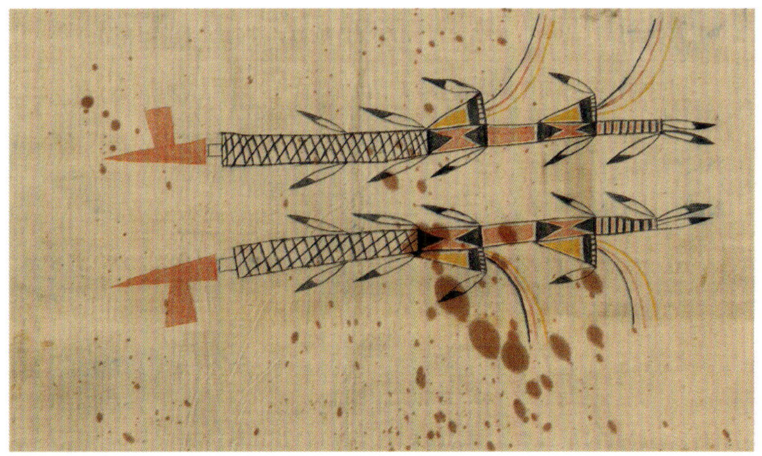

Muslin (details), ca. 1890. Painted by Siyosapa (Yanktonai Nakota, ca. 1845–ca. 1902), ca. 1890. Montana. Muslin, ink, paint; 216.4 × 89.5 cm. 2/3304

The two pipes and stems at the bottom of the painting are more difficult to interpret in this context. Each has a red stone or catlinite bowl and a long wooden stem wrapped with porcupine-quill decoration and strung with pendants, some made of eagle feathers and others of horsehair. Holy men like Siyosapa customarily possessed pipes. As Sword told Walker, "Each shaman may have a ceremonial pipe. He keeps it and uses it only when he is performing an important ceremony."[15] Sword also instructed Walker on how such a ceremonial pipe is consecrated, usually by a group of senior holy men after a prospective spiritual leader has fasted in isolation and received a vision from spirit beings.[16] Siyosapa splattered the images of the two pipes with red paint. Sacred red paint, customarily vermillion or red ochre called *wasé*, is applied to faces and hands to anoint individuals for the Sun Dance and other purposes. "Red is the color of the sun. . . . A man who paints red is pleasing to the spirits," explained Oglala holy man One Star to Walker in 1897.[17] The red splatters reinforce the notion that the pipes in Siyosapa's painting are sacred, but the significance of an identical pair remains a mystery. Were paired pipes, like paired drums, part of the sacred prerogatives stemming from his unique visions and practice?

This painting is one of several scattered in different museum collections. Most of them present the same kind of imagery. Siyosapa also made painted drums, at least one model shield, and smaller paintings on muslin featuring images of thunder beings such as the horned thunderbird shown on his other painting at NMAI. Undoubtedly museums around the world hold more of his works that have not yet been identified. It is possible to determine, through scant documentation or inference, that between 1880 and 1900 painted muslins and drums were sold to officials, military officers, and visitors at Fort Peck Agency. Although prolific, his work remained narrow in scope, consistently featuring images and themes presumably drawn from his own visions, practice, and experience. His artistic productivity, assertive pursuit of sales, and self-referential subject matter all seem calculated to extend his renown and influence beyond his home and out into the colonialist, modern world that had grown to overwhelm and control his community. While one should acknowledge an entrepreneurial motivation for his efforts, he may also have had other, more

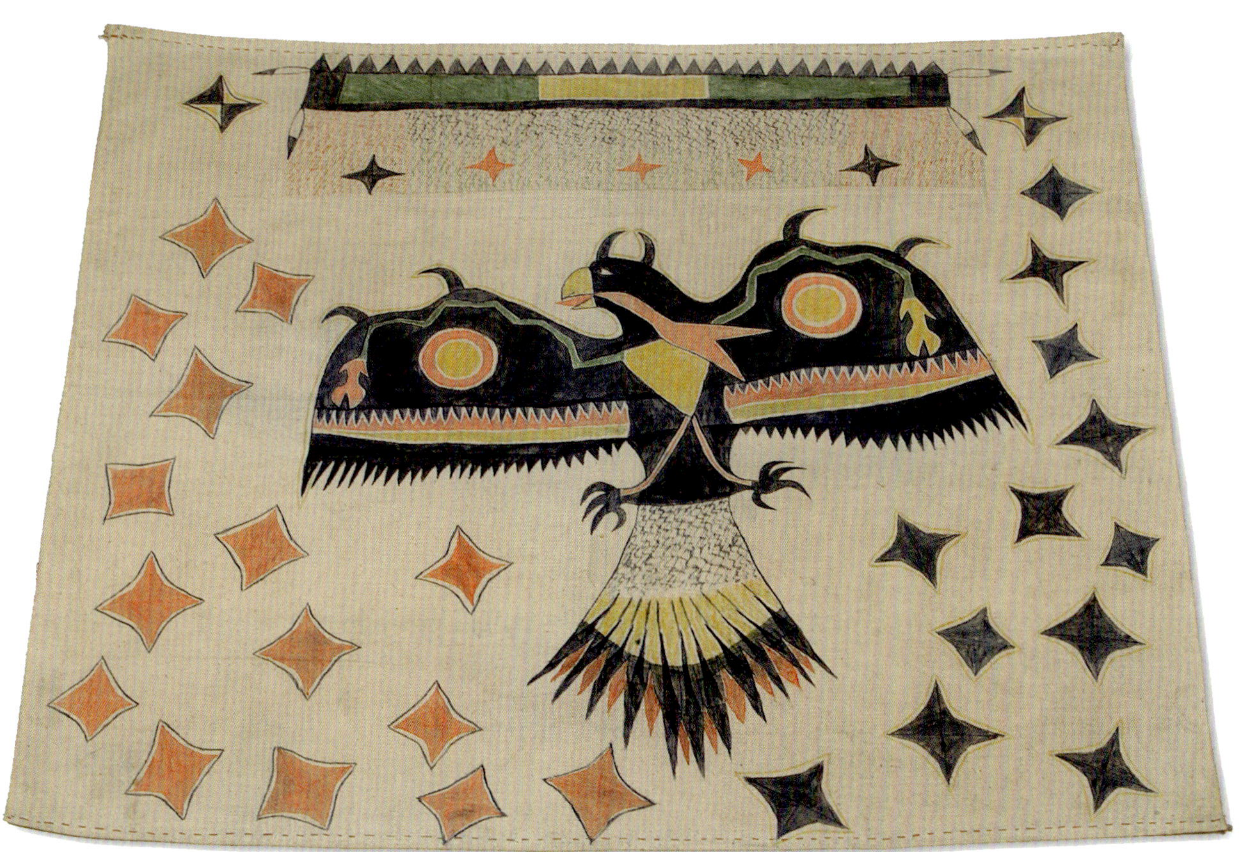

Muslin, ca. 1890. Painted by Siyosapa (Yanktonai Nakota, ca. 1845–ca. 1902). Montana. Muslin, paint; 77 × 91.3 cm. 2/3132

instrumental considerations. Creating and selling his works offered a means of engaging and, to some extent, influencing the powerful outsiders.[18]

Ironically, once his creations left Siyosapa, they rarely remained associated with him. The Sun Dance muslin at NMAI can only be attributed to Siyosapa on the basis of its style and subject matter. There is no collection history that ties the work to his authorship. The same is true for most of his other paintings now in museum collections. The only firm documentation of Siyosapa's muslin painting known to date is attached to a pair of paintings "presented by 'Black Chicken,' a Sioux Chief of the Oglala Tribe [*sic*] to Major General Lloyd Wheaton stationed at the Fort Peck Indian Agency." As a captain, Wheaton was posted to Camp Poplar River, the agency's military garrison, in 1886 and left as a major and the commanding officer when the post closed in 1893. A descendant, Dr. Clarence L. Wheaton, donated the two paintings to the Chicago Historical Society in 1923.[19] Perhaps the misidentification of "Black Chicken" as an Oglala chief stems from the younger Wheaton's faulty memory three decades later when recalling the family account of the gift.

When the ethnographer Stewart Culin visited Siyosapa at Fort Peck in 1900, he established Siyosapa's Hunkpapa origins, collected his stones and other sacred items, commissioned from him rare and distinctive Hunkpapa gaming pieces for his research about North American Indian games, and wrote expansively about this experience in a report of his expedition for the Free Museum of Science and Art at the University of Pennsylvania, now the Penn Museum. In his account, Culin made a passing reference to Siyosapa selling "curios" at the agency post but wrote nothing about his paintings.[20] The collection record for Culin's expedition, however, indicates that he bought from Siyosapa two large "tent curtains," their dimensions corresponding broadly to his muslin paintings. Culin noted in the record a term Siyosapa used to describe them, *o'-zan o'-wa-pi*: "written or figured curtain," or "painted lodge curtain."[21]

Culin evidently failed to realize that in 1900 two of Siyosapa's paintings were already at the University of Pennsylvania, both ultimately destined for NMAI. They had been displayed prominently in the University Library until deinstalled in 1898 in anticipation of the opening of a new museum building the following year. In 1909, Philadelphia artist Emil W. Lenders sold these two paintings to collector George Gustav Heye, along with other items from the University Library installation, as part of a large collection of Plains Indian objects. Heye founded the Museum of the American Indian in 1916, which later became the present-day National Museum of the American Indian. During the preceding seven years, he was affiliated with the University of Pennsylvania museum, storing his collections in Philadelphia and sponsoring expeditions and purchases. But he kept his own collections separate, including his purchases from Lenders.[22]

Lenders, a Philadelphia resident since 1886 or 1887, sold thousands of heritage items to museums in Germany and the United States between 1904 and 1910. Heye was just one of his many customers. When writing to prospective buyers in Germany, Lenders's associate, fellow artist Frederick Weygold, characterized Lenders as a "private hobby collector" who "occasionally [bought] whole collections from private individuals and bulk shipments from traders on reservations."[23]

In 1907, Lenders had convinced the University of Pennsylvania museum to engage in a large transaction involving the museum's "Black Chicken group, Yankton Sioux, from Fort Peck, Mont." This collection included the sacred stones, ritual equipment, gaming pieces, and the two muslin paintings that Stewart Culin had purchased from Siyosapa in 1900. Once he had secured the Siyosapa collection, Lenders offered it to the Ethnologisches Museum Berlin, with Weygold describing the "tent curtains" as

> two large strips of canvas, each one about 1,50 m wide and 3 to 4 m long. Rather new (clean) canvas. These are curtains from the tipi of Black Chicken. . . . The paintings represent pipes (ceremonial, hung with feathers), and common forms (that according to J. Mooney may represent war parties) and numerous horses probably stolen from another tribe.[24]

The offer to the Ethnologisches Museum Berlin also included at least one of the Siyosapa paintings from the old University Library installation, although it was not attributed to Siyosapa. Weygold sent a sketch of it with this annotation, "A

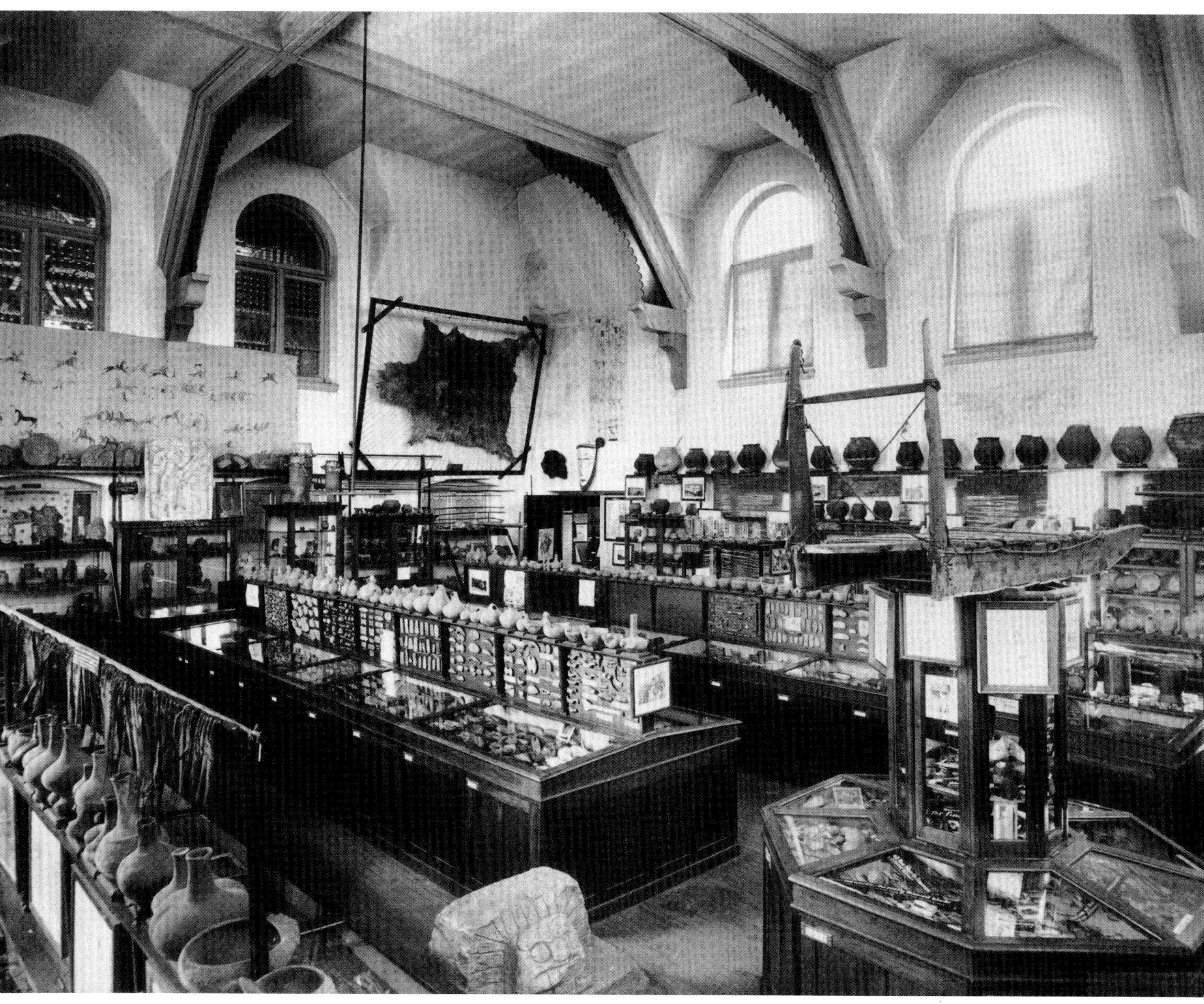

The *American Section–Material Culture* exhibit in the University of Pennsylvania's University Library (Furness Building), 1898. Courtesy of Penn Museum, Image No. 153359

Siyosapa's painting of a Sun Dance, now at the National Museum of the American Indian, hangs on the far wall, to the right of the buffalo hide.

colored drawing on canvas of a large horned thunderbird (eagle), very carefully done, (from the Crow). Old."[25] The Ethnologisches Museum declined to act until 1911, when it purchased the sacred stones and other ritual items but not the "tent curtains" or the thunderbird painting. Lenders had sold the latter to Heye in the meantime. The whereabouts of the "tent-curtain" muslin paintings Siyosapa sold to Culin remain unknown. Almost certainly, their connection to the Culin collection history has been lost.

Heye evidently remained curious about the two University Library paintings he had purchased from Lenders, however, and in 1925 Museum of the American Indian curator Robert Utley sent photographs of them to one of the museum's field collectors, William Wildschut, who was working among the Apsáalooke in Montana. "The Crows I consulted about this specimen are convinced that this specimen is not of Crow origin," he wrote of the thunderbird painting. As for Siyosapa's Sun Dance painting, he reported, "This piece is also not of Crow origin. The Crows to whom I showed this photograph told me that it was a Shoshone piece, depicting the Sun Dance in the upper part of the picture, and the visions received in the Sun Dance, in the lower part."[26] The paintings remained catalogued as, respectively, of unknown origin and Shoshone origin for more than fifty years. It wasn't until the 1990s that Smithsonian curator John C. Ewers recognized them as the work of Siyosapa, based on stylistic comparisons with the paintings that Clarence Wheaton had donated to the Chicago Historical Society.[27]

It may seem surprising that Lenders was unable to make the connection between the various Siyosapa pieces he handled, but he clearly was not looking for such connections. The episode lays bare the attitudes toward and mechanisms for anthropological collecting from American Indians at the turn-of-the-last-century moment that, in aggregate, separated millions of items from their communities and erased any traces of connection to makers and original owners. The pipeline was fed by assimilationist policies—forced residential school education, suppression of ceremony through Courts of Indian Offenses, and poverty—all contributing to Lenders-type "bulk shipments from traders on reservations," as coercively administered reservation residents gave up their belongings. This was the circular logic of salvage ethnography: to collect the remnants of such destruction in an effort to preserve them in faraway museums in urban centers of the modern world. Museums sought "old," "rare," and "difficult to find" pieces, judging them for their "scientific value" as samples, specimens, or artifacts.

Many Native artists such as Siyosapa, however, responded to the market in ethnographic items by creating objects not only for sale but also as powerful, personal interpretations of cultural experiences and histories. When these creations found their way into the collection pipeline, they were mixed in with heritage items, with no effort to distinguish them. On the contrary, the anthropology of the time considered most of the items made expressly for non-Native buyers to be less authentic and of less scientific value, characterizing them as "curios" or touristic creations. In Stewart Culin's eyes, Siyosapa's identity as a traditional holy man, a wicasa wakan, contributed more scientific value to his sacred stones and his informed re-creations of then obsolete games than to his paintings. His "tent curtains" represented for Culin a material cultural category as artifacts, rather than individualistic creations.

This is unfortunate, since large o'-zan o'-wa-pi, or painted lodge curtains, had grown into a far more expansive medium for visual expression during the last decades of the nineteenth century, and many were intended for sale to outsiders. Arguably, they were made and sold to represent Native perspectives, as pictorial expressions of cultural experience and knowledge. As syncretic productions of "auto-ethnography," muslin paintings tend to be didactic, culturally illustrative, and modernist, in the sense that the artists were responding to the modernity of the settler colonial marketplace and to collectors' ethnographic and historical curiosity. Anthropology museums of the day, however, almost invariably failed to notice.

Many large and elaborate muslin paintings in museum collections today remain unidentified. Consider, for example, several large and impressive o'-zan o'-wa-pi made by Standing Bear (Minneconjou, 1859–1933), a veteran of the Battle of the Greasy Grass, also known as the Battle of Little Bighorn. He created at least five large muslin paintings representing the battle, based on his own observations and the experiences of his peers. His daughter recalled how, after completing a painting, Standing Bear would invite guests to a feast and pipe ceremony to confirm the accuracy of his representations. Some of these important paintings ended up in museums in Chicago, Tulsa, Germany, South Dakota, and New York by means that erased their origins with Standing Bear. Reestablishing that connection waited on the considerable efforts of his great-grandson, the artist Arthur Amiotte, who only in the 1980s was able to recognize the paintings' stylistic connections to a series of drawings Standing Bear had produced for John Neihardt's book *Black Elk Speaks*.[28] The documentation, like that for Siyosapa's paintings, had been lost or neglected.

Lenders included two additional large o'-zan o'-wa-pi, along with Siyosapa's Sun Dance and horned thunderbird paintings, in the sale to Heye in 1909, but they remain unattributed to an individual artist. Hundreds of others are scattered throughout museum collections around the world. If the work of Siyosapa and Standing Bear is any indication, the paintings were produced with deliberation and care to communicate to everyone the artists' substantial cultural knowledge and experience. But without awareness of their authorship, they remain largely mute, unable to communicate their creators' intentions. Like messages in a bottle drifting at sea, they await discovery, and reconnection with their particular histories.

FROM PAST TO PRESENT

Viewed together, Plains narrative artworks of the past and present reflect a strong sense of cultural identity. Hallmarks of the style are events shown in sequence, representational figures, stylized symbols, and strong solid colors. As life on the plains changed, nineteenth-century artists used pictorial storytelling to record the past and preserve their cultures. Today's narrative artists—employing a wide array of approaches, subjects, and media—also express the resilience of their communities. Whether working 150 or five years ago, they have used the form to tell important stories about their personal and communal lives.

A winter count is an illustrated calendar history in which a drawing of an important or unusual event represents each year. The annual cycle is marked from winter to winter, hence the calendar's name. Each Plains community may have kept its own winter count. Most often, respected members of the community determined which event should represent the entire year. An artist-historian illustrated the event. Since winter counts can span several decades, usually more than one artist-historian contributed.

This winter count begins in 1798 and ends in 1902. The artists are unknown, but the Hunkpapa Lakota chief Long Soldier described the drawings for an interpreter. The calendar is known as the Long Soldier Winter Count. The first year appears in the upper left corner. Subsequent years move inward in a clockwise direction.

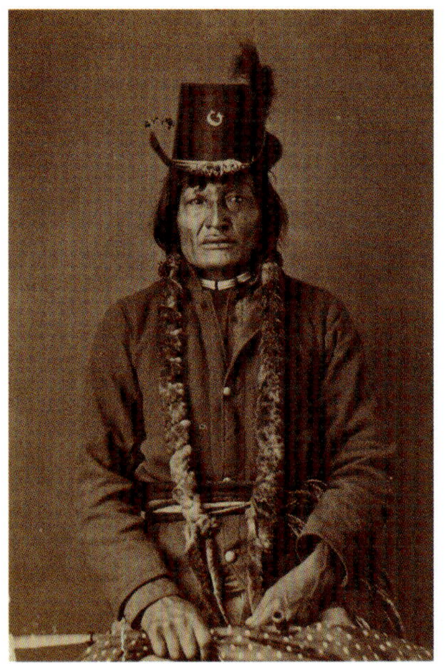

Long Soldier, ca. 1877. Photo by Orlando Scott Goff. P17005

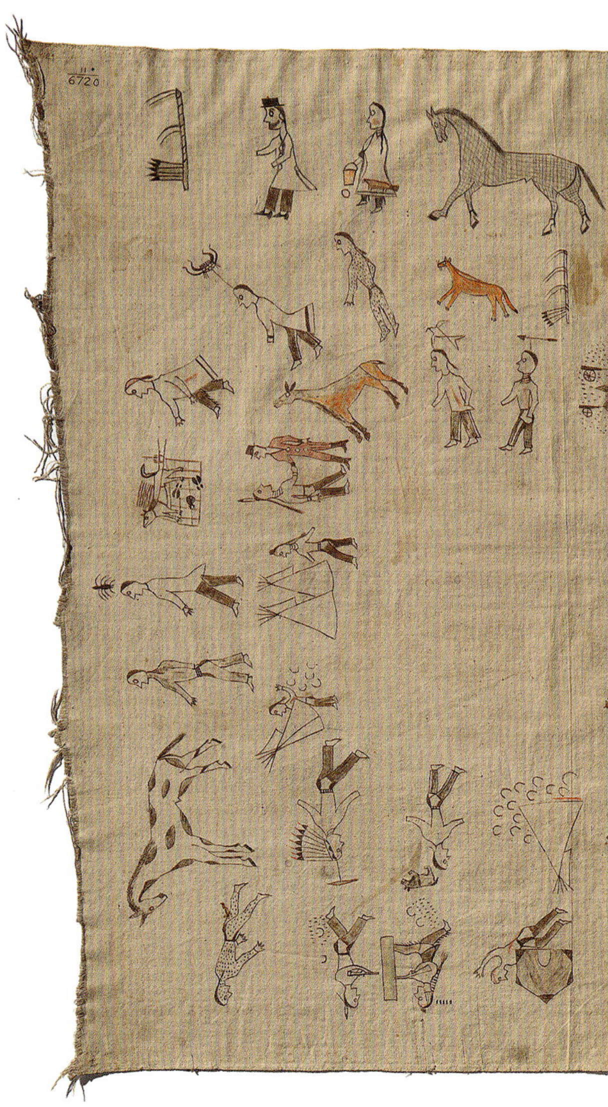

Long Soldier Winter Count, ca. 1902. Artists unknown. North Dakota. Muslin, paint; 88 × 181 cm. 11/6720

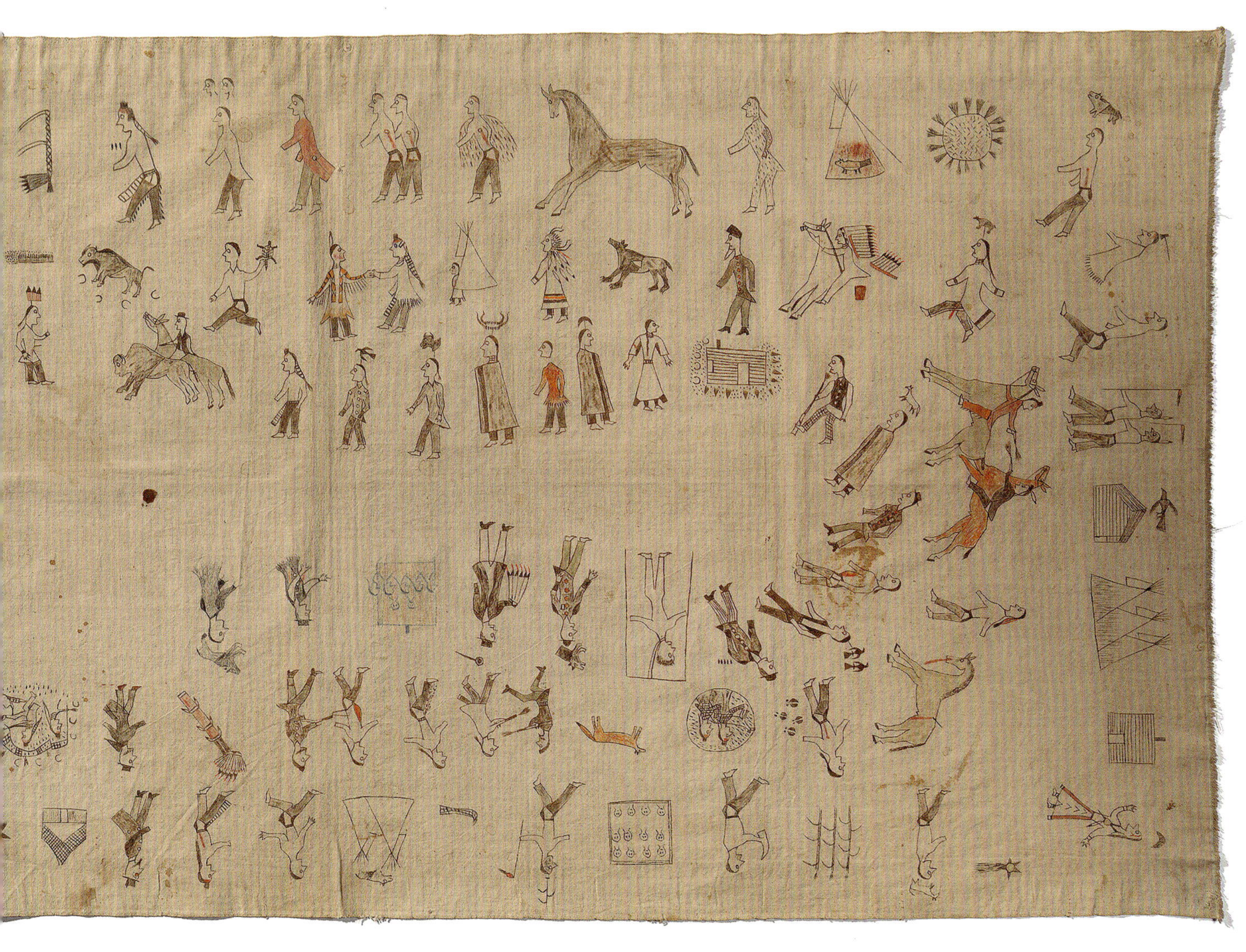

In his work, Martin E. Red Bear (Oglala/Sicangu Lakota) seeks to integrate contemporary life with his tribal identity. This winter-count calendar, a modern version of a Plains traditional method of recording history, is no exception. Here, Red Bear illustrates significant events from 1980 to 2004. Beginning in the lower right corner, the illustrations for each year can be read from right to left and then left to right, in alternating rows.

Events shown in winter counts do not necessarily date to the same month each year. Some recall personal occasions, such as the illustration here for 1983, which shows Red Bear and his family watching a lunar eclipse. Other drawings relate to significant community events, such as President Bill Clinton's 1999 visit to the Pine Ridge Reservation. ◊

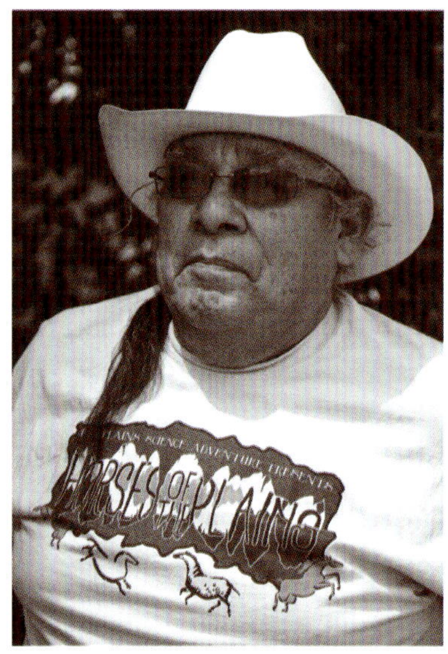

Martin E. Red Bear, 2015. Photo by NMAI staff

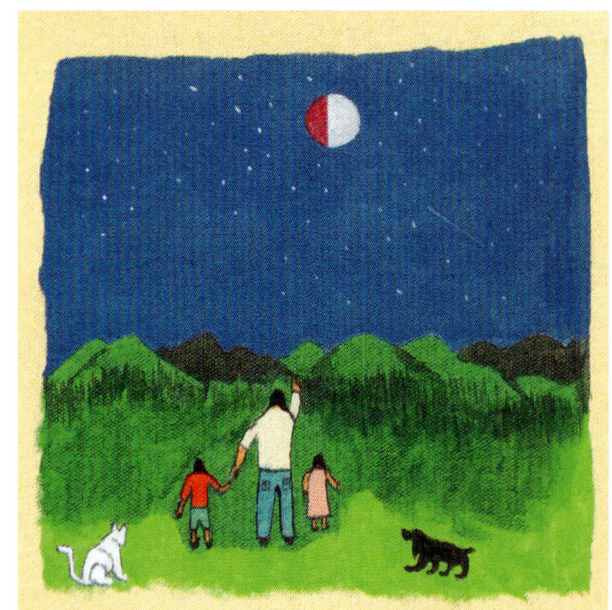

Martin E. Red Bear (Oglala/Sicangu Lakota, b. 1947). *Red Bear's Winter Count* (detail), 2004. Canvas, acrylic paint; 116.5 × 116 cm. 26/8020

Red Bear, his children, and their pets watch a lunar eclipse.

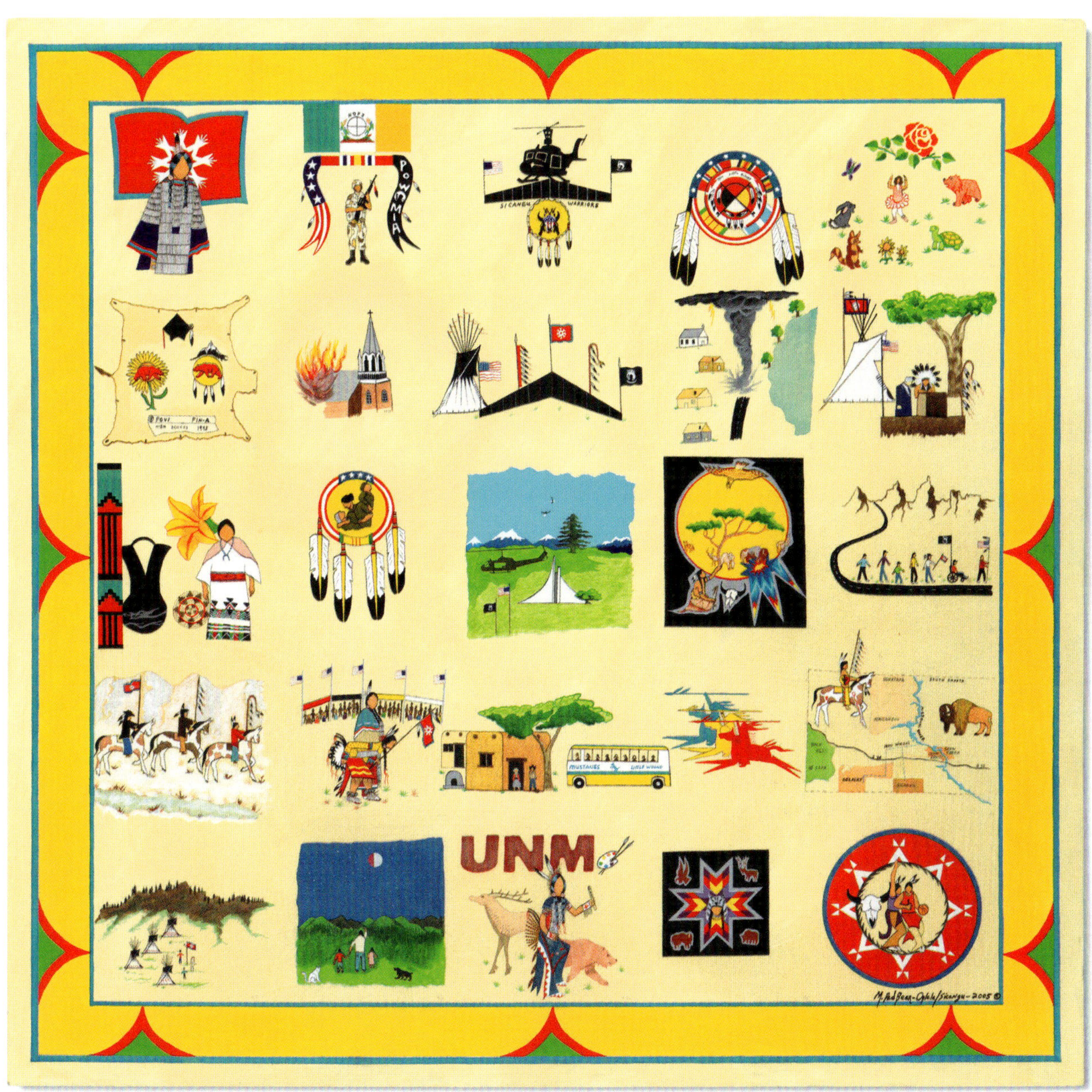

Martin E. Red Bear (Oglala/Sicangu Lakota, b. 1947). *Red Bear's Winter Count*, 2004. Canvas, acrylic paint; 116.5 × 116 cm. 26/8020

This elkskin robe records the war honors of Mountain Chief, a Piikuni, or Blackfeet, chief. His accomplishments are among those most often depicted on Plains robes and panels. Mountain Chief is known to have led battles against Sioux, A'aninin, Cree, and Assiniboine enemies. As shown on this robe, he led horse raids and war parties against his enemies and killed bears (painted in blue in the lower left corner). Each inverted U-shape indicates a war party effort. The nearby crescent symbols with an S-shape extending downward from the center record Mountain Chief's success as a scout discovering enemy camps.

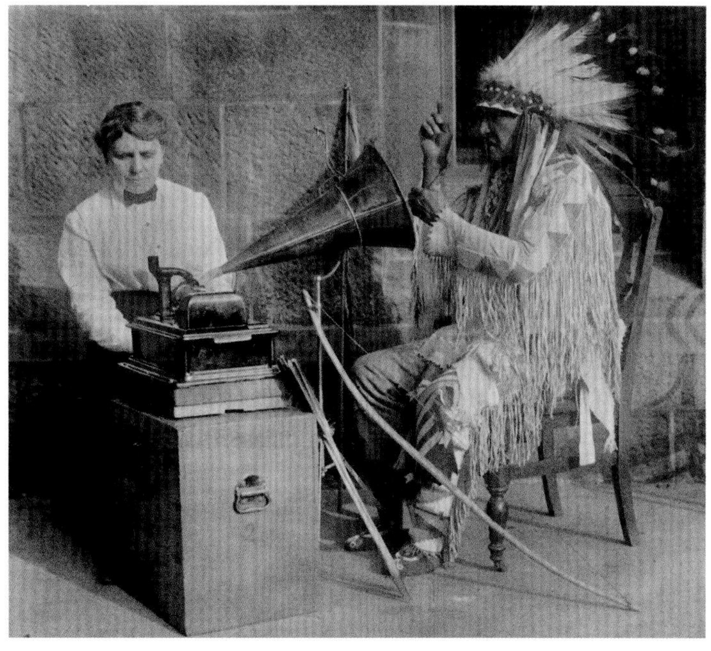

Frances Densmore records Chief Mountain Chief for the Bureau of American Ethnology, 1916. Photo by Harris & Ewing

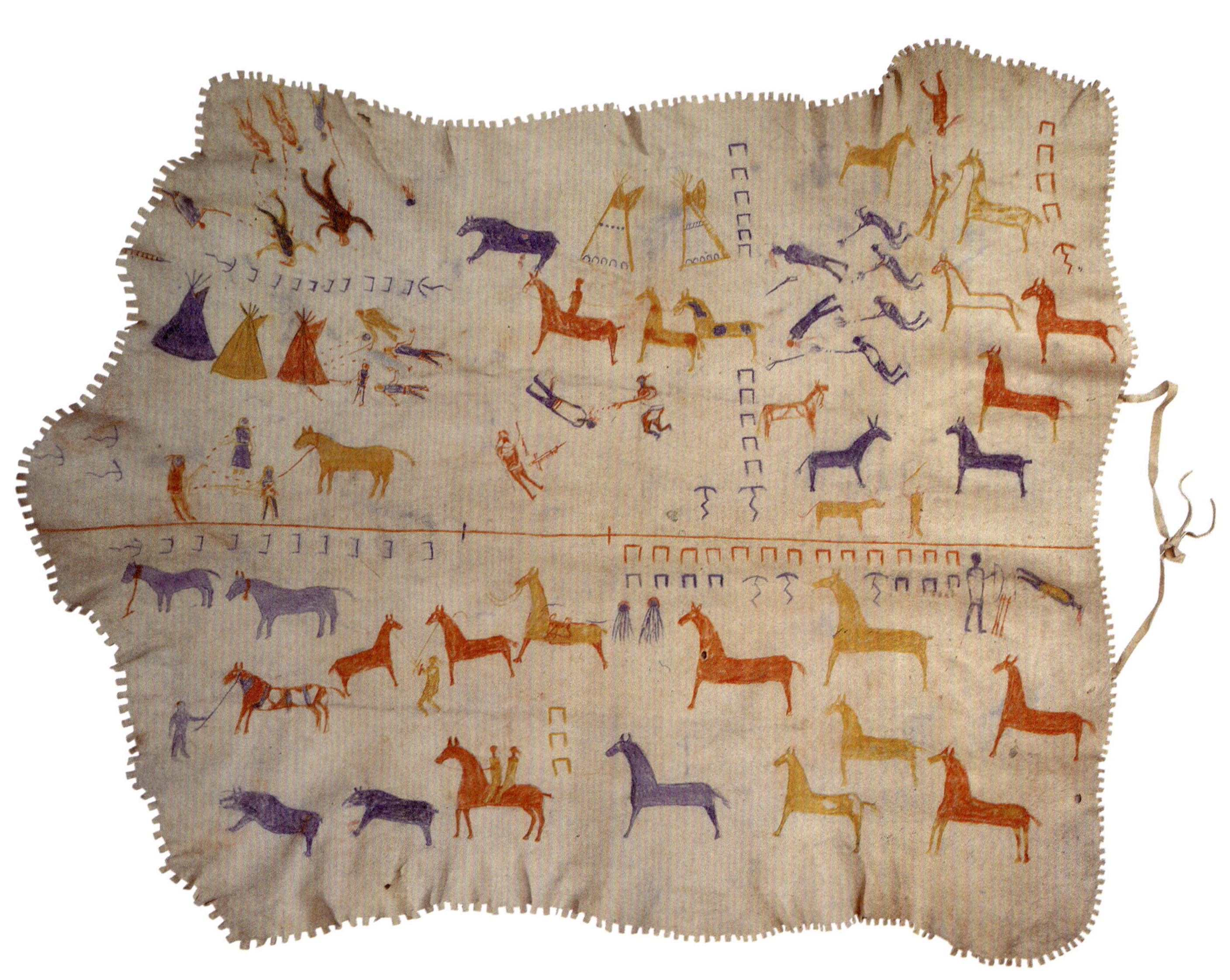

Elkskin robe, ca. 1920. Attributed to James White Calf (Piikuni [Blackfeet], ca. 1860–1969). Elkhide, paint; 173 × 155 × 5.5 cm. 22/1878

Artist David Dragonfly painted this elkhide with six scenes of war deeds achieved by his great-grandfather Little Calf. Little Calf was the head chief of the Piikuni, or Blackfeet, in the mid-1800s. Born in Kalispell, Montana, and raised on the Blackfeet Reservation, Dragonfly often draws upon his Blackfeet and Assiniboine heritage in his designs. ◊

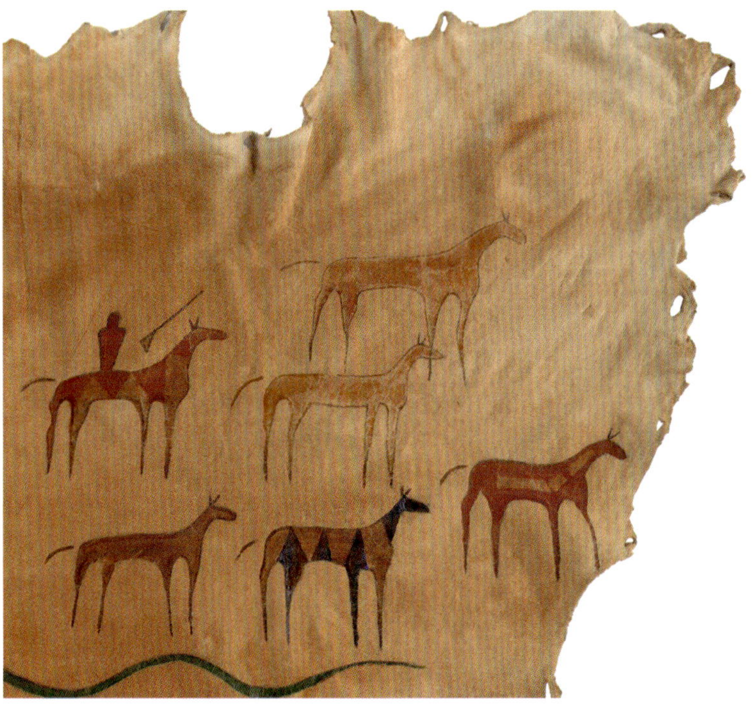

David Dragonfly (Blackfeet/Assiniboine, b. 1956). *Little Calf's War Record* (detail), 2010. Smoked elkhide, earth paints; 193.5 × 161.6 cm. 26/8014

Little Calf captures five enemy horses.

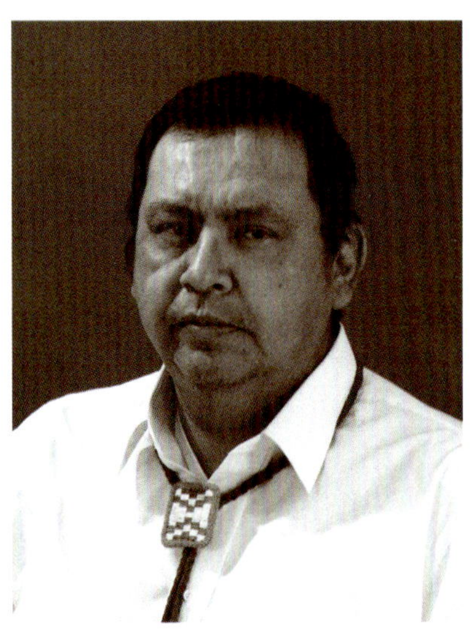

David Dragonfly, 2012. Photo by Angelica Harden Norman

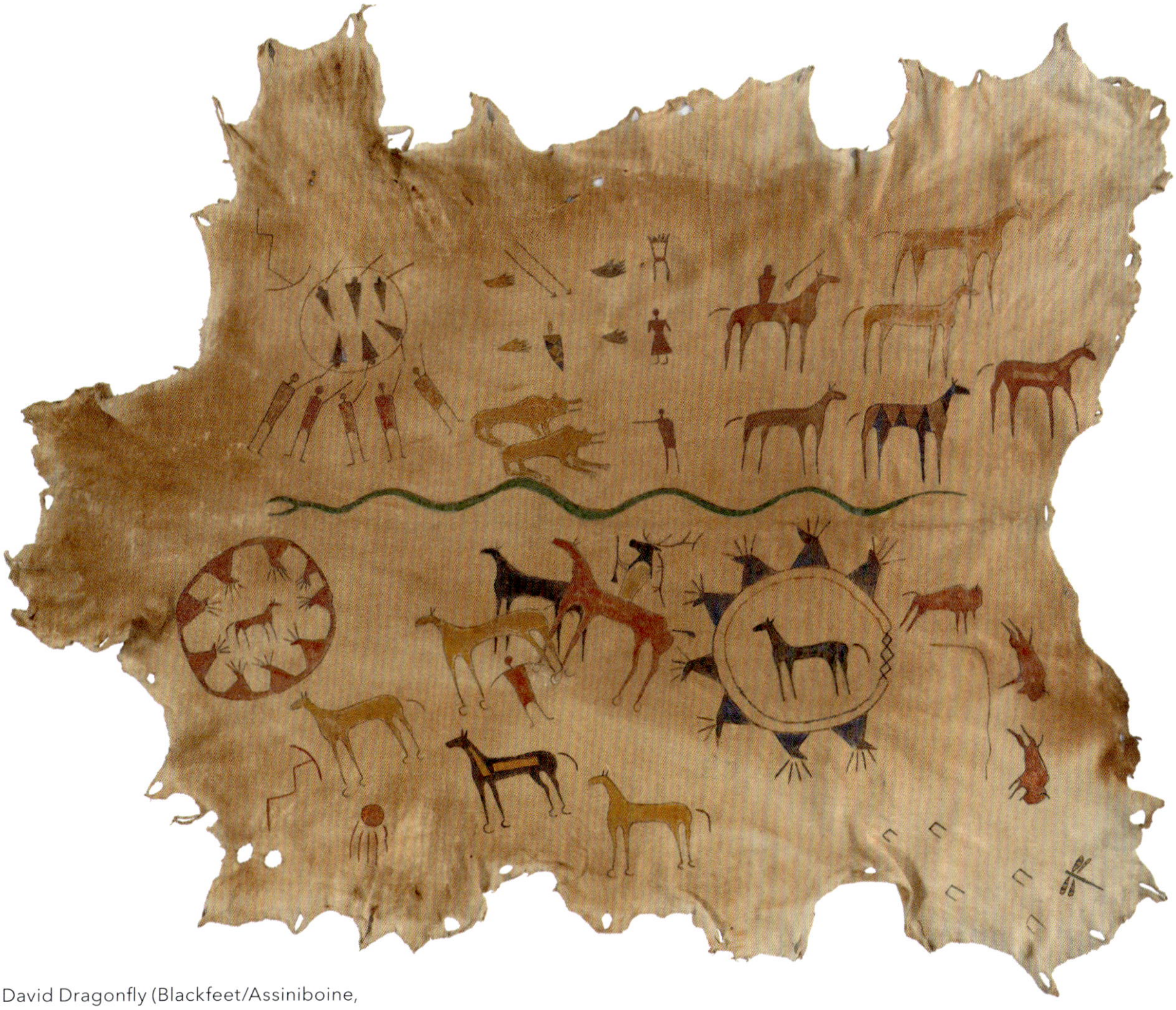

David Dragonfly (Blackfeet/Assiniboine, b. 1956). *Little Calf's War Record*, 2010. Smoked elkhide, earth paints; 193.5 × 161.6 cm. 26/8014

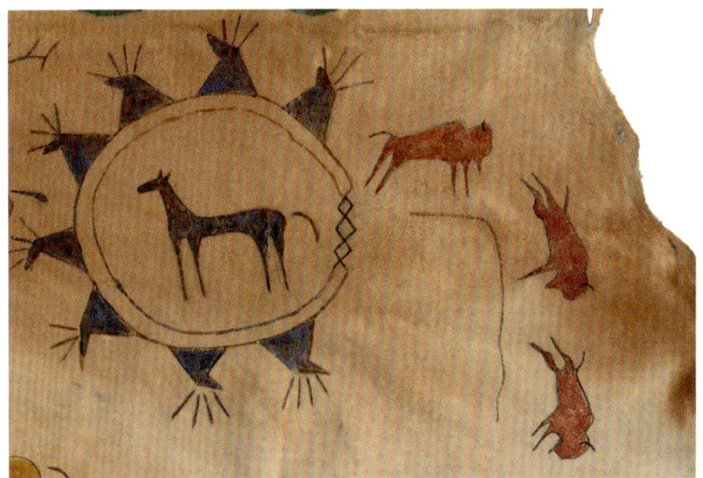

David Dragonfly (Blackfeet/Assiniboine, b. 1956). *Little Calf's War Record* (detail), 2010. Smoked elkhide, earth paints; 193.5 × 161.6 cm. 26/8014

Buffalo are driven over a cliff during a hunt. The best buffalo-hunting horses were kept in the center of the camp.

CHILD'S PLAY

Lakota children likely used this model tipi as a toy. Battle scenes decorate it, just as they would a full-sized painted tipi. The scenes depicted here may feature a close relative of the child for whom the toy was created.

Lakota painted model tipi, ca. 1890. North Dakota or South Dakota. Hide, wood, porcupine quills, tin cones, feathers, horsehair, paint, sinew, twine; 72 × diam. 56 cm. 2/9535

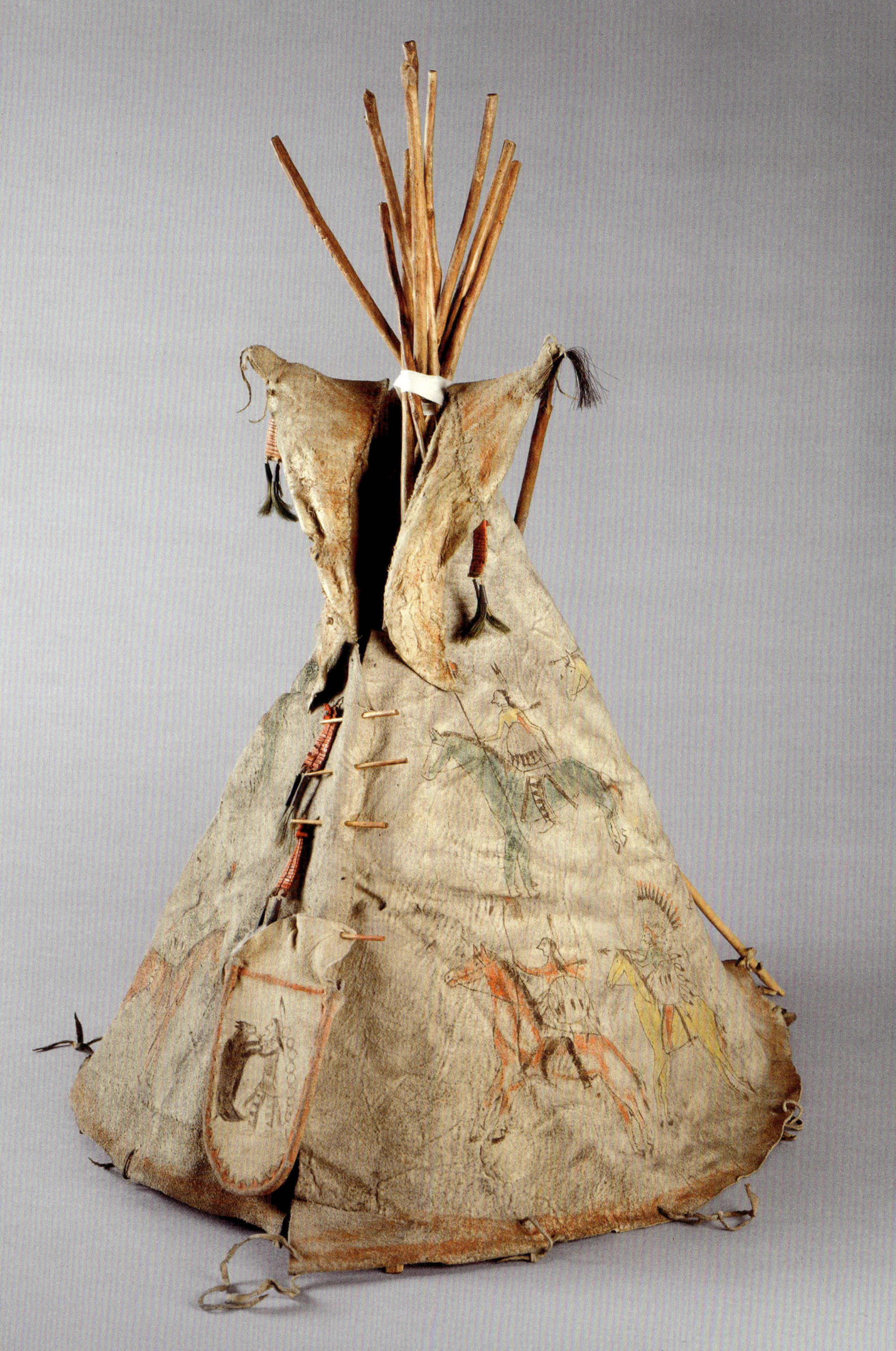

As an artist who experiments with mixed media, James Yellowhawk (Cheyenne River Lakota) was attracted to this mid-1900s Coleman model tent, which he saw in an antique shop. "I had this idea that it would be really nice to carry something from the old again to the new . . . to take designs from an old tipi and put them on a new, contemporary tent," he says. The illustrations tell the story of a buffalo hunt, with the top depicting the night sky. ◊

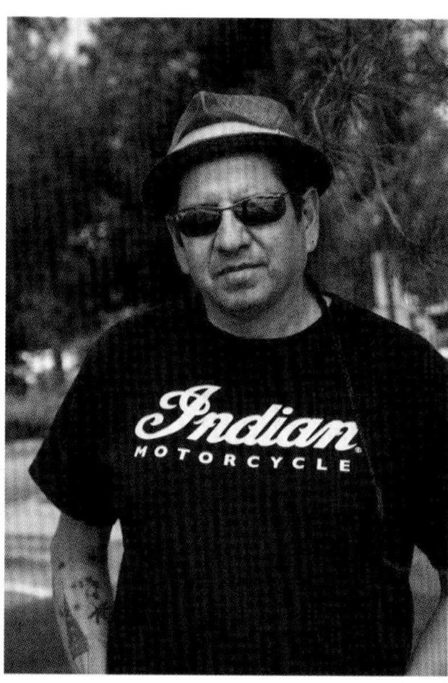

James Yellowhawk, 2015. Photo by NMAI staff

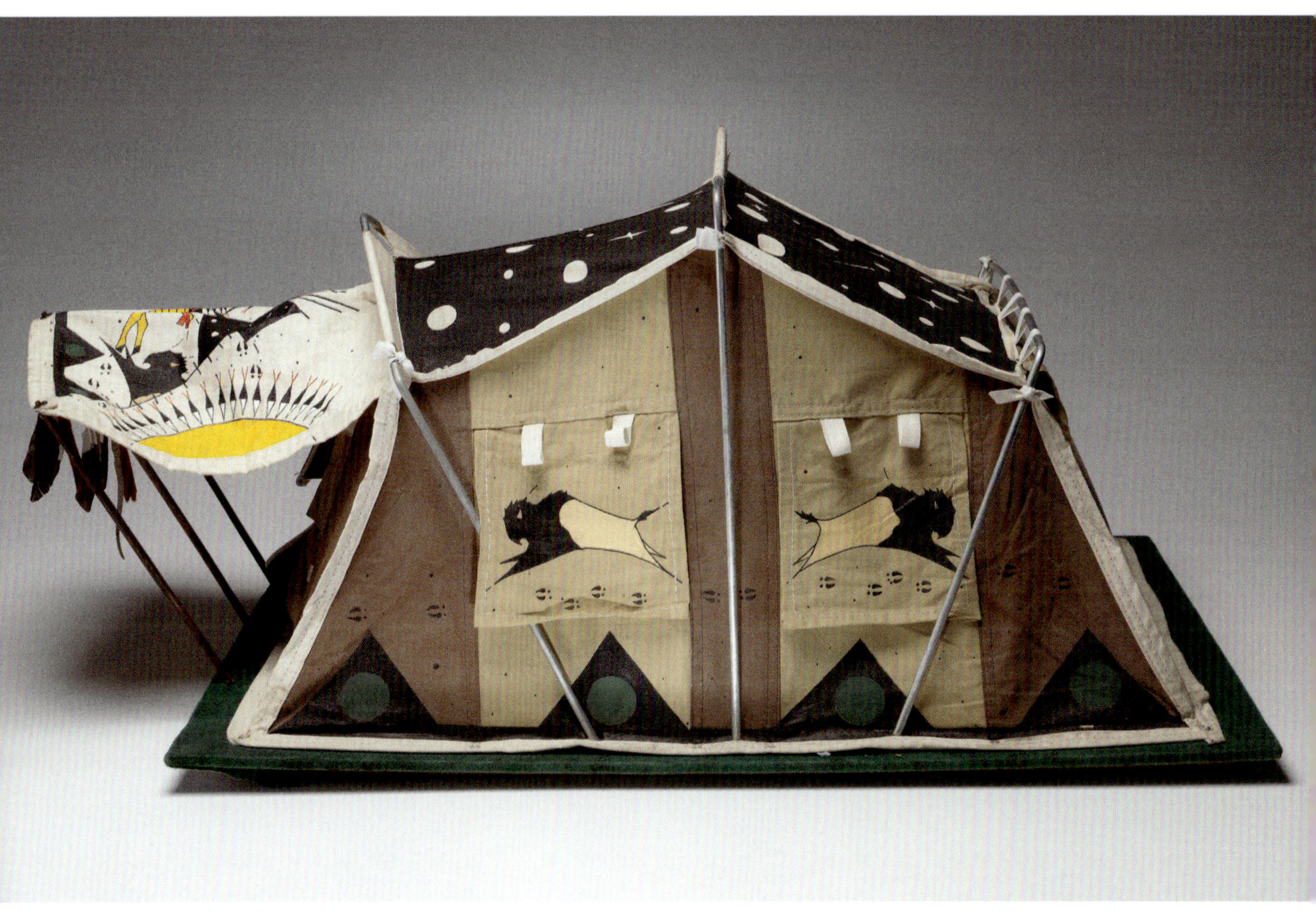

James Yellowhawk (Cheyenne River Lakota, b. 1958). *Wacipi Oti*, 2012. Cotton cloth, fabric webbing, aluminum, metal, zipper, thread, hide, wool felt, feathers, wood, velveteen, cotton tape, ink, acrylic paint; height 41 × width 87 × depth 51 cm. 26/9167

Only women whose relatives had been killed in battle could wear these decorated dresses. This dress was probably painted by Running Antelope. It depicts exploits in Hunkpapa Lakota battles with the Arikara. Dresses of this type are rare. A similar dress can be seen in this photograph of Ini'laon'win, or Silent Woman. Her younger brother was killed by the Apsáalooke (Crow).

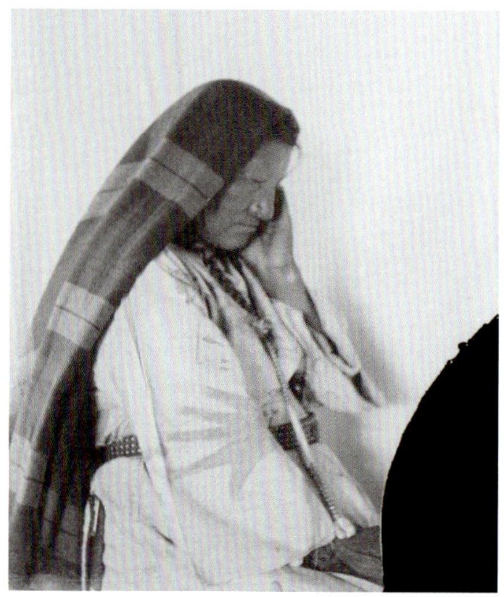

Ini'laon'win, or Silent Woman, 1913. Photo by Frances Densmore. National Anthropological Archives, Smithsonian Institution 03373E

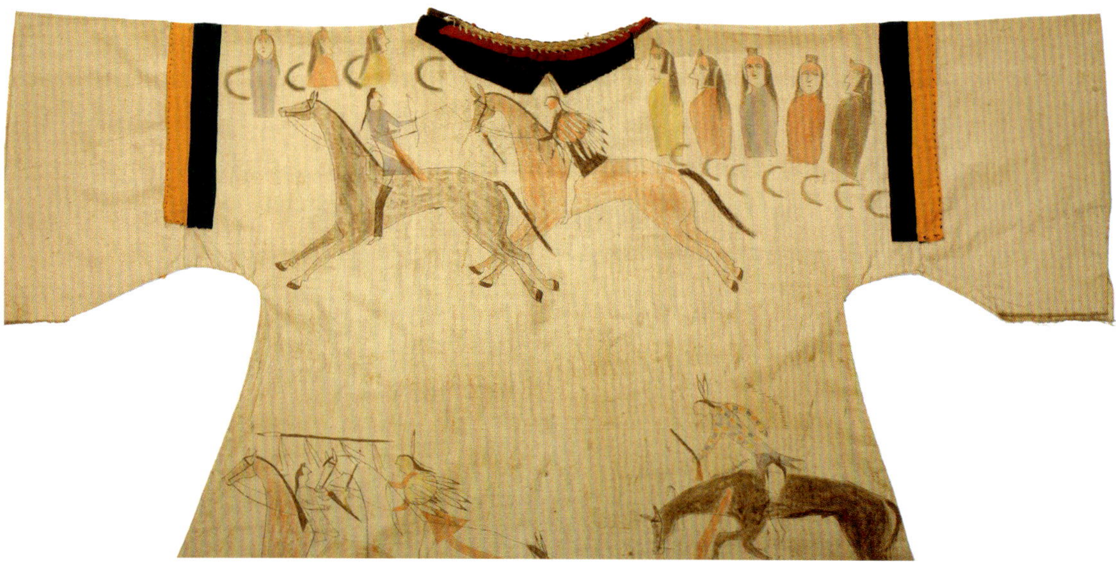

Hunkpapa Lakota dress (detail from front of dress), ca. 1880. North Dakota or South Dakota. Muslin, wool cloth, silk ribbon, thread, paint; 141.5 × 128.4 cm. 21/3665

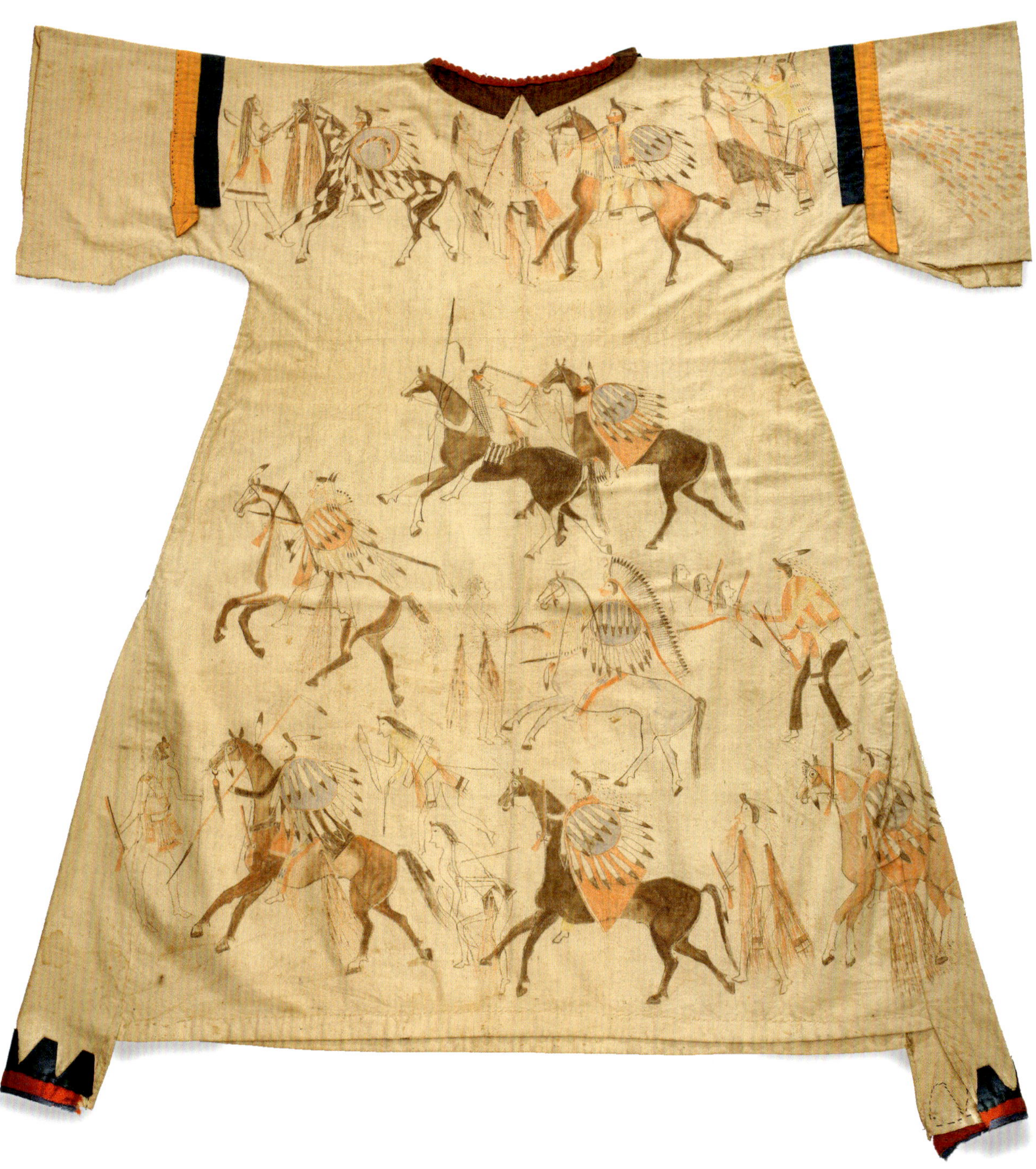

Hunkpapa Lakota dress (back), ca. 1880. North Dakota or South Dakota. Muslin, wool cloth, silk ribbon, thread, paint; 141.5 × 128.4 cm. 21/3665

Lauren Good Day (Arikara/Hidatsa/Blackfeet/Plains Cree) painted this dress to honor the achievements of her late grandfather Emery Good Bird Sr., or Blue Bird. "My grandfather was a real culture bearer, and he made a big impact on my life," she says. In illustrating the dress, she is reviving a traditional art that honors the war deeds of male relatives.

Around the bottom portion of the dress are stories that relate to Blue Bird's time in the Vietnam War. Before he deployed, his father invited Chief Drags Wolf to their house. The chief presented Blue Bird with a special feather, a medicine plume, to protect him. He kept it in his helmet. One day, under heavy fire, he lost both helmet and feather.

Blue Bird wrote to his father, explaining what had happened. Blue Bird's father wrote back to tell his son that he already knew about the lost plume. Chief Drags Wolf, who by then had passed away, had appeared to him in a dream. In the dream, he returned the feather to Blue Bird's father, saying that it had come back to the tribe and his son also would come home.

Later, Blue Bird gifted the name of his story, "Plume Comes Home," to one of his great-grandsons. ◊

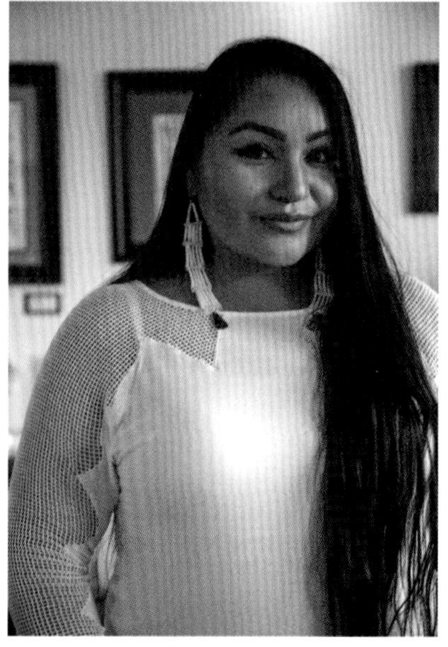

Lauren Good Day, 2015. Photo by NMAI staff

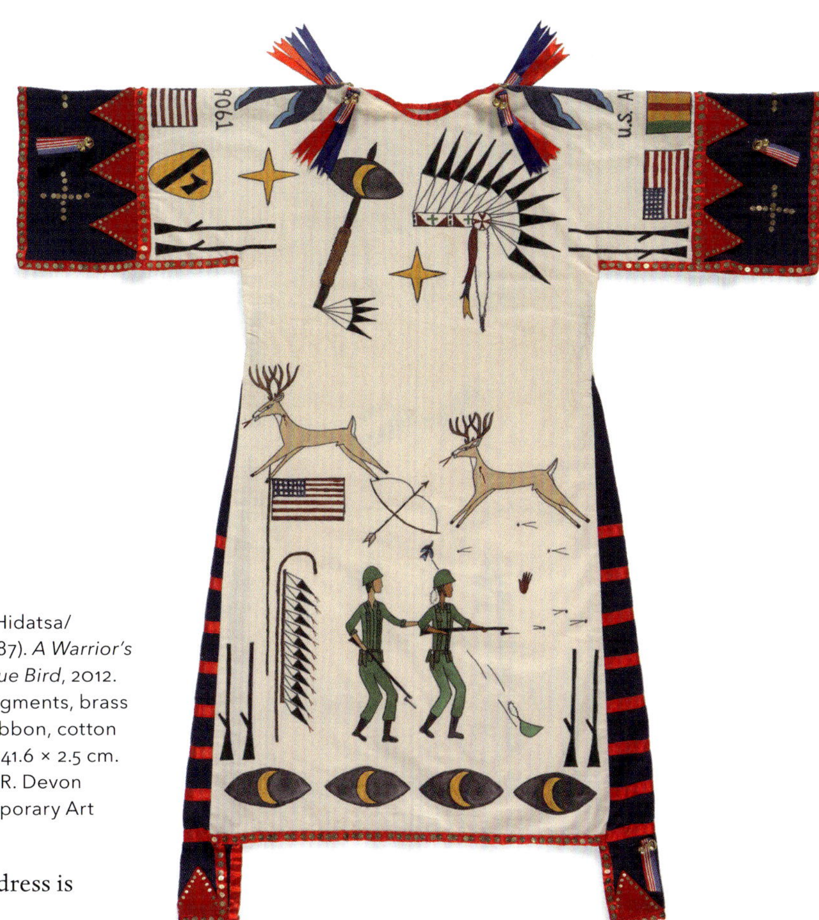

Lauren Good Day (Arikara/Hidatsa/Blackfeet/Plains Cree, b. 1987). *A Warrior's Story, Honoring Grandpa Blue Bird*, 2012. Muslin, dyed wool fabric, pigments, brass sequins, brass bells, satin ribbon, cotton thread, acrylic sinew; 151 × 141.6 × 2.5 cm. Purchase supported by the R. Devon Hutchins Memorial Contemporary Art Fund. 26/8817

The reverse side of the dress is pictured on page 116.

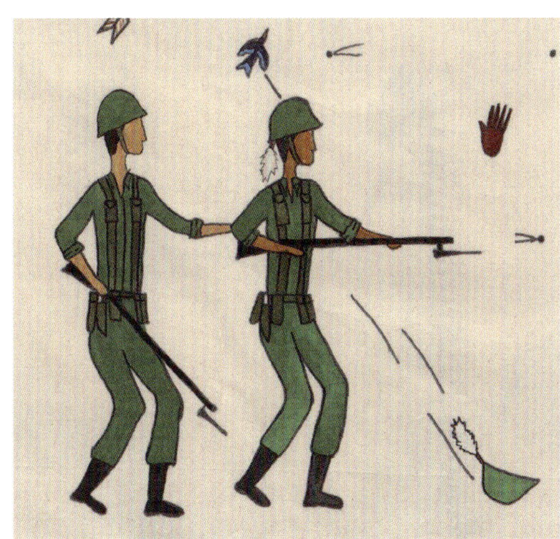

(detail) Blue Bird loses his helmet and medicine plume in battle. The red hand near him shows he was wounded.

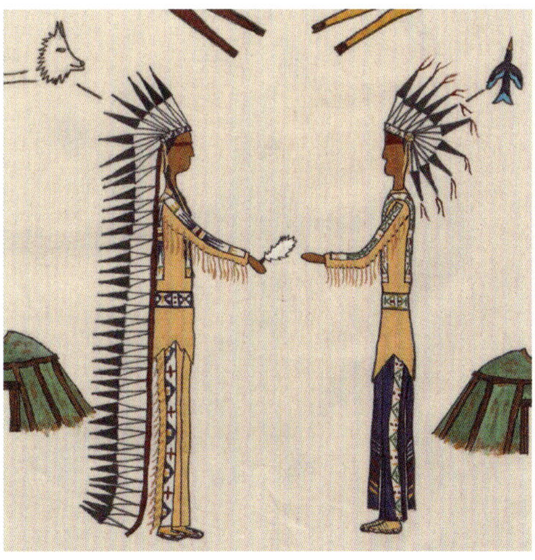

(detail from reverse side of dress) Chief Drags Wolf visits Blue Bird's father in a dream to return the lost medicine plume.

AN ENDURING TRADITION

Southern Plains Narrative Art, Fort Marion, and the Legacies of Bear's Heart, Zotom, and Sherman Chaddlesone

Michael Paul Jordan

Drawings produced by Cheyenne, Arapaho, and Kiowa artists imprisoned at Fort Marion in St. Augustine, Florida, between 1875 and 1878 are among the best-known examples of Southern Plains narrative art. These warrior-artists, however, were part of a longstanding artistic tradition. Beginning in the 1830s and 1840s, if not earlier, Southern Cheyenne and Kiowa men, like warriors in other Plains Native nations, celebrated their bravery and martial prowess in hide paintings that depicted their exploits. When paper and colored pencils became more widely available, artists adopted these new media, filling the pages of bound volumes with scenes of combat and courtship.[1] These drawings on paper are frequently referred to as ledger art, as some of them appeared on the lined pages of account books.[2] Inspired by the work of the Fort Marion prisoners and others, contemporary artist Sherman Chaddlesone (Kiowa, 1947–2013) helped revive this artistic tradition. Developing his own version of the ledger art style, Chaddlesone created drawings and paintings that celebrated the culture and history of his people.

SOUTHERN PLAINS ART FROM FORT MARION

In 1875, following the end of the Red River War, seventy-two members of Southern Plains nations were exiled to Fort Marion. During their incarceration, the Kiowa, Cheyenne, and Arapaho prisoners created drawings chronicling their experiences in Florida as well as their lives on the southern plains. Since the 1970s, their work

Bear's Heart (Southern Cheyenne, 1851–1882). *Indian Guard Ft. Marion – Marching On.* From Bear's Heart's drawing book, ca. 1875. Paper, graphite, colored pencil, ink; 17 × 23 cm. 20/6231

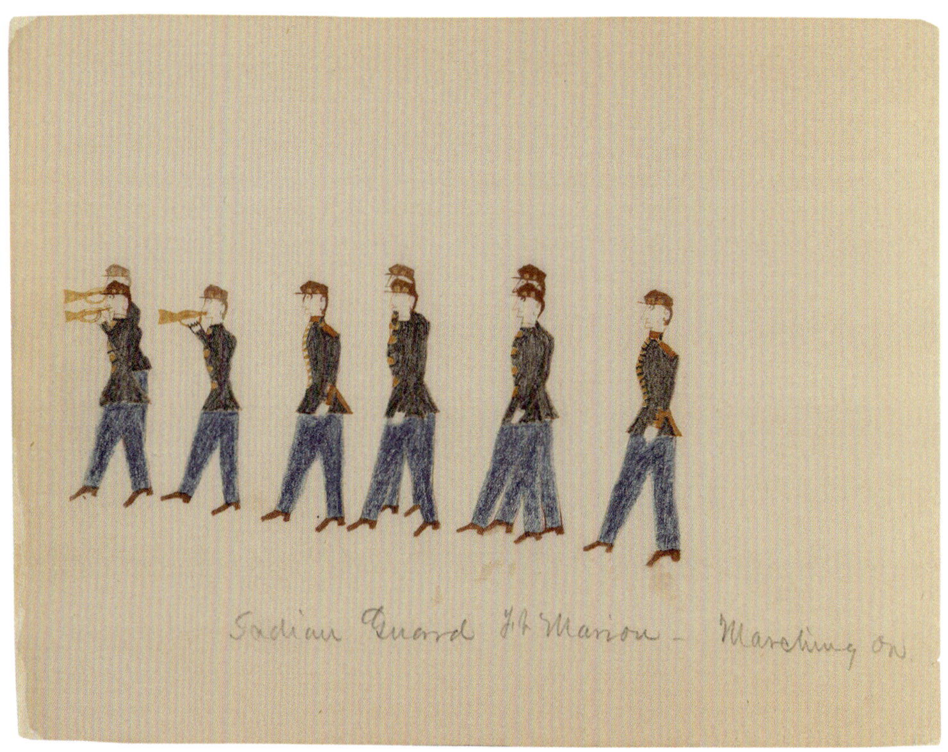

has attracted a tremendous amount of scholarly interest. The National Museum of the American Indian (NMAI) is fortunate to have in its collection two books of the drawings created at Fort Marion. The books are attributed to Zotom (Kiowa, 1853–1913) and Bear's Heart (Southern Cheyenne, 1851–1882). The set of drawings attributed to Zotom, however, includes a two-page drawing of the Maussaum, or Animal Dance, a Cheyenne religious rite. Almost certainly, a Southern Cheyenne artist created this particular drawing.

The prisoners began producing drawings shortly after their arrival at Fort Marion in May 1875. Lieutenant Richard H. Pratt, the army officer in charge of the prisoners, encouraged this activity, providing them with sketchbooks, colored pencils, and other supplies. The artists earned money by selling their art to tourists who visited the fort. In addition, Pratt bestowed bound volumes of the prisoners' drawings on prominent government officials and philanthropists whom he hoped would support his work at Fort Marion.

INSIDE THE PRISON WALLS: DOCUMENTING THE FORCES OF ASSIMILATION

Pratt, an ardent proponent of cultural assimilation, sought to eradicate Native American cultural practices. Through education and religious indoctrination, he hoped to transform the Fort Marion prisoners into Christian farmers and tradesmen. In 1892, Pratt reflected on the educational philosophy that had guided him at Fort Marion, stating that his goal was to "kill the Indian . . . and save the man."[3]

In several drawings, Bear's Heart documented the assimilationist forces Pratt and others brought to bear. One of them depicts what appears to be a formation of soldiers, but the title, *Indian Guard Ft. Marion – Marching On*, reveals that the uniformed men are prisoners rather than soldiers. Soon after the prisoners arrived at the fort, Pratt sought to transform their physical appearance, ordering that their hair be cut short and that they be clothed in military uniforms.[4] One of the buglers depicted in the drawing is most assuredly the Kiowa artist Zotom. When Pratt organized the prisoners into a military company, he appointed Zotom to serve as a bugler.[5]

Seeking to instill military discipline, Pratt required the men to drill and perform calisthenics. He also conducted regular military inspections.[6] Bear's Heart depicted such an inspection in at least two of his drawings. In the one included in the book at NMAI, an officer wearing a dress uniform, likely Pratt, reviews the assembled prisoners, who stand at attention. Zotom also drew prisoners standing in formation during inspections.[7]

Several of Bear's Heart's drawings depict some of the white American activists who eagerly volunteered to assist with the prisoners' education and assimilation. One features Episcopal bishop Henry B. Whipple addressing the prisoners, while a seated army officer, presumably Pratt, looks on. Whipple, a Minnesotan, spent the winter of 1875–76 in St. Augustine. He taught the prisoners twice a week and led religious services on Sundays.[8] Given the number of prisoners shown in the drawing, Whipple is likely delivering a sermon rather than a classroom lecture.

In another drawing, Bear's Heart provides a glimpse inside one of Fort Marion's classrooms. The prisoners, seated on benches, listen attentively as a teacher

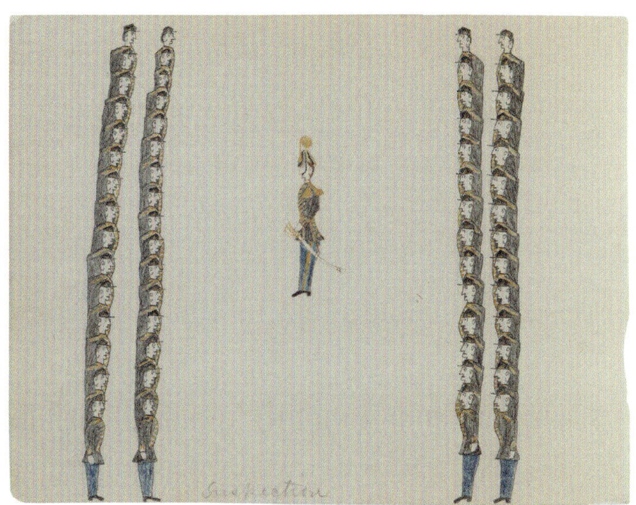

Bear's Heart (Southern Cheyenne, 1851–1882). *Inspection.* From Bear's Heart's drawing book, ca. 1875. Paper, graphite, colored pencil, ink; 17 × 23 cm. 20/6231

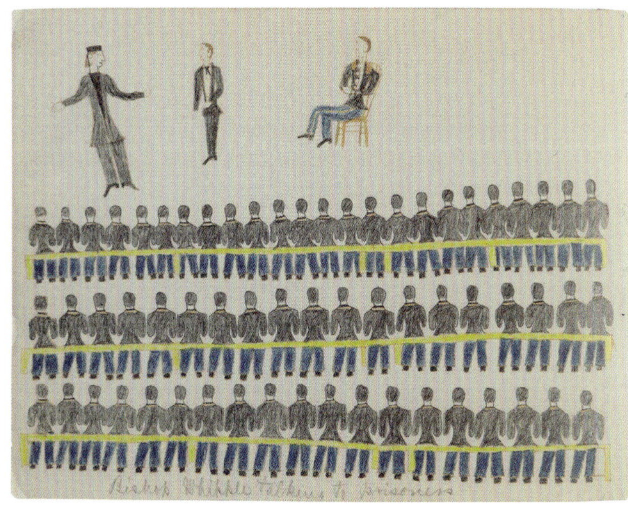

Bear's Heart (Southern Cheyenne, 1851–1882). *Bishop Whipple Talking to Prisoners.* From Bear's Heart's drawing book, ca. 1875. Paper, graphite, colored pencil, ink; 17 × 23 cm. 20/6231

Bear's Heart (Southern Cheyenne, 1851–1882). *Miss Nannie Burts Class of Indian Prisoners Ft. Marion.* From Bear's Heart's drawing book, ca. 1875. Paper, graphite, colored pencil, ink; 17 × 23 cm. 20/6231

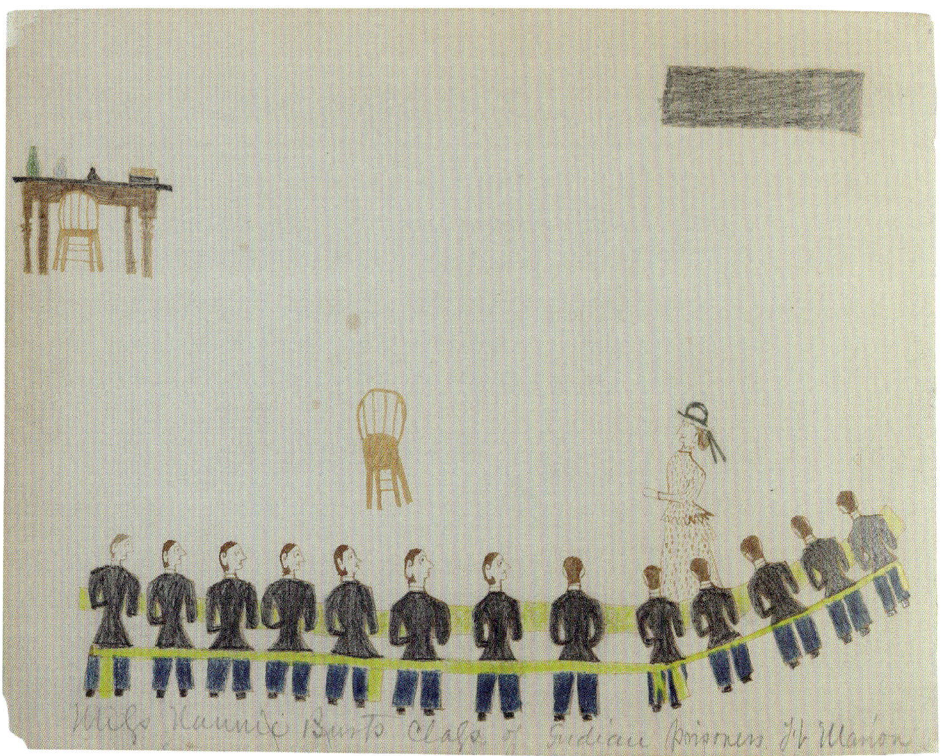

named Nannie Burt lectures, her desk and a blackboard visible in the background. Burt was one of several women who volunteered as an instructor at Fort Marion. Under their tutelage, Bear's Heart and his fellow prisoners completed lessons in spelling, grammar, phonetics, and handwriting as well as geography and arithmetic. Eventually, the prisoners grew proficient enough in the English language that translators were no longer required.[9] Indeed, Bear's Heart's signature on the first page of his drawing book testifies to his mastery of an alien language and writing system. This classroom drawing is one of several created by Fort Marion artists that depict similar scenes.[10]

OUTSIDE THE PRISON WALLS: DEPICTIONS OF LEISURE ACTIVITIES

In contrast to scenes of military inspections and classroom instruction, others portray the leisure activities in which the prisoners were permitted to engage. In one drawing, Bear's Heart depicts a shark-fishing expedition. Several prisoners pull the shark onto the beach, while another man moves in with an axe to dispatch it. The civilian helping to land the shark is likely Mr. Pacetti, a local hired guide. On one expedition, the prisoners caught five sharks, which they called water buffalo. One shark weighed an estimated 1,200 pounds.[11] For men accustomed to pursuing bison and pronghorn, shark fishing provided a welcome diversion from the monotony of prison life.

The Fort Marion artists evinced a great deal of interest in boats and sailing. In *Going to Camp*, Bear's Heart depicts nineteen prisoners and an officer in a sailboat piloted by a civilian. The boat appears to be the same one shown in the shark-fishing scene, which, according to the inscription, depicts an event that transpired in July 1875. If so, *Going to Camp* likely records one of the prisoners' first times aboard a sailboat. A drawing by Zotom titled *Boating St. Augustine* features seven people aboard a sailboat. They are not wearing military uniforms and may not be prisoners. In any case, many of the men eventually learned to sail. They had access to vessels, and sailing became a popular pastime. The prisoners even operated a charter business, offering sailing excursions to tourists.[12]

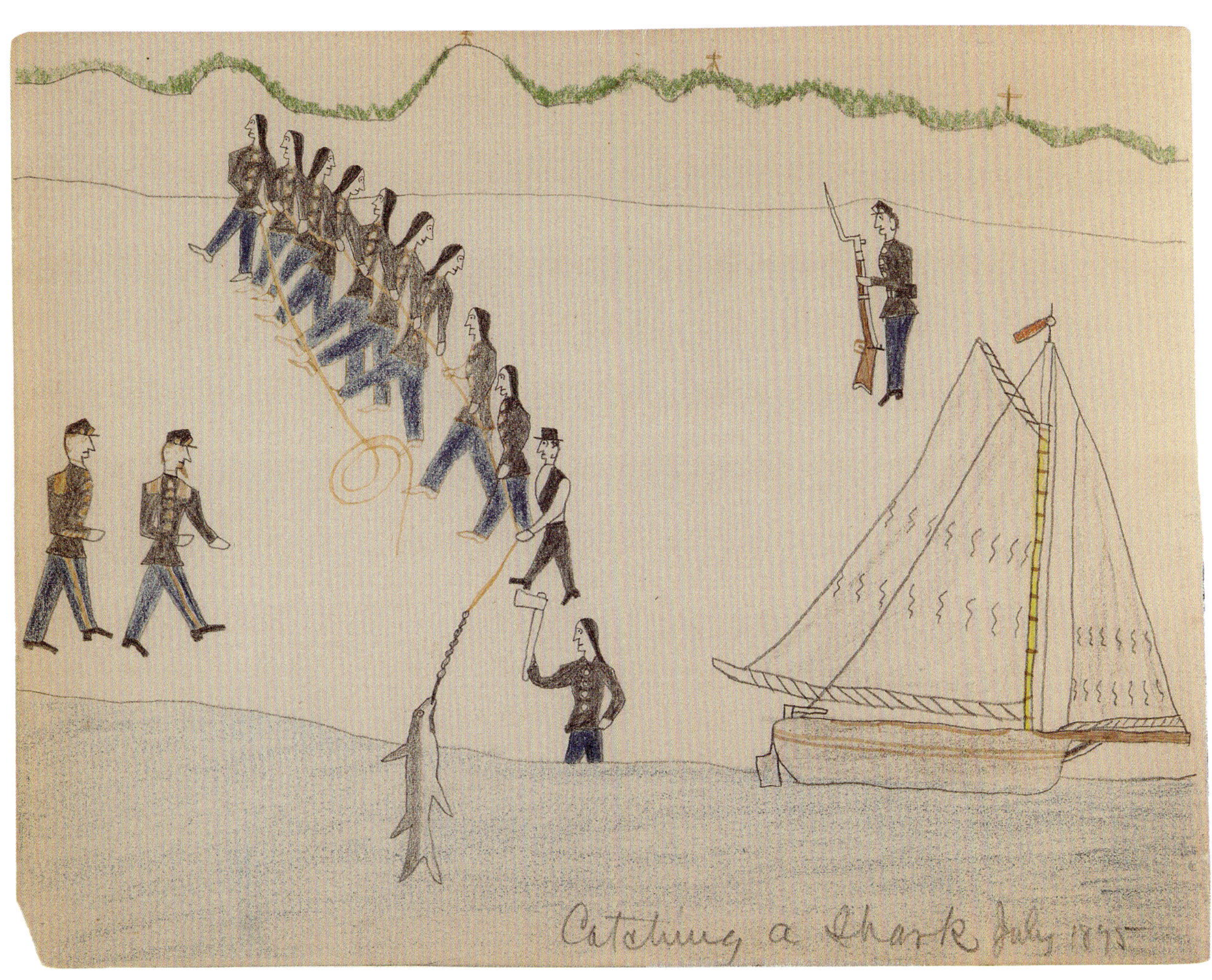

Bear's Heart (Southern Cheyenne, 1851–1882). *Catching a Shark July 1875*. From Bear's Heart's drawing book, ca. 1875. Paper, graphite, colored pencil, ink; 17 × 23 cm. 20/6231

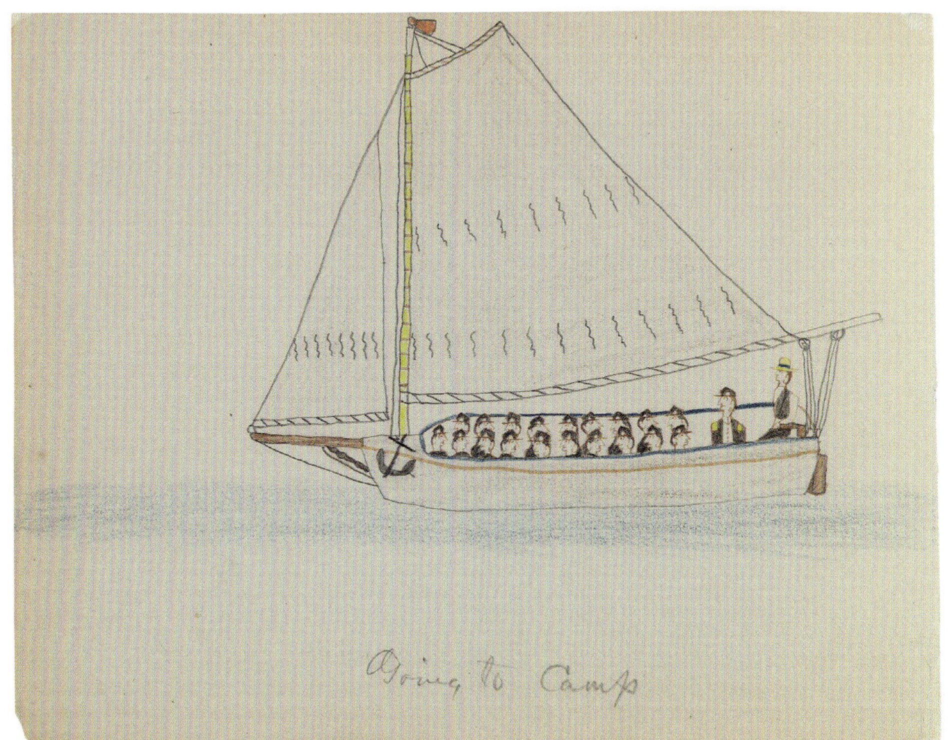

Bear's Heart (Southern Cheyenne, 1851–1882). *Going to Camp.* From Bear's Heart's drawing book, ca. 1875. Paper, graphite, colored pencil, ink; 17 × 23 cm. 20/6231

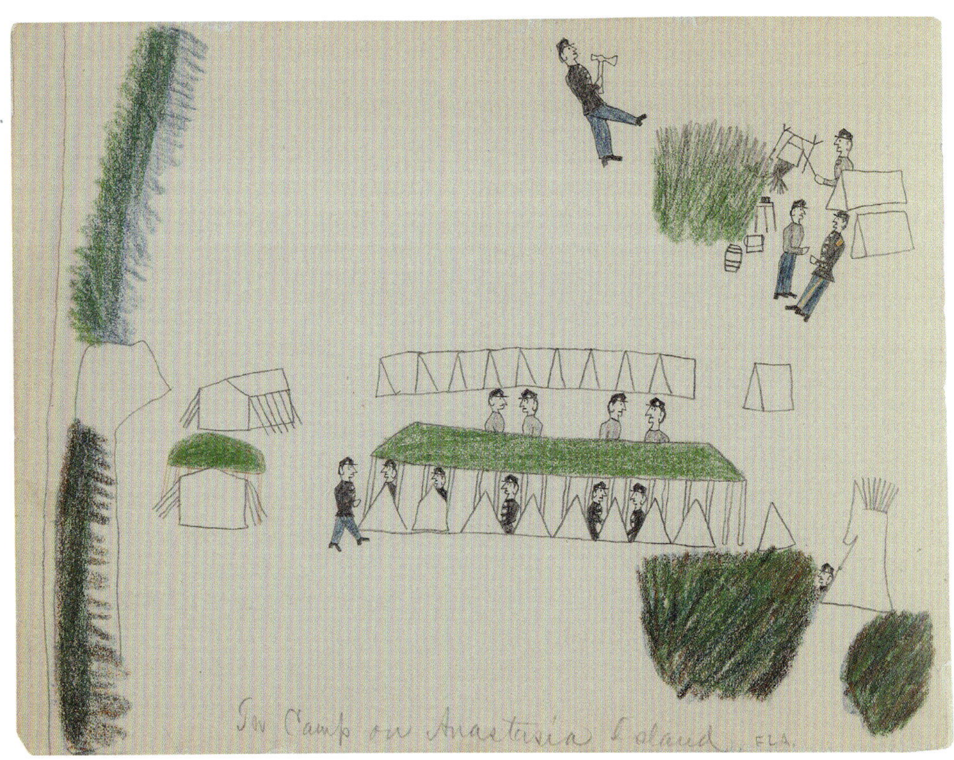

Bear's Heart (Southern Cheyenne, 1851–1882). *In Camp on Anastasia Island FLA.* From Bear's Heart's drawing book, ca. 1875. Paper, graphite, colored pencil, ink; 17 × 23 cm. 20/6231

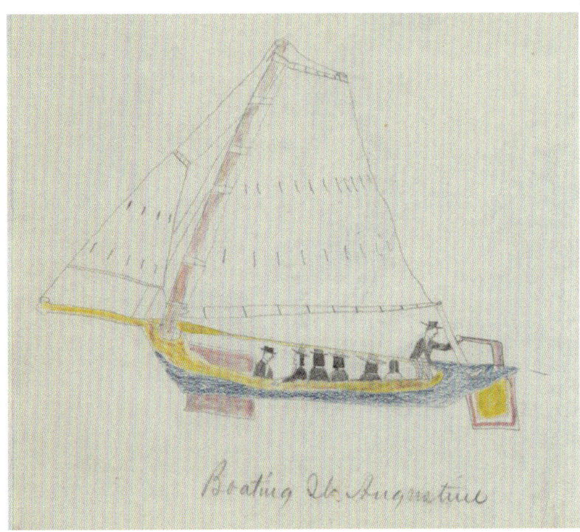

Zotom (Kiowa, 1853–1913). *Boating St. Augustine* (detail). From Zotom's drawing book, ca. 1875. Paper, graphite, colored pencil; 19.8 × 26.3 cm. 20/6238

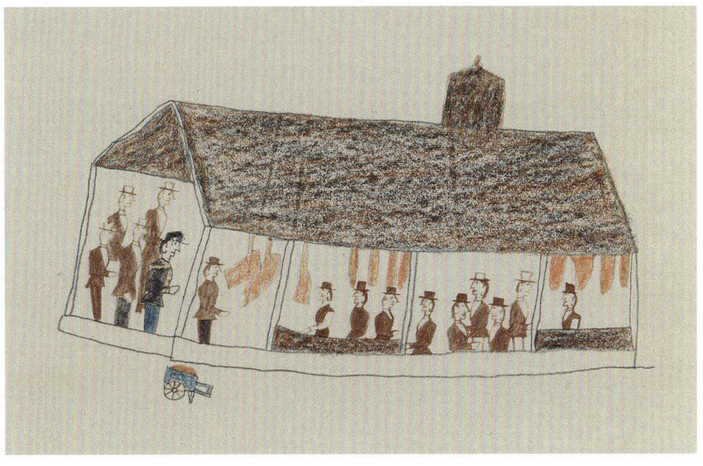

Bear's Heart (Southern Cheyenne, 1851–1882). *Meat Market St. Augustine* (detail). From Bear's Heart's drawing book, ca. 1875. Paper, graphite, colored pencil, ink; 17 × 23 cm. 20/6231

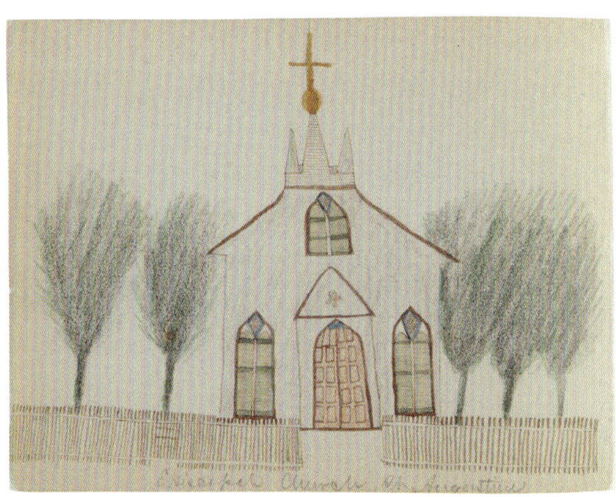

Bear's Heart (Southern Cheyenne, 1851–1882). *Episcopal Church St. Augustine*. From Bear's Heart's drawing book, ca. 1875. Paper, graphite, colored pencil, ink; 17 × 23 cm. 20/6231

From Fort Marion, the artists could see Anastasia Island, a barrier island located across Matanzas Inlet from the fort. From October 1 to 25, 1875, the prisoners camped there.[13] In one of Bear's Heart's scenes, which depicts either this outing or a subsequent visit, the men's tents as well as shades or arbors are visible. The prisoners perform camp chores or mill about. One of them converses with an officer, likely Pratt. As historian Herman Viola notes, the island "became something of a sanatorium for ailing prisoners. On the advice of the medical officer, small parties went there to recuperate by fishing, hunting, and beachcombing."[14] For the prisoners, these outings were a break from their daily routine and a much-needed change of scenery.

Eventually the prisoners were allowed to explore the town of St. Augustine. The men patronized local businesses, purchasing goods with money earned in part through the sale of their drawings.[15] Bear's Heart depicts a prisoner, possibly himself, shopping at a St. Augustine meat market. Dressed in his uniform, the prisoner stands alongside the townspeople, waiting to make his purchase. During his brief visits to town, the artist recorded other sights, including two local houses of worship, Trinity Episcopal Church and the Cathedral of St. Augustine.

SCENES OF LIFE ON THE PLAINS

In addition to recording scenes of their captivity, both Bear's Heart and Zotom produced drawings that recall tribal life on the southern plains. Scholars have attributed the many Fort Marion pieces that focus on the prisoners' lives before their incarceration to feelings of nostalgia and homesickness.[16] Yet the artists may have been expressing not only longing for traditional ways of life but also pride in them. The selection of certain subjects may have served as subtle acts of resistance, enabling prisoners like Bear's Heart and Zotom to assert their identities as Southern Cheyenne and Kiowa men.

Hunting scenes, for example, appear frequently in drawings from Fort Marion. Artists depicted the pursuit of bison, pronghorn, and elk, as well as other species.[17] In one drawing, Bear's Heart conveyed the excitement of a bison hunt: six mounted hunters pursue a herd of bison, their arrows having already struck several of the animals. In such scenes, the prisoners could emphasize their role as hunters and providers.

While hunting scenes far outnumber those of battle in Fort Marion drawings, artists occasionally broached the subject of warfare.[18] Zotom produced a two-page drawing depicting intertribal warfare. Rather than focusing on the exploits of a single warrior, he provided an overview of an engagement between Kiowa and Navajo fighters. The enemy warriors wear red high-top moccasins, which frequently appear in Kiowa artists' depictions of the Navajo.[19] Kiowa calendar histories record numerous clashes with the Navajo. Particularly noteworthy engagements occurred in 1865, 1867, and 1868, so it is possible that Zotom participated in the conflict he depicted.[20] Regardless, the drawing reinforces the image of Kiowa men as warriors willing and able to do battle.

Zotom also rendered scenes of intertribal diplomacy. One drawing depicts a delegation from a visiting tribe. Although the men are armed, the way in which they hold their weapons conveys their peaceful intentions. While Pratt's inscription identifies the individuals as "Navajoes," the warriors' roached hair, front tab leggings, and beaded garters indicate they are Osage.[21]

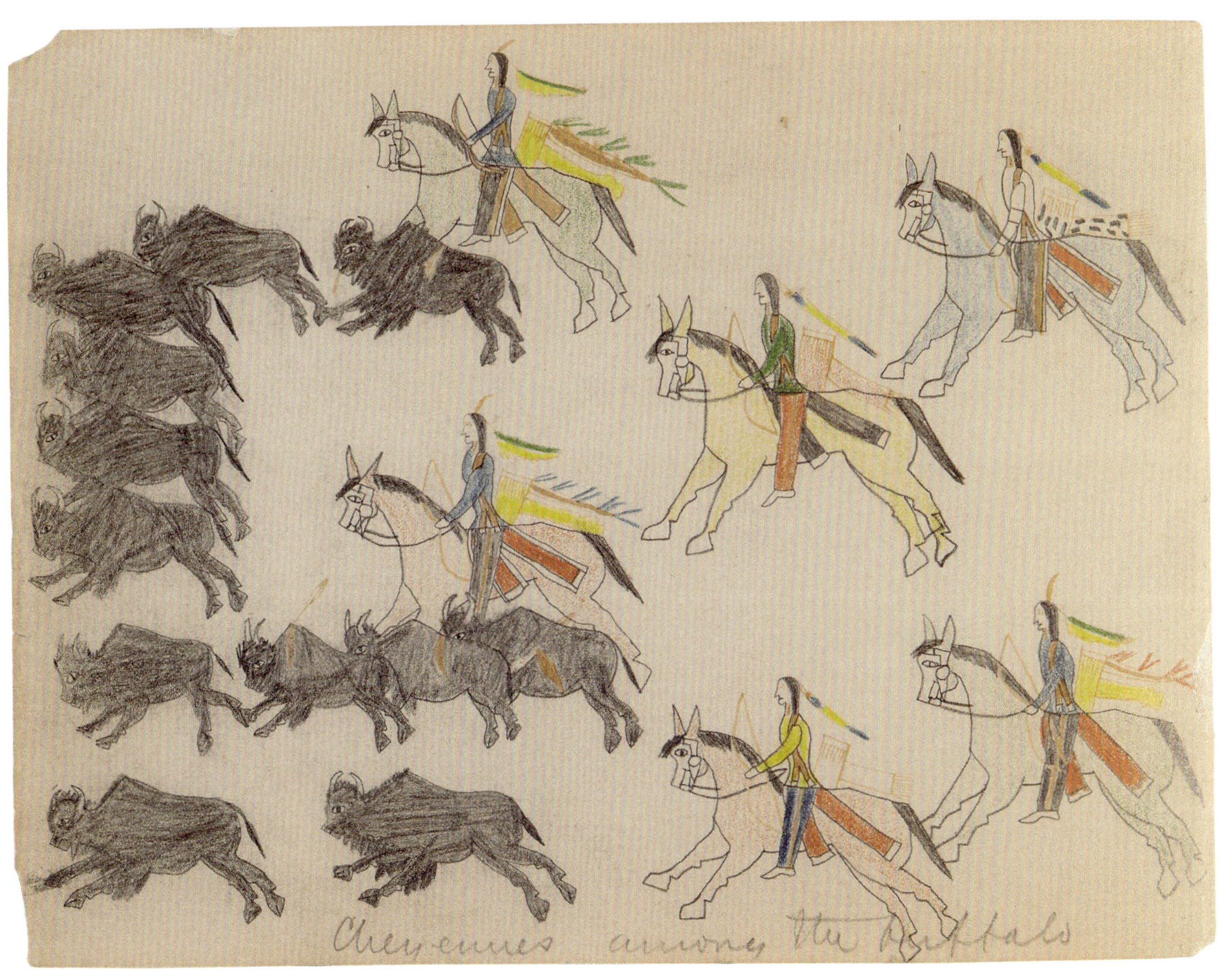

Bear's Heart (Southern Cheyenne, 1851–1882). *Cheyennes among the Buffalo.* From Bear's Heart's drawing book, ca. 1875. Paper, graphite, colored pencil, ink; 17 × 23 cm. 20/6231

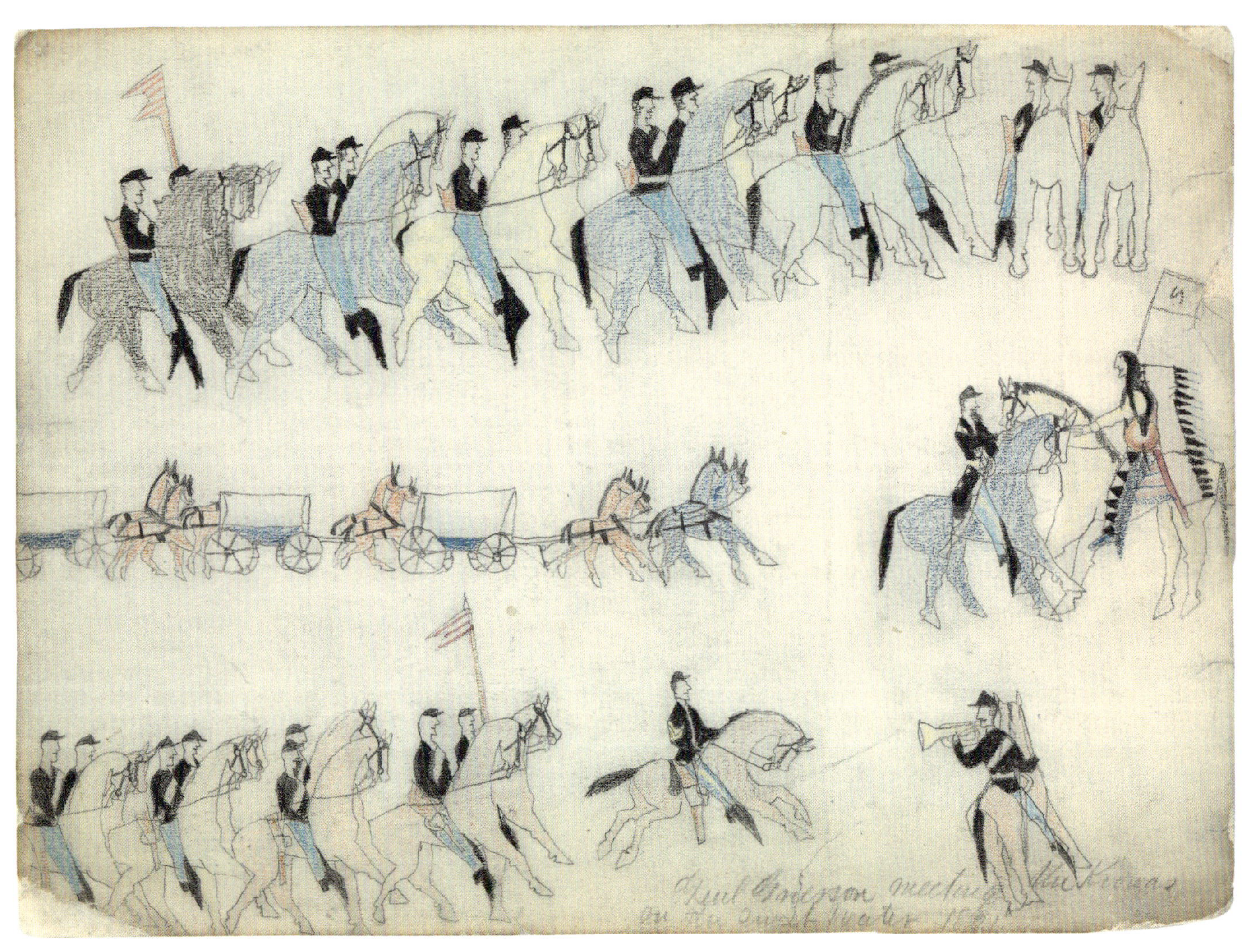

Zotom (Kiowa, 1853–1913). *Leut Grierson Meeting the Kiowas on the Sweet Water 1871*. From Zotom's drawing book, ca. 1875. Paper, graphite, colored pencil; 19.8 × 26.3 cm. 20/6232

Like other Kiowa artists, Zotom was a keen observer of the customs and dress of neighboring tribes. One of his drawings depicts what the title describes as an Osage war dance. The dancers' dress supports the identification. In the summer of 1872, Kiowa and Osage parties joined forces to attack a suspected surveying party in Kansas.[22] It is possible that the Kiowa observed their Osage allies performing the dance on this occasion. Regardless of when the Kiowa warriors witnessed the dance, the Osage dancers made a memorable impression on them. Several other Fort Marion artists also reproduced the dance.[23]

Another of Zotom's drawings evokes the longstanding trade relations that linked Southern Plains nations with New Mexico's Pueblo and Hispanic communities. Zotom shows a party of traders, wearing striped serapes, accompanied by five pack mules laden with goods. The scene may represent Pueblo and Hispanic traders who visited the Kiowa in the winter of 1872–73. This event was recorded by the Kiowa historian Settan. According to James Mooney, the traders wished to exchange eagle feathers and Pueblo bread for bison robes and horses.[24] The Pueblo bread was quite popular with the Kiowa.

Both Zotom's and Bear's Heart's drawings of the southern plains reveal the extent to which Euro-Americans had penetrated Kiowa and Southern Cheyenne territory during the latter half of the nineteenth century. The artists depicted U.S. Army operations as well as the military posts established within their homelands. Zotom drew an encounter that occurred along Sweetwater Creek, then in Indian Territory (present-day Oklahoma). A Kiowa warrior carrying a white flag greets a cavalry officer. The military column had been authorized to attack any Indians found outside the reservation boundaries. The Kiowa request for a parley proved to be a delaying tactic so that the women and children camped nearby, beyond the border, could safely relocate to reservation land.[25] The drawing speaks to the shifting balance of power on the southern plains. By the early 1870s, the Kiowa could no longer travel freely within their territory without risking military reprisal.

SHERMAN CHADDLESONE

Like Zotom and Bear's Heart, Sherman Chaddlesone was a warrior-artist. An enrolled member of the Kiowa Tribe of Oklahoma, he was a Vietnam veteran and a member of the Ton-Kon-Gah, or Kiowa Black Leggings Warrior Society (KBLWS), a Kiowa veteran's organization.[26] As his nineteenth-century predecessors had, he created works inspired by personal experiences. In several of them, he celebrated the traditions of the KBLWS. In one, he depicted his own participation in the society's then semiannual ceremonial.

Chaddlesone also drew inspiration from the Kiowa calendar keepers, artists who traditionally maintained pictorial records of tribal life. They depicted two memorable events each year, one each from summer and winter.[27] Chaddlesone was descended from the custodians of two such calendars. His great-grandmother, Annaun-Tay (Buffalo Tracks), maintained a calendar with entries spanning the years 1855 to 1945.[28] Her father, known as Agiati (Gathering Feathers), or Pakonkgya (Black Buffalo), had also served as a calendar keeper, a role inherited from his uncle Dohasan (Little Bluff), who is credited as the first Kiowa artist to maintain such a record.[29] Given this ancestry, as well as a deep and abiding interest in Kiowa history, it is not surprising that Chaddlesone was drawn to the calendar records.

Many of Chaddlesone's works, including two in NMAI's collection, depict aspects of nineteenth-century Kiowa life. In one drawing, a bison hunt featuring three mounted hunters pursuing the herd fills a piece of art paper cut in the shape of a bison robe. Around the perimeter, Chaddlesone painted a border that incorporates geometric designs similar to those that adorn Kiowa parfleches and women's robes.[30] The drawing evokes Bear's Heart's hunting scene. Both pay homage to the central role bison played in the lives of the Southern Plains tribes, while conveying the thrill of the mounted chase.

Bison are also referenced in another of Chaddlesone's drawings. This one focuses on the first day of the Kado, the Kiowa Medicine Lodge or Sun Dance, a religious ceremony central to Kiowa culture. Pursued by a "hunter" wielding a firebrand, tribal members dressed as bison are driven into the Sun Dance lodge,

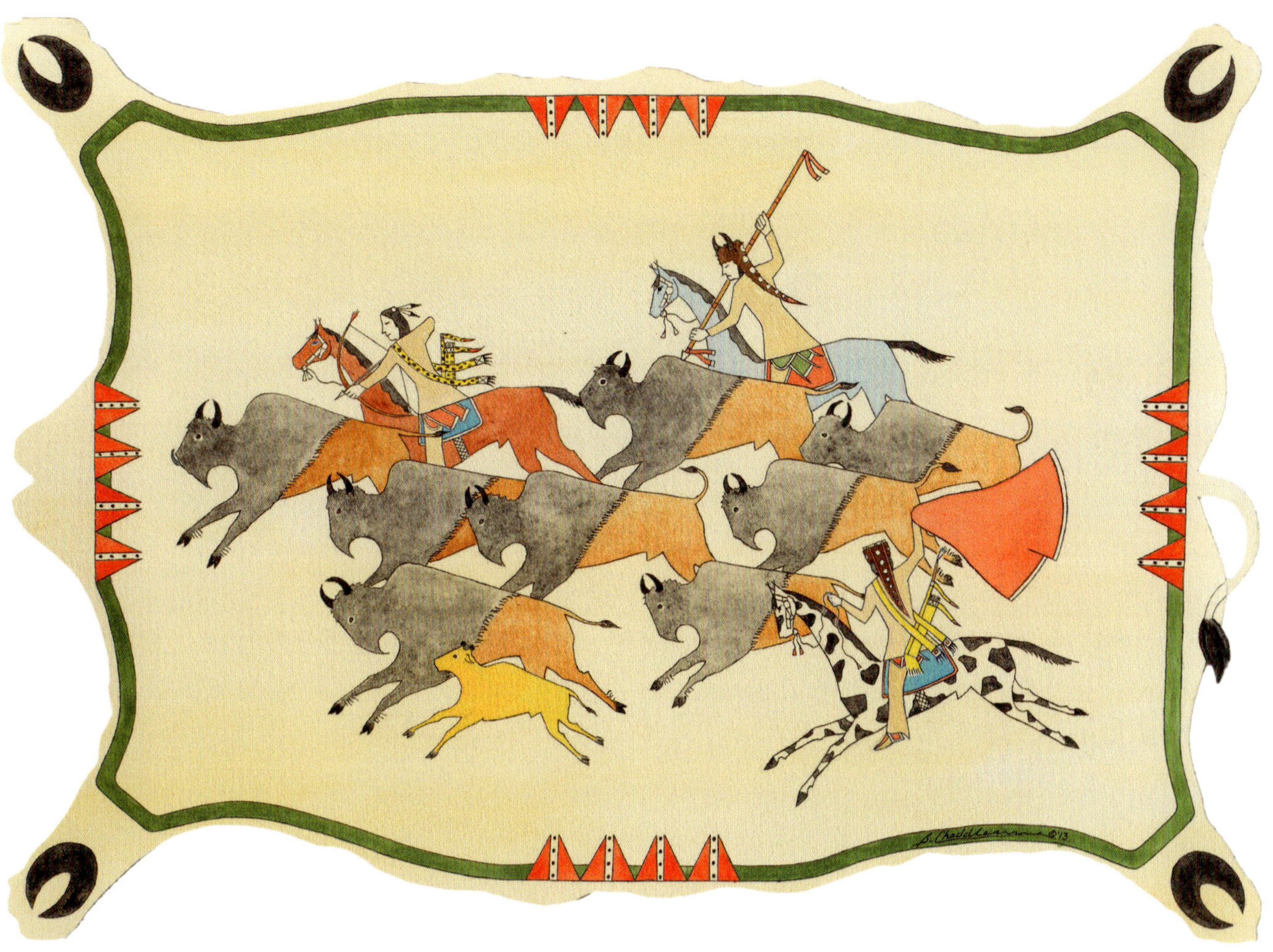

Painting of a buffalo hunt, 2013.
Made by Sherman Chaddlesone
(Kiowa, 1947–2013). Paper, graphite,
ink, watercolor; 56.5 × 76 cm.
26/9180

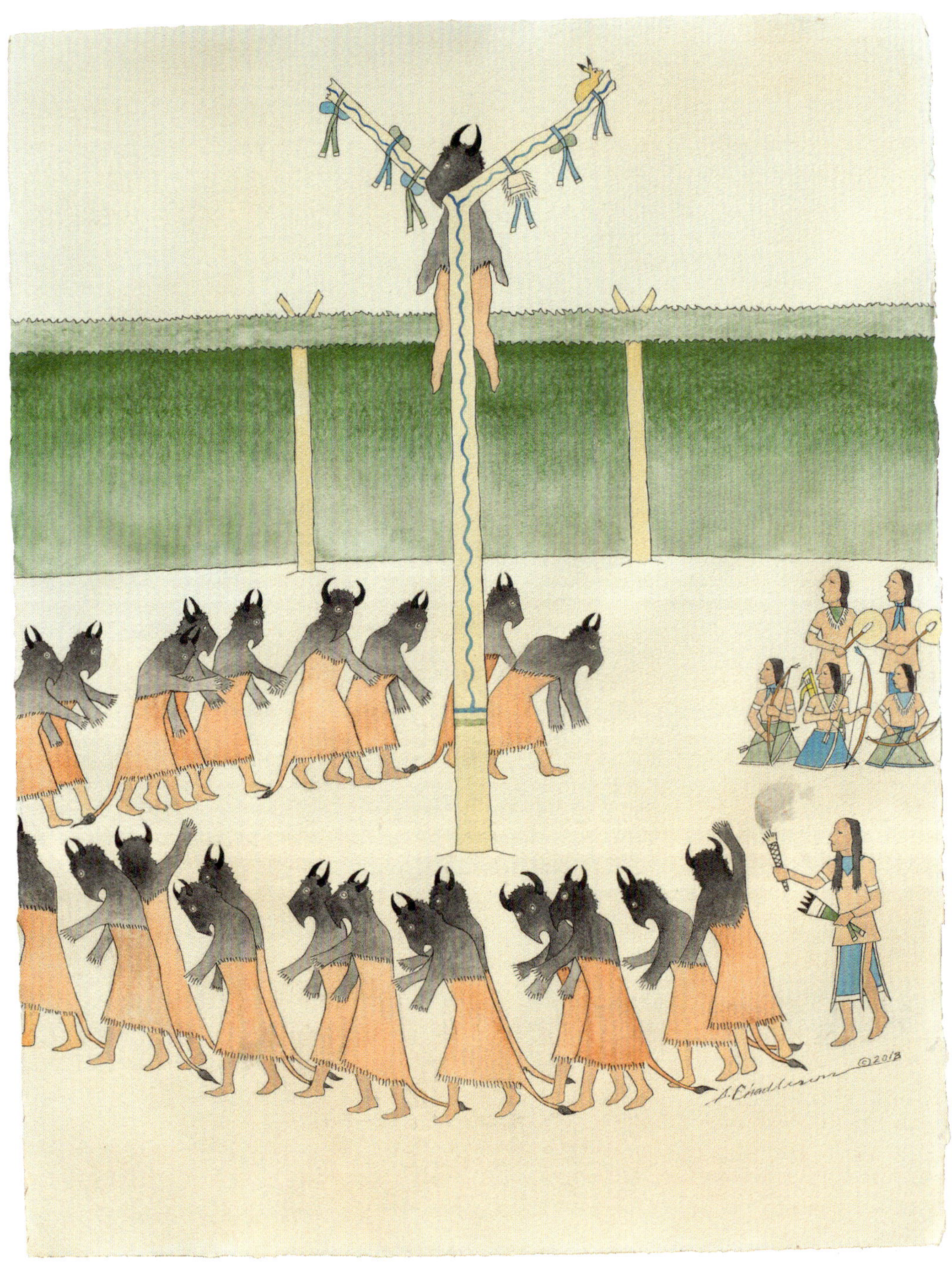

Painting of a Sun Dance, 2013. Made by Sherman Chaddlesone (Kiowa, 1947–2013). Paper, watercolor, graphite, ink; 76.5 × 57 cm. 26/9181

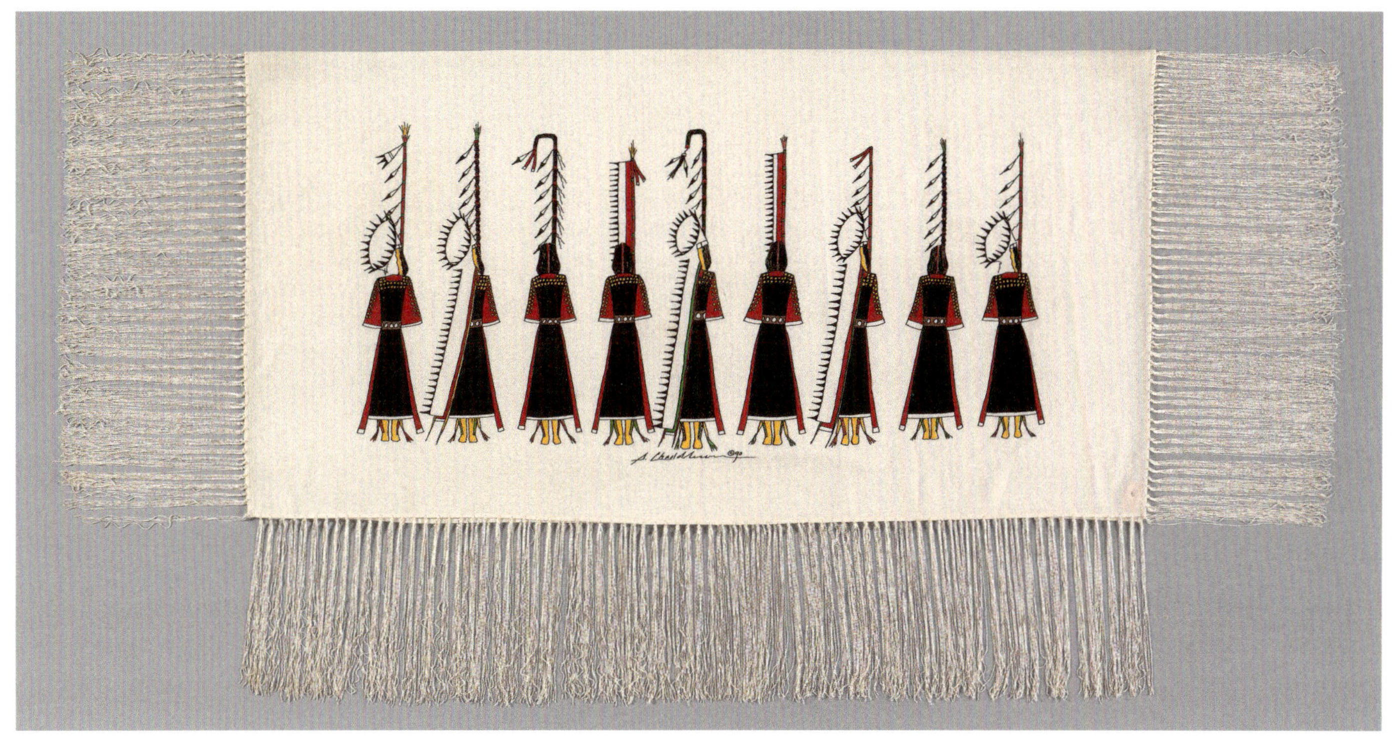

Painting of a Ton-Kon-Gah, or Kiowa Black Leggings Society, Victory Dance, 1990. Made by Sherman Chaddlesone (Kiowa, 1947–2013). Synthetic fabric (folded), nylon fringe, ink, acrylic paint, cotton thread; 159.5 × 146 cm. 26/9178

where they circle the center pole.[31] Several of the Kiowa artists imprisoned at Fort Marion drew scenes of the Sun Dance. Indeed, a drawing by an unidentified artist focuses on the same portion of the ceremony that Chaddlesone represented.[32]

Another of Chaddlesone's drawings adorns a woman's dance shawl. The shawl depicts Kiowa women participating in a Victory Dance. Historically, during Kiowa Victory and Scalp Dances women honored their male relatives' exploits in battle by wearing their kinsmen's headdresses and carrying their weapons.[33] Nineteenth-century Kiowa artists, including one unidentified Fort Marion artist, depicted women scalp and victory dancing.[34] In Chaddlesone's drawing, the women, likely members of the Kiowa Veterans Auxiliary, carry lances that belong to their male relatives. Several of them also wear eagle-feather bonnets. Each of the women wears a red and black *màunkàugúlhòldà* (red-sleeve dress). Numerous nineteenth-century Kiowa drawings feature women wearing similar dresses.[35] Today, these dresses are often referred to as victory dresses or battle dresses, and they have become closely associated with the Kiowa Veterans Auxiliary.[36]

One of Chaddlesone's most personal and poignant pieces is a drawing that he began but was unable to complete before his death in 2013. It features members of the KBLWS dancing alongside the society's distinctive tipi. In 2008, Chaddlesone had been one of the artists selected to paint a new version of the tipi to mark the fiftieth anniversary of the warrior society's revival. Chaddlesone painted four battle scenes (not shown) on the north side of the tipi. They commemorate the 1864 Battle of Adobe Walls, as well as Kiowa service in World War I, World War II, and the Iraq War.[37]

Chaddlesone included himself in his 2013 drawing.[38] The central figure, he wears a roach, beaded leggings, and a set of hair plates as well as a red cape and a black shawl, two important symbols of the Ton-Kon-Gah. He and other society members carry firearms. During the Xàkóigácùngà (the Turn Around or Reverse Dance), which marks the culmination of the ceremonial, dancers frequently fire blanks to simulate the sound of combat.[39] In the drawing, Chaddlesone celebrates his status both as a warrior and a proud member of the Ton-Kon-Gah. Like countless Southern Plains men before him, Chaddlesone used art to record his personal accomplishments.

CONCLUSION

In his paintings, Sherman Chaddlesone left an enduring legacy that honors the vibrant culture and history of the Kiowa people and pays homage to nineteenth-century warrior-artists such as Zotom and Bear's Heart. In a very real sense, Chaddlesone's work speaks to the resilience of Southern Plains cultures in the face of assimilationist forces. During their incarceration at Fort Marion, Bear's Heart and Zotom confronted these forces. Both men used their drawings to navigate fraught cross-cultural encounters. Standing on the parapet of Fort Marion, exiled far from their homes, one wonders if they envisioned that, more than a century later, artists such as Sherman Chaddlesone would be creating art that celebrates the cultural survival of their people.

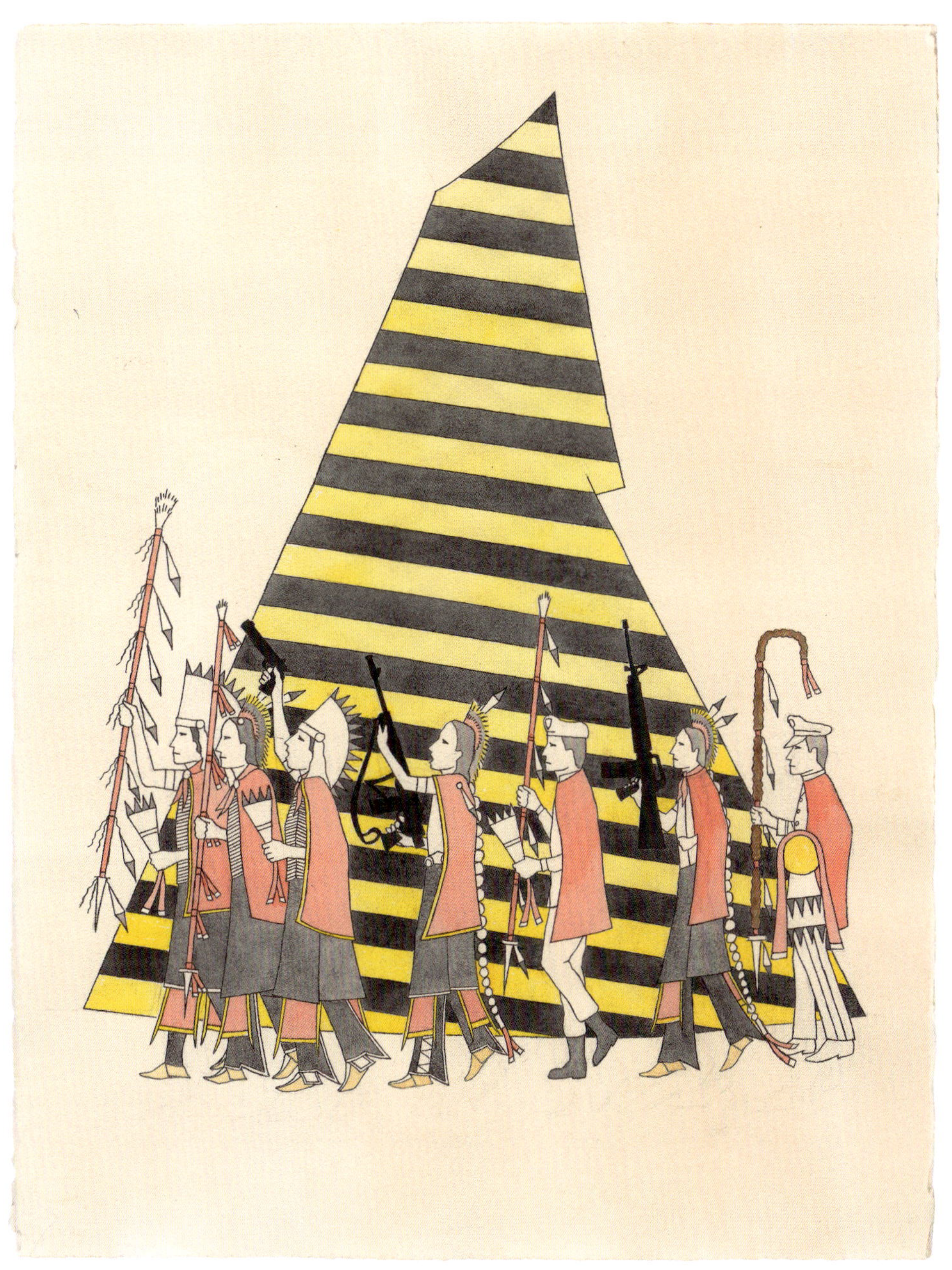

Painting of a Ton-Kon-Gah, or Kiowa Black Leggings Warrior Society, dance, 2013. Made by Sherman Chaddlesone (Kiowa, 1947–2013). Paper, graphite, watercolor, ink; 77 × 58 cm. 26/9402

The drawings by Bear's Heart and Zotom that illustrate this essay come from books of each artist's work in the National Museum of the American Indian's collection. Lieutenant Richard H. Pratt (1840–1924), who supervised the Native prisoners at Fort Marion, sent the books to General William T. Sherman (1820–1891) to solicit his support for Pratt's efforts to assimilate American Indians. Sherman's granddaughter, Eleanor Sherman Fitch (1876–1959), donated them to the Museum of the American Indian (the National Museum of the American Indian's predecessor institution) in 1943. Lieutenant Pratt titled the drawings in both books.

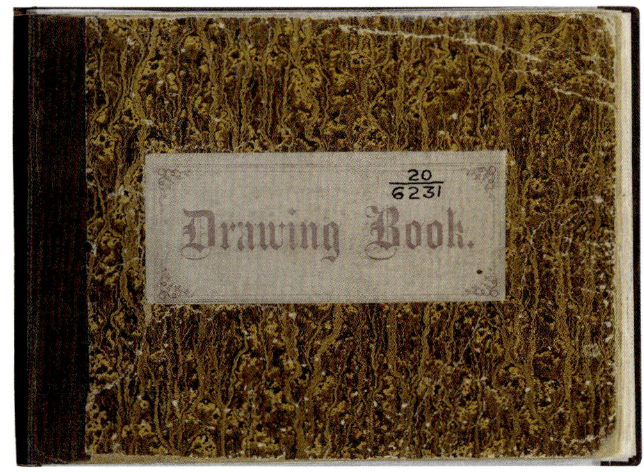

Bear's Heart (Southern Cheyenne, 1851–1882). Drawing book, ca. 1875. Paper, graphite, colored pencil, ink; 17 × 23 cm. 20/6231

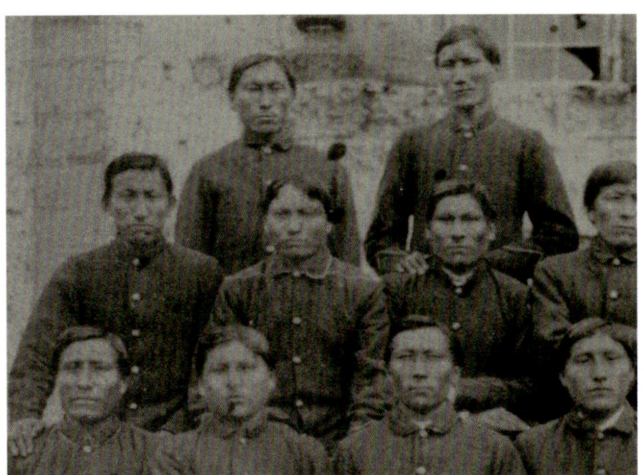

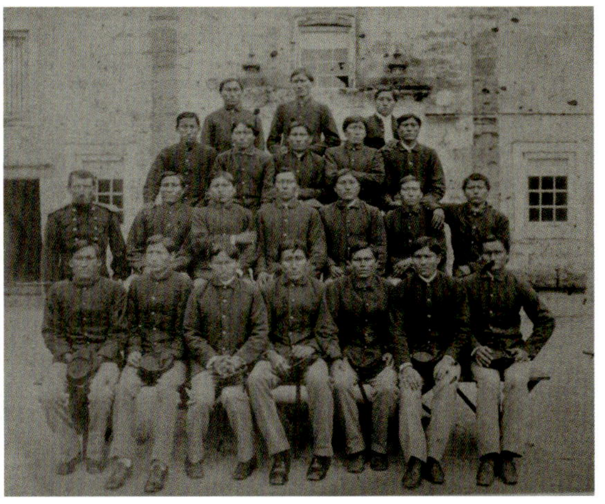

Bear's Heart (third row, far left) and other Indian prisoners with Lieutenant Richard H. Pratt, Fort Marion, St. Augustine, Florida, 1878. Photographer unknown. National Anthropological Archives, Smithsonian Institution 54546

Bear's Heart was a Southern Cheyenne warrior who, after three years in prison at Fort Marion, spent another three years in the East. He studied at Hampton Normal Agricultural Institute in Virginia. In 1881, he returned to the Cheyenne Arapaho Agency in Oklahoma but died of tuberculosis only a few months later.

Zotom, 1880. Photographer unknown. Yale Collection of Western Americana, Beinecke Rare Book and Manuscript Library 1041021

After his release from Fort Marion, the Kiowa warrior-artist Zotom remained in the East. He was ordained as an Episcopal deacon in 1881, but by 1889 he had returned to Oklahoma and Plains spiritual traditions.

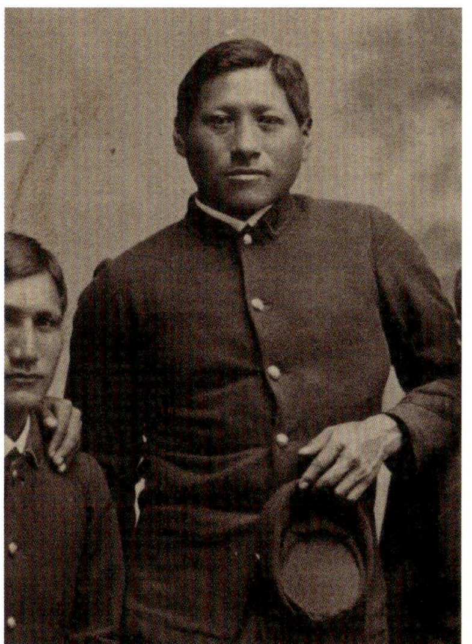

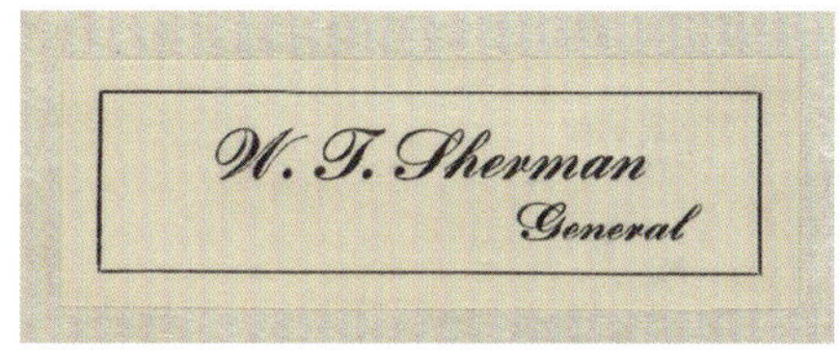

Zotom (Kiowa, 1853–1913). Drawing book (detail), ca. 1875. Paper, graphite, colored pencil; 19.8 cm × 26.3 cm. 20/6232

The nameplate on Zotom's drawing book shows that it once belonged to General William T. Sherman.

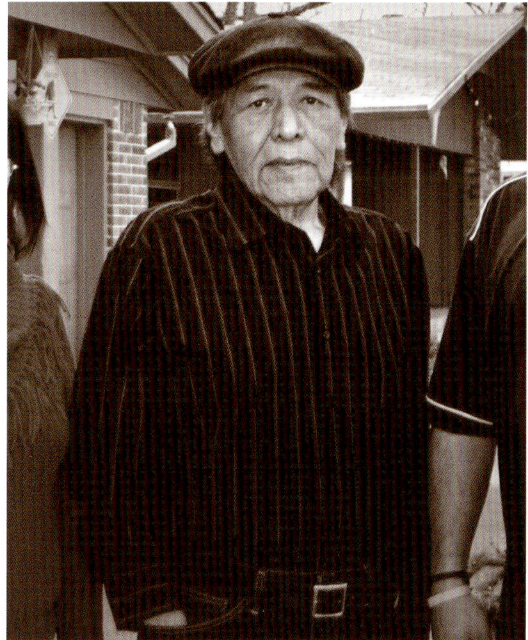

Sherman Chaddlesone, 2013. Photo by Boots Kennedye

Taught the basics of anatomy, portraiture, pencil sketching, and screen printing by his father, Sherman Chaddlesone (1947–2013) became a full-time painter and sculptor in his mid-thirties. He worked in a variety of media, including acrylic, watercolor, pastel, stone, and bronze. Most of his art focuses on Kiowa tribal history and cultural traditions. A descendant of the famous Kiowa war chief Satanta (White Bear), Chaddlesone was a veteran of the Vietnam War.

CONTEMPORARY EXPRESSIONS

Today both men and women narrative artists draw upon their cultural traditions, personal experiences, and artistic sensibilities as they continue to shape and expand on the Plains narrative style. As artist Dallin Maybee states, "One of the strengths of our culture has been our ability to adapt to and evolve in an ever-changing technological landscape. Our art has reflected that evolution."

DWAYNE WILCOX (Oglala Lakota)

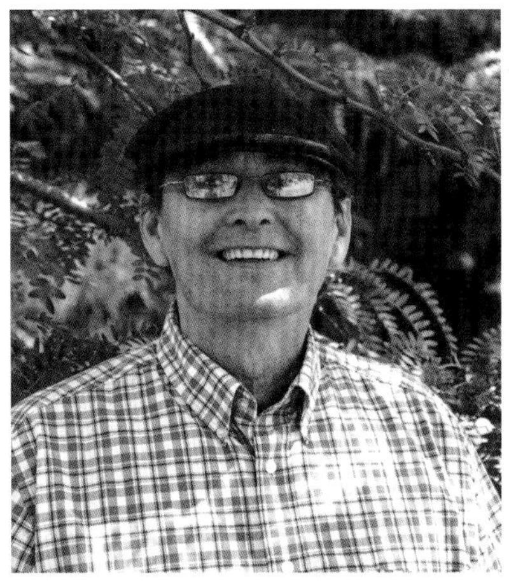

Dwayne Wilcox, 2015. Photo by NMAI staff

"For as long as I can remember, I've been able to draw funny things and make people laugh."

Dwayne Wilcox describes his sensibility as akin to that of Jon Stewart or Stephen Colbert. He uses his art to bring out the humor in modern Native life. This sense of levity is rooted in the Lakota Heyoka, or Sacred Clown, figure.

In his recent work Wilcox has focused almost exclusively on themes of modern life. "In the 1800s our ancestors did what they had to do to preserve things for us," he says. "They very eloquently covered everything from that period. They don't need my help with that. Our lives are just as important as our ancestors' lives."

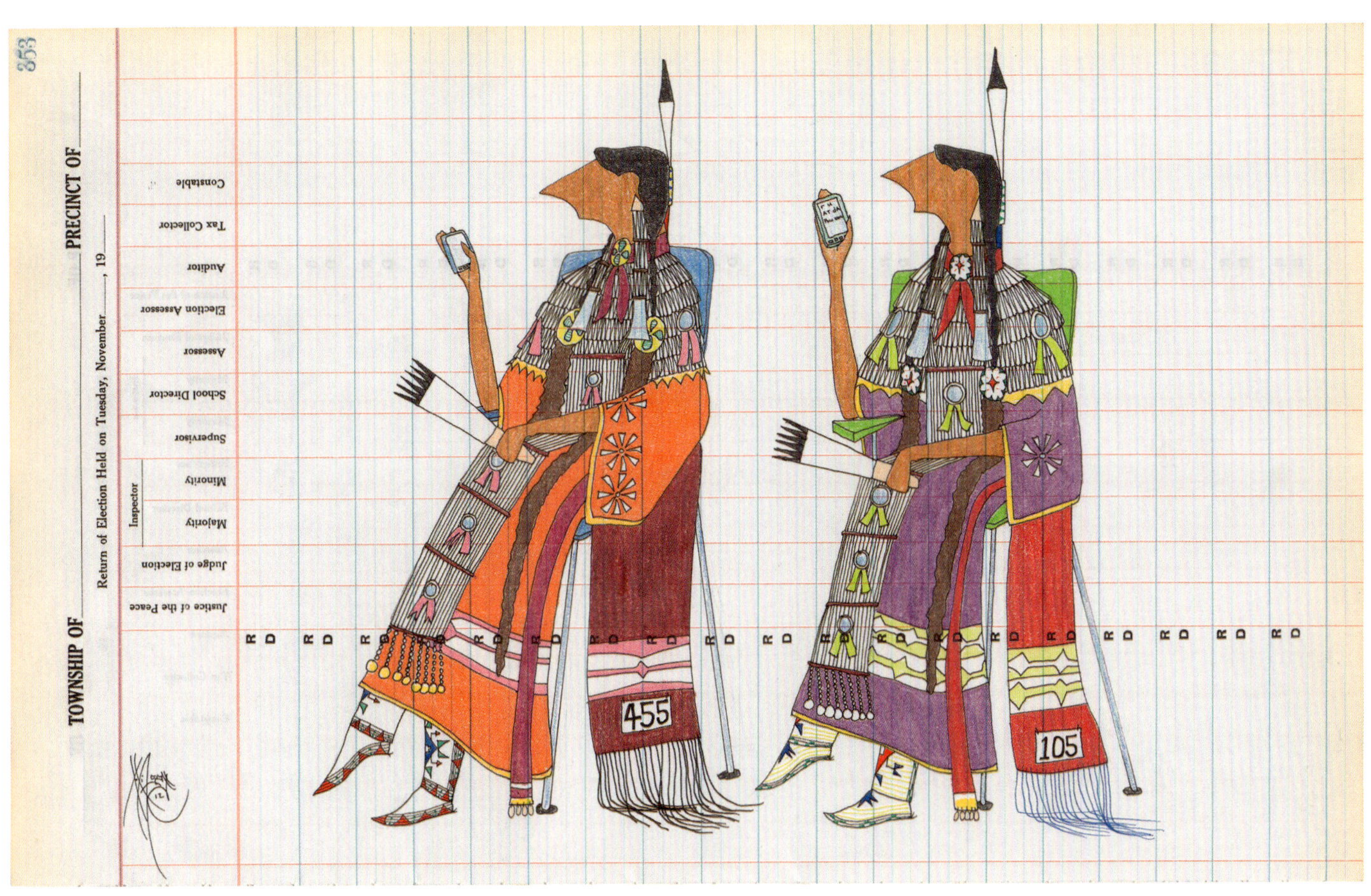

Dwayne Wilcox (Oglala Lakota, b. 1954). *4G Better than One-G*, 2012. Antique ledger paper, graphite, colored pencil, ink; 28.8 × 45 cm. 26/8952

Wilcox includes smartphones in this depiction of a powwow, in part to show how modern technology is present in Native life and culture. The title is a play on the Lakota word for the number one, *wáŋči* (pronounced ONE-gee).

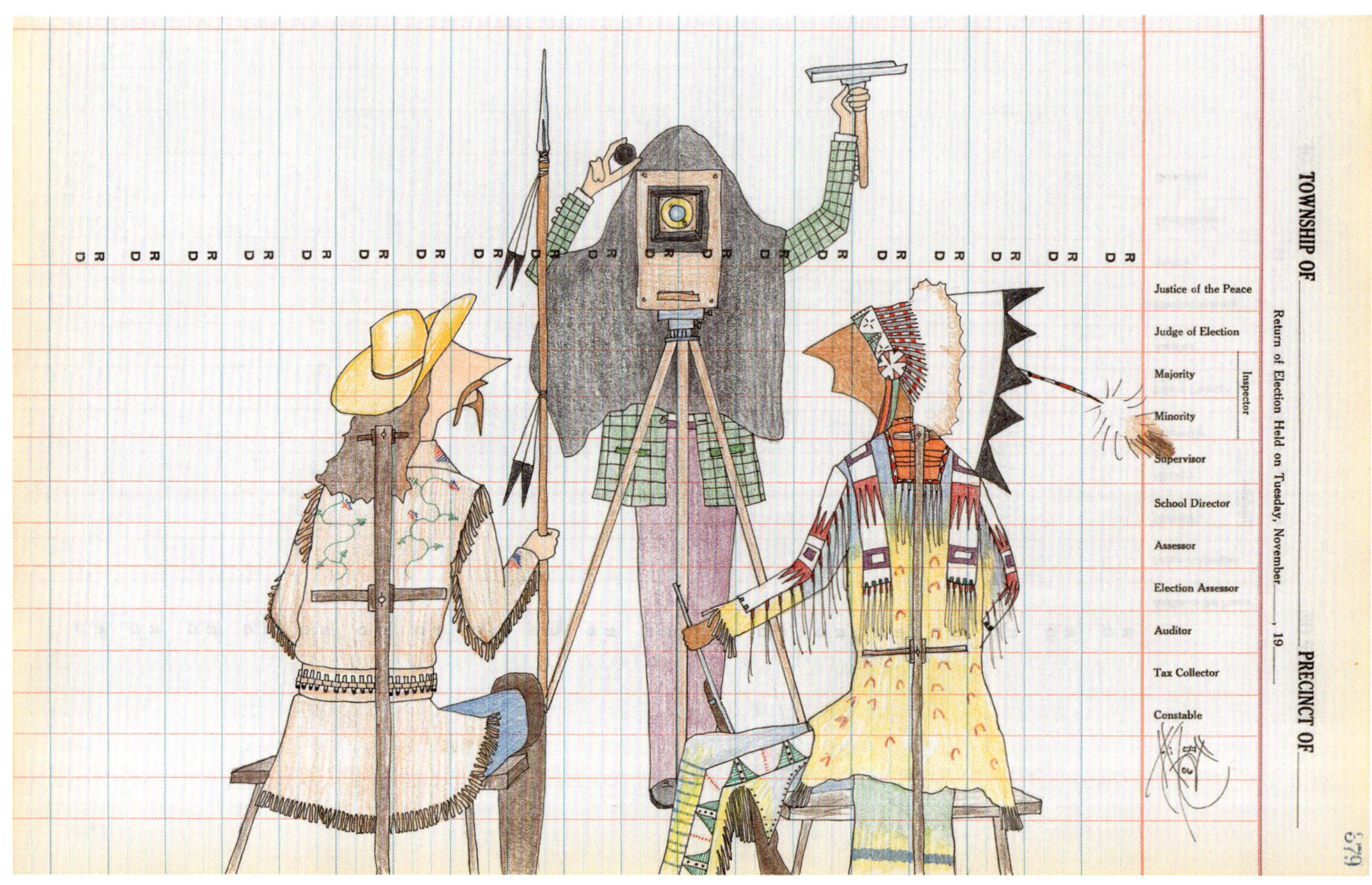

Dwayne Wilcox (Oglala Lakota, b. 1954). *In Studio*, 2012. Antique ledger paper, graphite, colored pencil, ink; 28.8 × 45.1 cm. 26/8951

Buffalo Bill Cody and an Indian performer sit for a photo-portrait. One of Wilcox's ancestors traveled with Cody's Wild West show in the late 1800s.

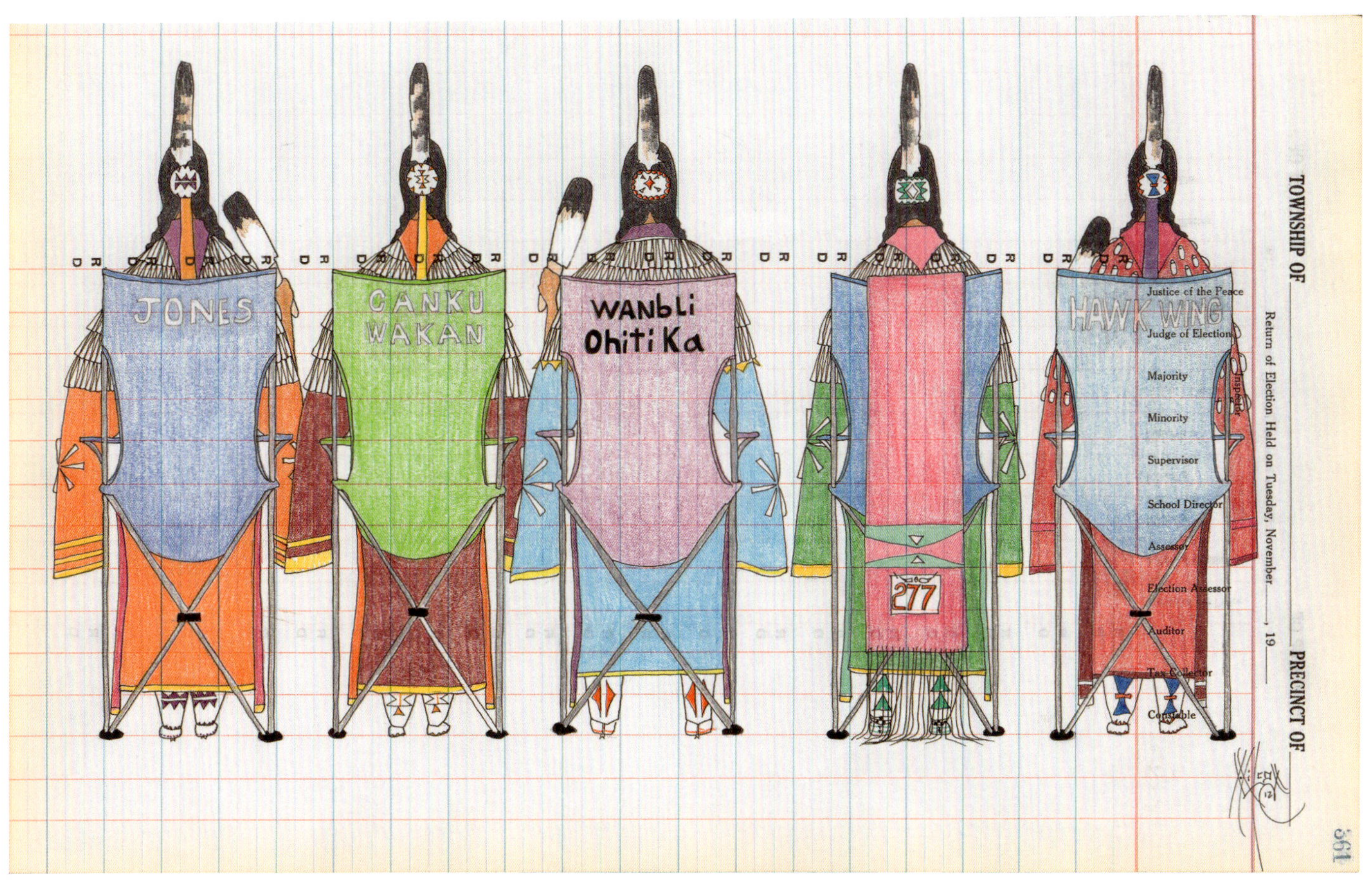

Dwayne Wilcox (Oglala Lakota, b. 1954). *Front Row Seats*, 2012. Antique ledger paper, graphite, colored pencil, ink; 28.8 × 45 cm. 26/8953

Lakota last names and English versions of Native names identify female dancers waiting to participate at a powwow. It is common for people to bring lawn chairs to outdoor events. "It's kind of odd, considering our ancestors used to just sit on the ground," Wilcox muses.

NORMAN FRANK SHERIDAN SR. (Southern Cheyenne/Arapaho)

Nearly four decades ago, Norman Frank Sheridan Sr. brought some mismatched, multicolored beads to his mother and asked her to teach him to bead. For the rest of his life, he practiced art. In addition to beadwork, he produced vibrant, colorful drawings that depict Cheyenne history and ceremonial life.

Beyond his art, Sheridan served as a community intervention specialist with the Indian Health Service. A distinguished scholar, he lectured for the Association of American Indian Physicians on spiritually based therapies, and he mentored many Native artists.

Sheridan was an active member of the Cheyenne traditional community, participating most years in the renewal ceremony, the Sun Dance. He signed much of his work with his traditional name, Pipe Woman.

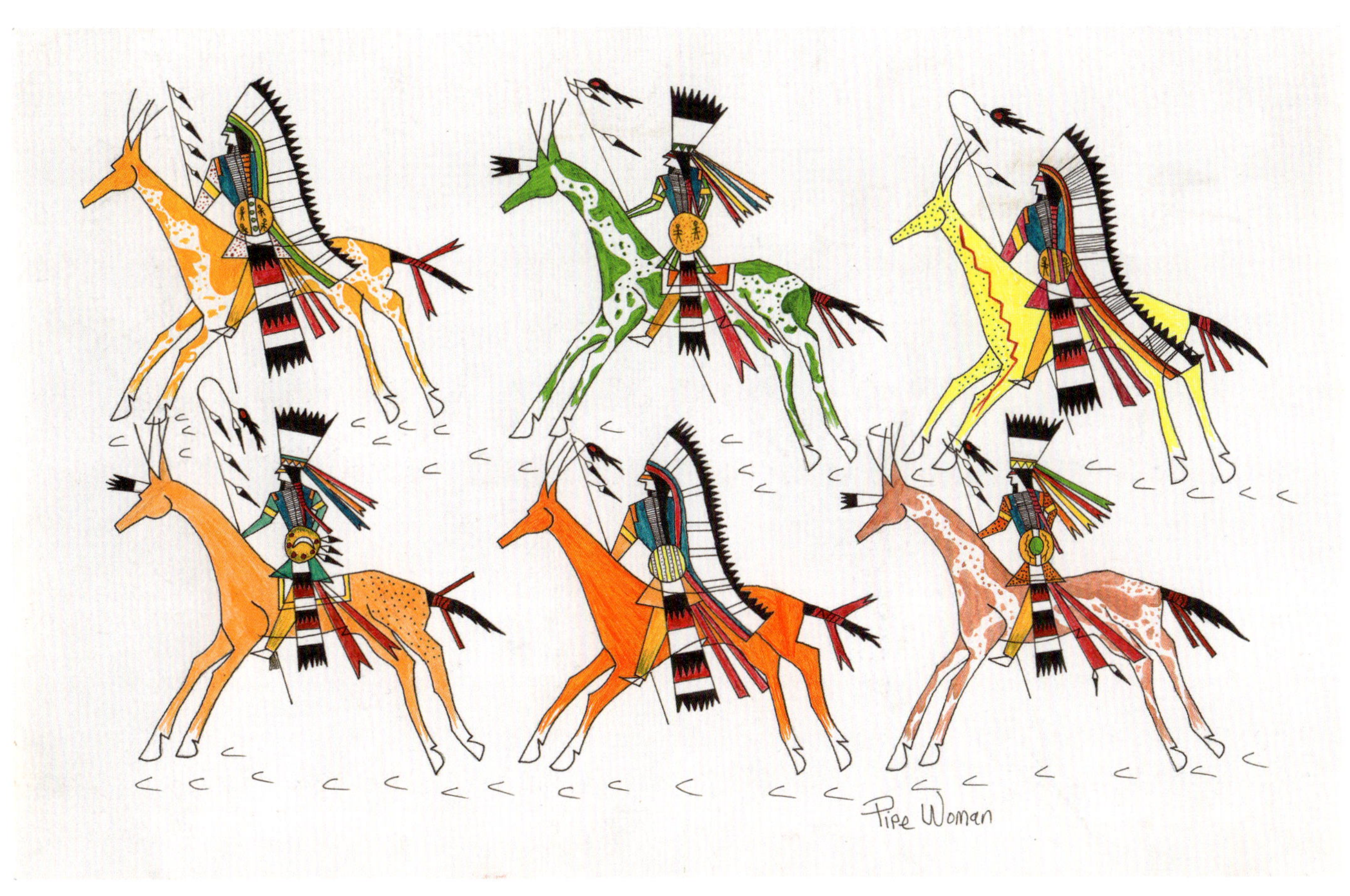

Drawing of a war party, 2012. Made by Norman Frank Sheridan Sr. (Southern Cheyenne/Arapaho, 1950–2014). Paper, graphite, ink, colored pencil, felt-tipped marker; 32.8 × 50.3 cm. 26/8948

Since each feather on a headdress represents an accomplishment, the length of these warriors' headdresses indicates their prowess. They also carry staffs adorned with feathers and enemy scalps. The horses' tails are tied in a fashion associated with a war party.

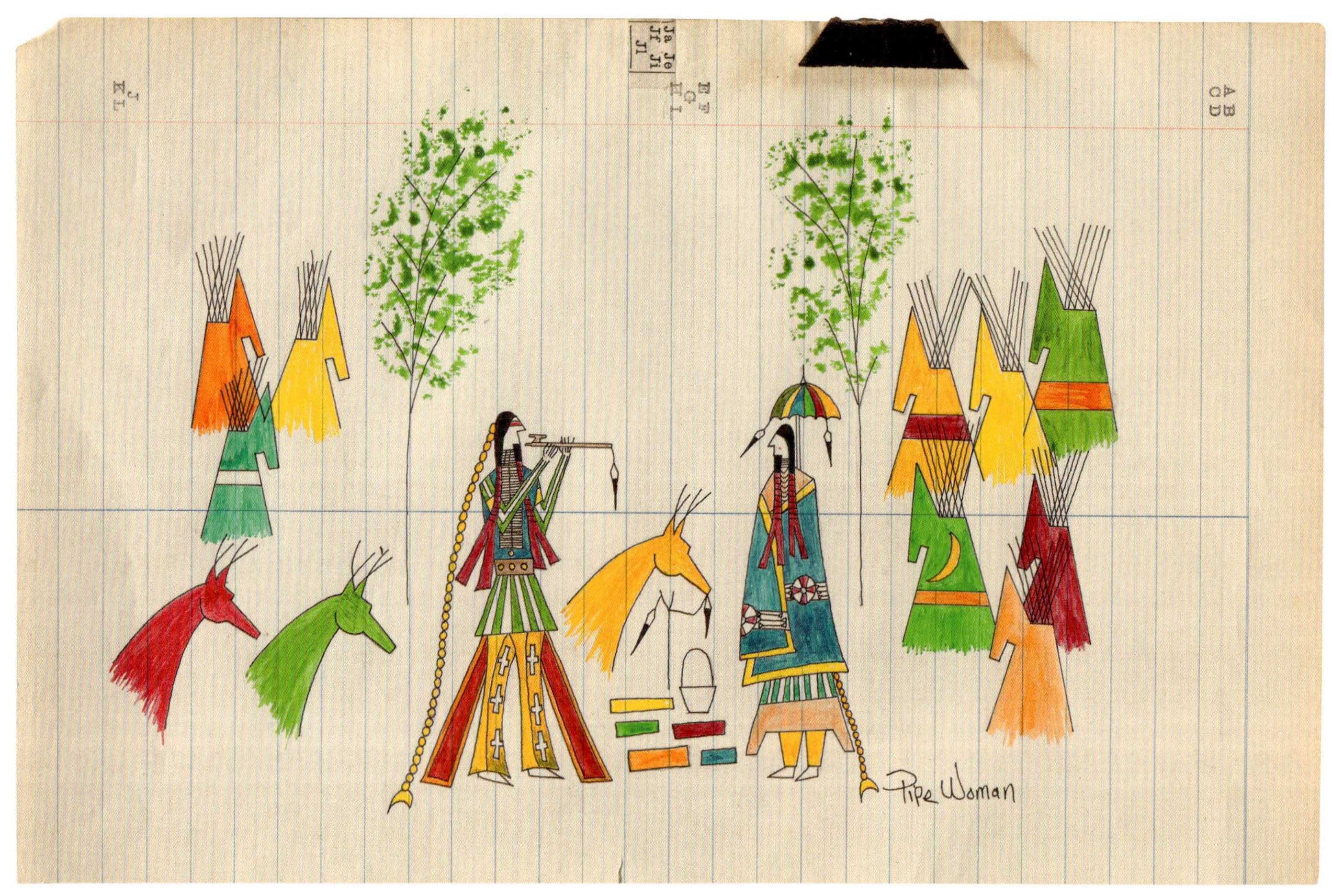

Drawing of a courting scene, 2012. Made by Norman Frank Sheridan Sr. (Southern Cheyenne/Arapaho, 1950–2014). Antique ledger paper, graphite, colored pencil, felt-tipped marker, ink, leather; 25.3 × 37.6 cm. 26/8947

The bucket suggests that this woman was on her way to fetch water when her suitor surprised her and serenaded her with a flute. The number of horses behind him indicates his interest in marrying her.

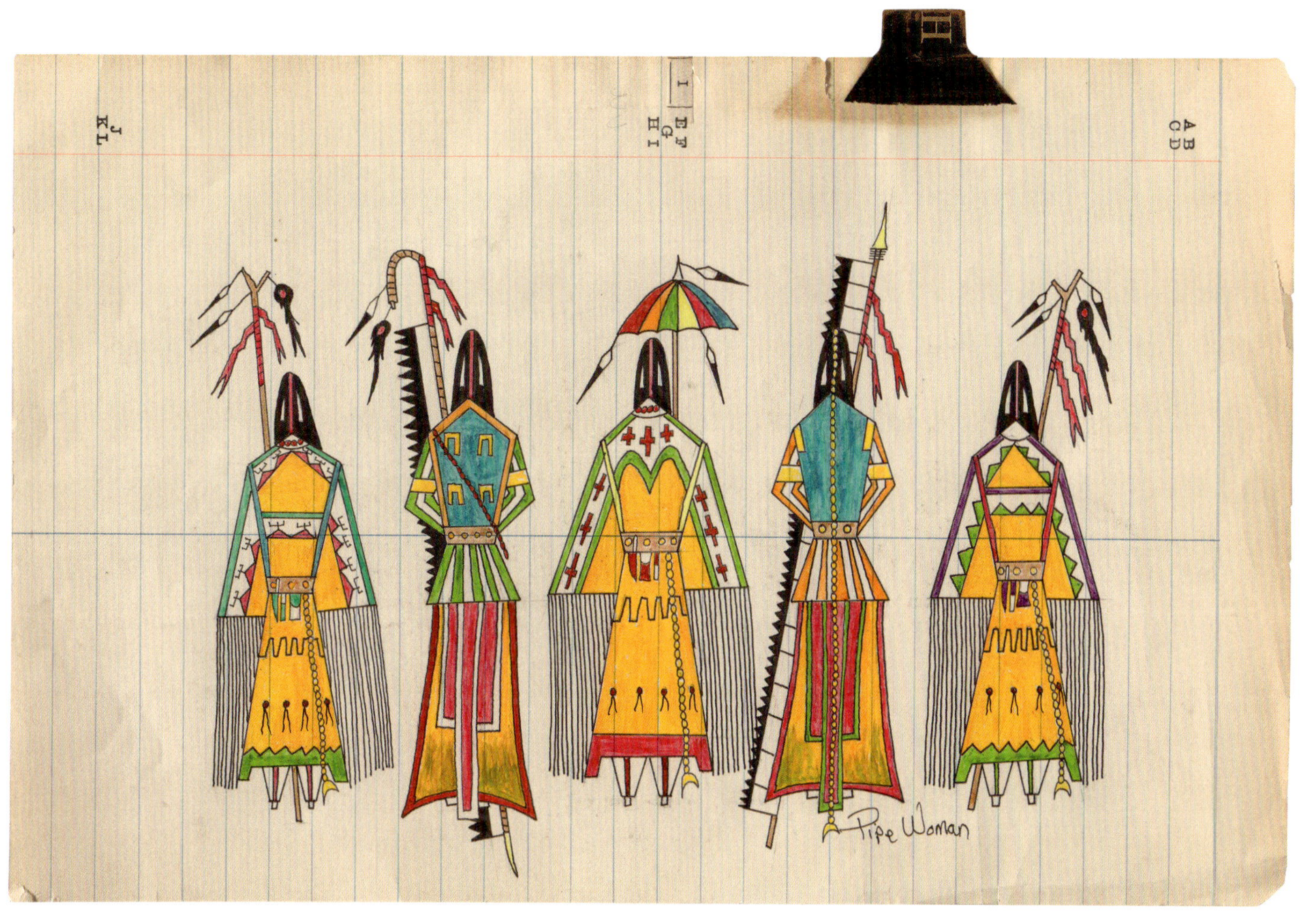

Drawing of a Victory Dance, 2012. Made by Norman Frank Sheridan Sr. (Southern Cheyenne/Arapaho, 1950–2014). Antique ledger paper, graphite, colored pencil, felt-tipped marker, ink, leather; 27 × 38 cm. 26/8946

Here, Sheridan depicts the lavish finery of a ceremonial Victory Dance. Several of the participants dance with staffs that are decorated with eagle feathers and enemy scalps.

JOEL PULLIAM (Oglala Lakota)

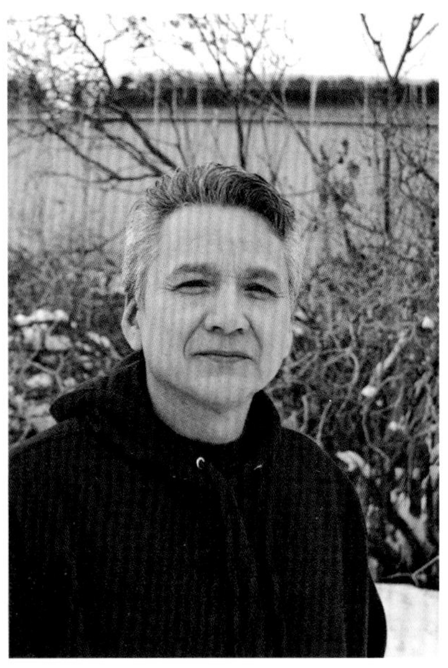

Joel Pulliam, 2015. Photo by NMAI staff

Joel Pulliam is a ledger artist and freelance graphic designer living on the Pine Ridge Reservation in South Dakota. He was introduced to ledger art in 2009. While researching the pictographic tradition in Amos Bad Heart Bull's *Pictographic History of the Oglala Sioux*, he became fascinated with its history. Like artists of the 1800s, Pulliam seeks to use his art to further cultural knowledge for future generations. He studies the regalia of traditional warriors and spiritual leaders.

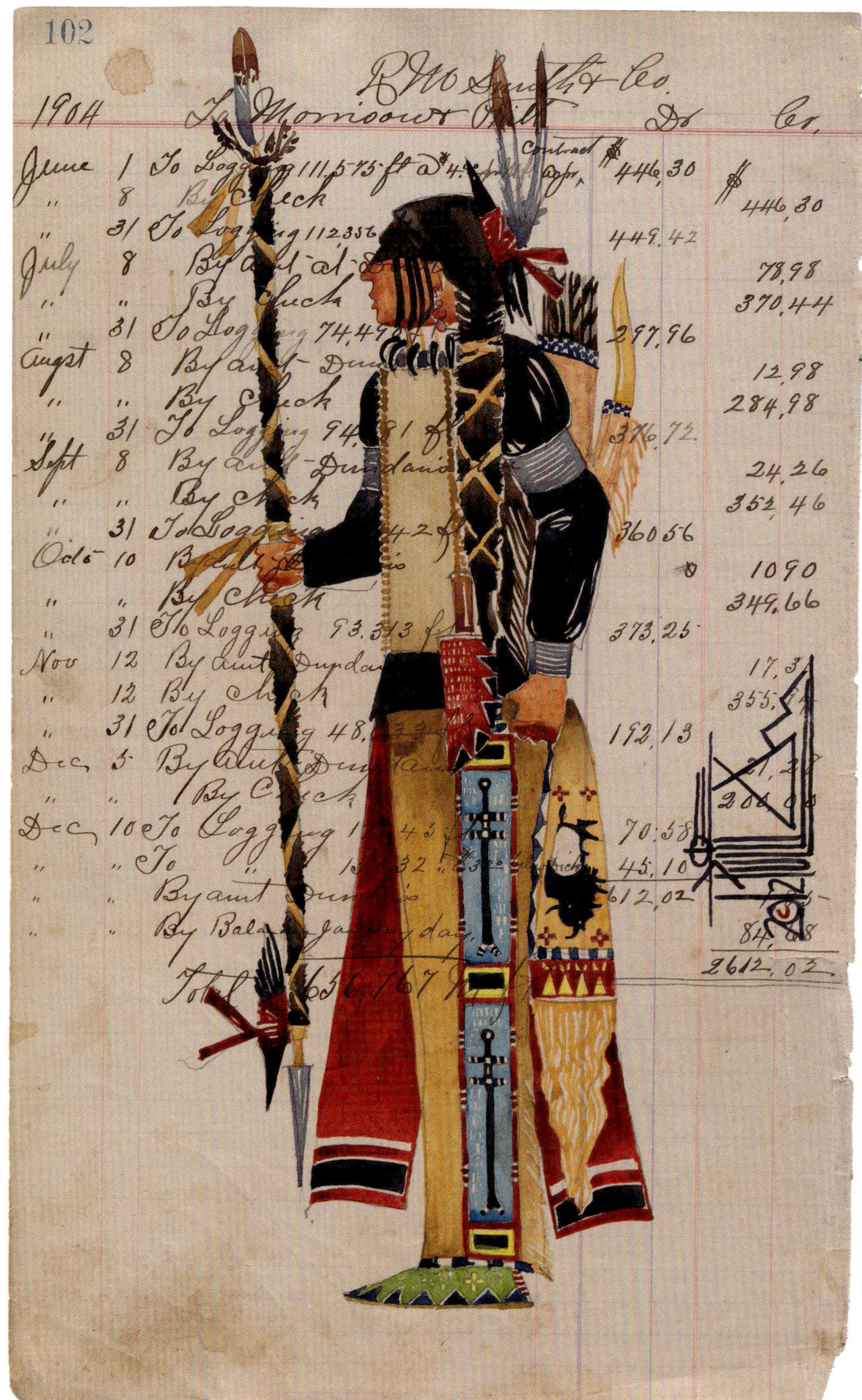

Joel Pulliam (Oglala Lakota, b. 1968). *Crow Owners Society Short Lance Carrier*, 2012. Antique ledger paper, watercolor, graphite, ink; 31.7 × 19 cm. 26/8954

Pulliam created this painting based on research into this Oglala Lakota society, which no longer exists. The regalia and lance are considered typical of the group.

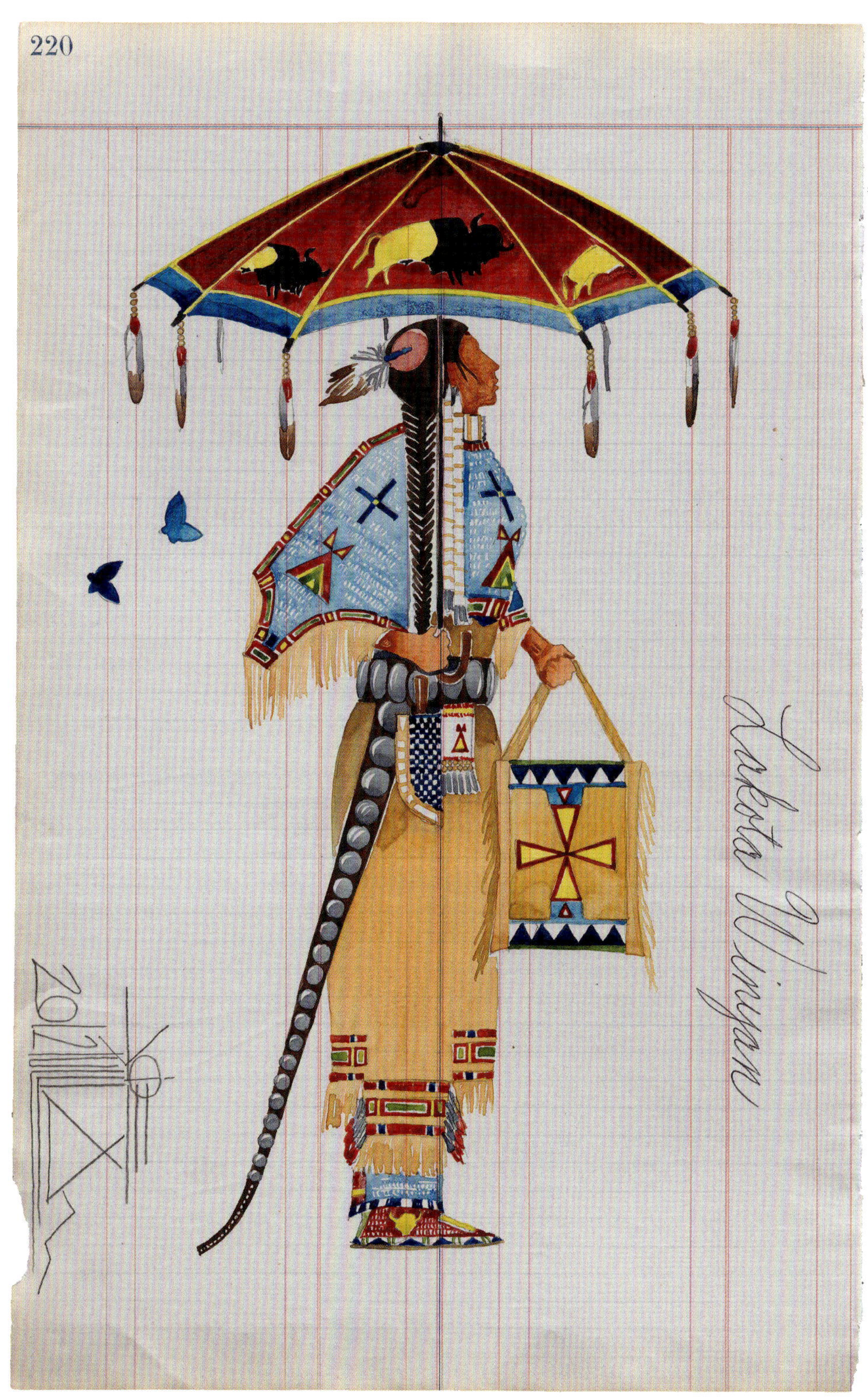

Joel Pulliam (Oglala Lakota, b. 1968). *Lakota Winyan,* 2012. Antique ledger paper, watercolor, graphite, ink; 39.3 × 24.2 cm. 26/8956

The finery on this woman indicates her prominence. In the 1800s parasols were a desired item acquired through trade. Native people often adapted them, adding their own designs, as seen here.

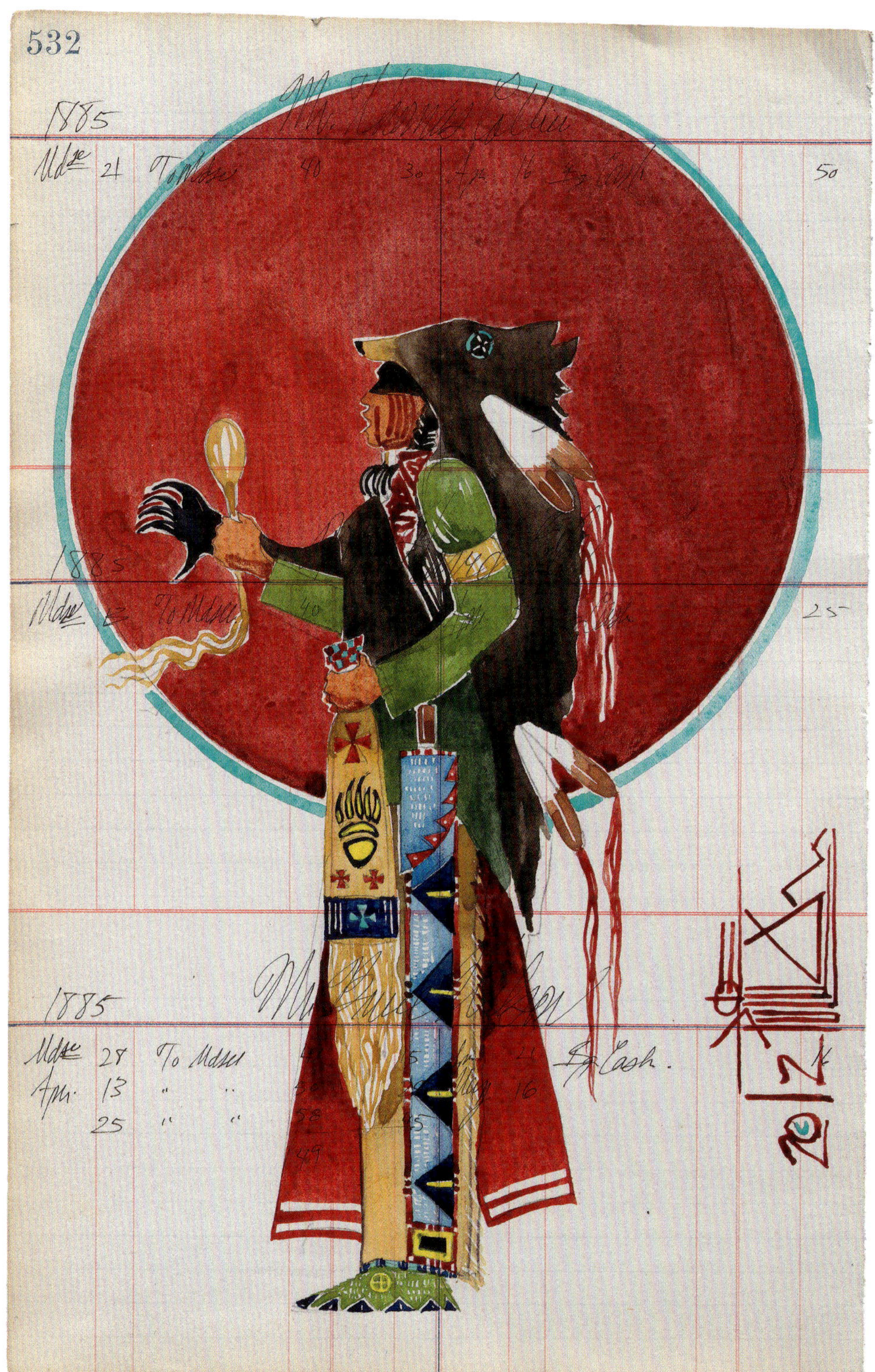

Joel Pulliam (Oglala Lakota, b. 1968). *His Bear Medicine,* 2012. Antique ledger paper, watercolor, graphite, ink; 31.8 × 20 cm. 26/8955

The bear headdress, claw, and footprint design all indicate that this man is a healer who gains his medicine power through an association with the bear. The animal's power has been transferred to him through a dream.

TERRANCE GUARDIPEE (Blackfeet)

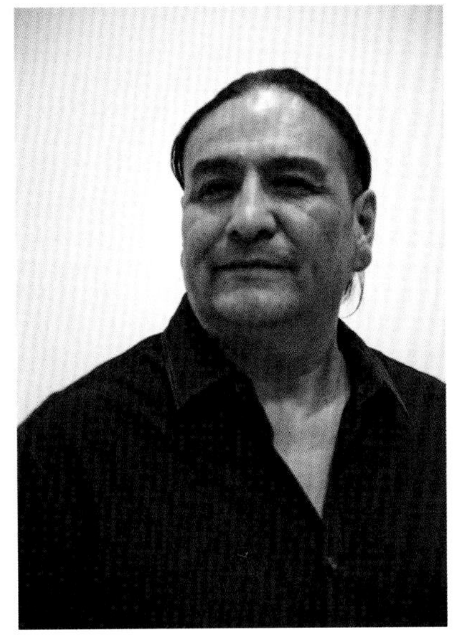

Terrance Guardipee, 2015. Photo by NMAI staff

"When I left Browning, Montana, I took twenty paintings, a one-way ticket to Seattle, and maybe a hundred and fifty bucks in cash. I knew I was going to be a good artist and share my culture in a true and accurate way."

Terrance Guardipee is a renowned ledger artist and painter. His powerful art reflects the strength and honor of his Blackfeet heritage. He uses bold, bright color combinations and blends contemporary style with traditional topics and symbols. Guardipee is well known for painting and drawing horse riders, warriors, spiritual leaders, society ceremonies, and tipis. As background media, he uses antique ledger paper, receipts, checks, music paper, and maps.

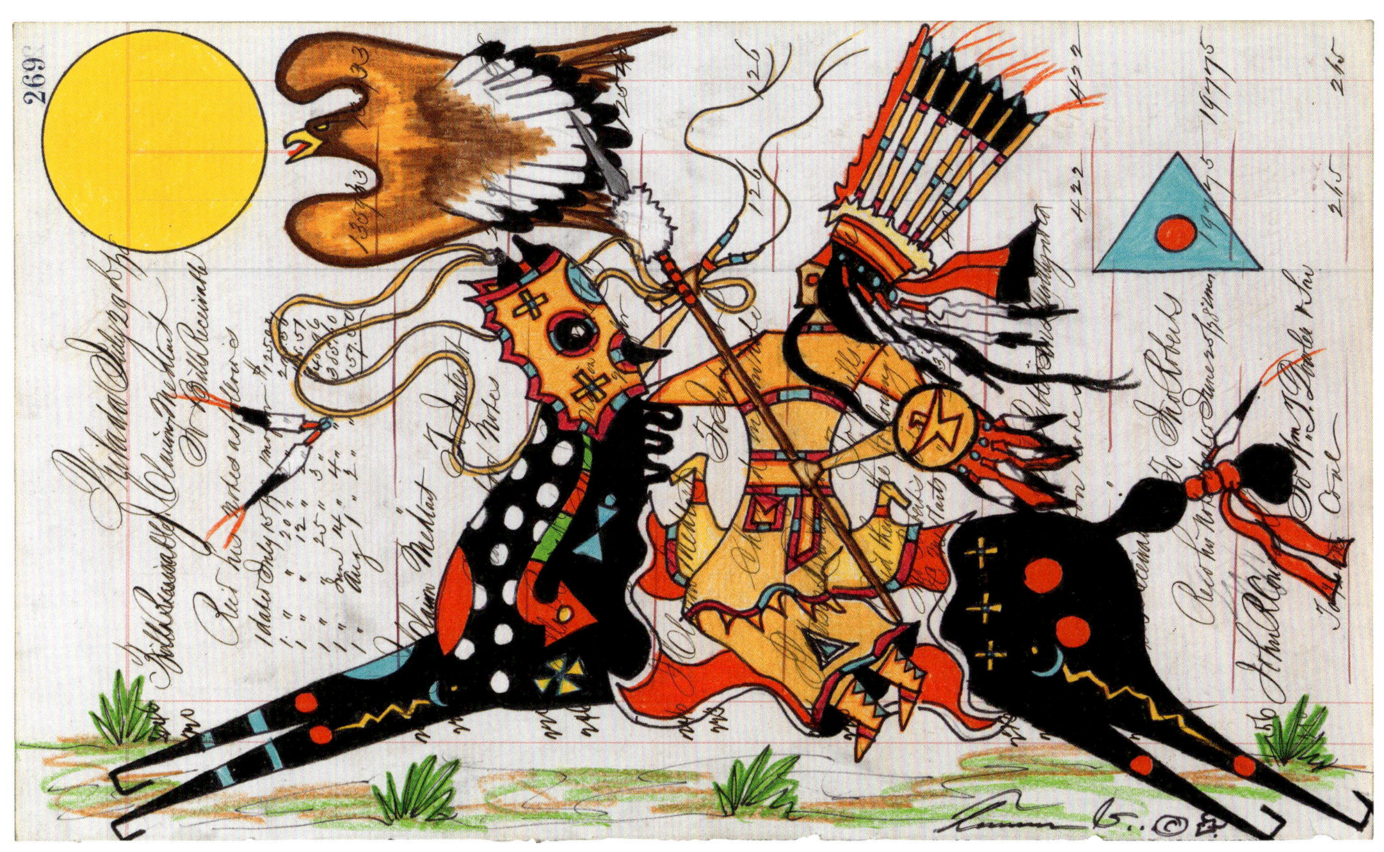

Terrance Guardipee (Blackfeet, b. 1968). *Running Eagle–Blackfeet Warrior Woman,* 2012. Antique ledger paper, colored pencil, graphite, ink; 21.2 × 34.7 cm. 26/8906

Running Eagle was a powerful Blackfeet warrior in the early 1800s. She was a war chief in the previously all-male Crazy Dogs Warrior Society. The blue disks on the horse's mask, front legs, and back legs indicate female power associated with Mother Moon.

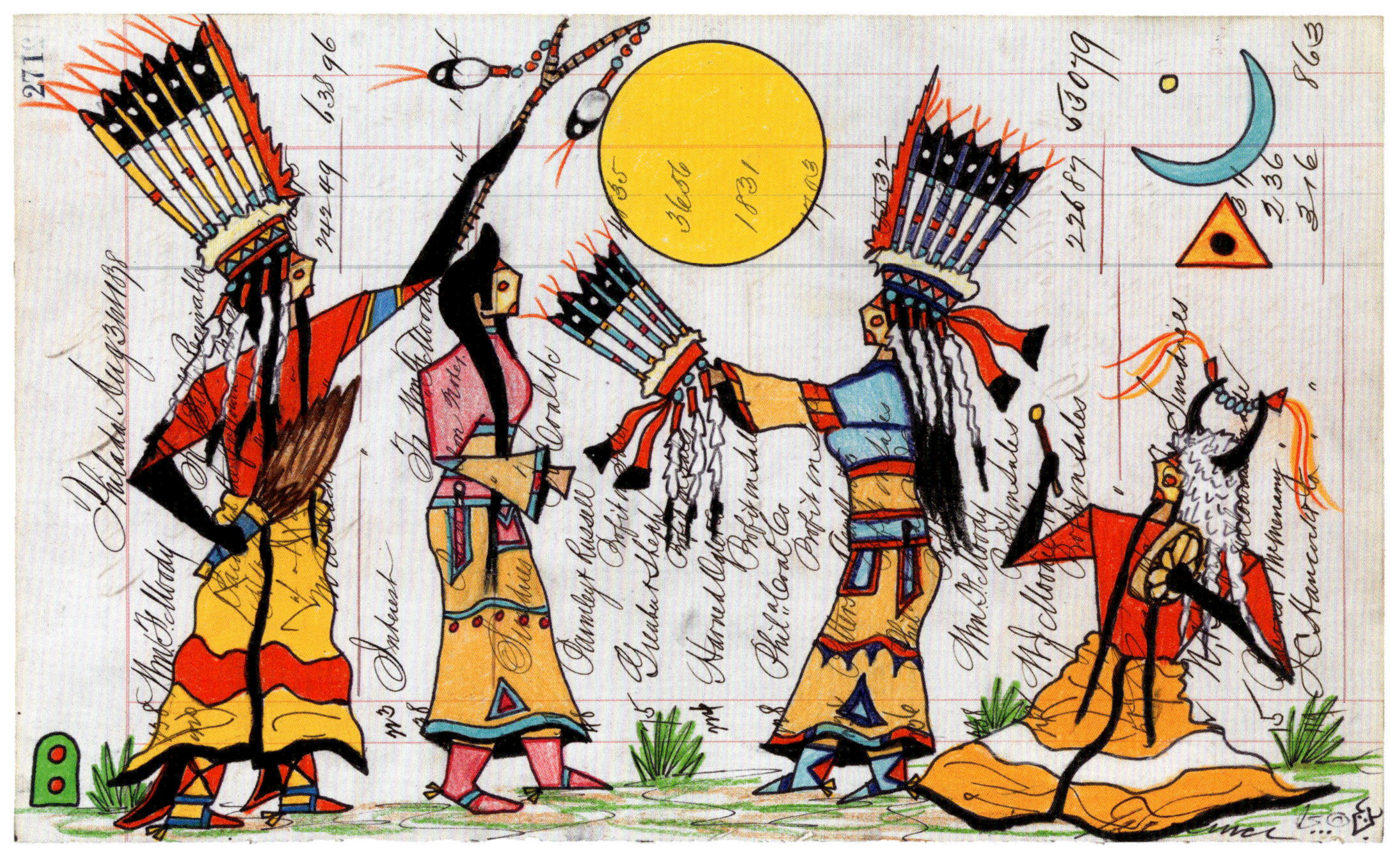

Terrance Guardipee (Blackfeet, b. 1968). *Blackfeet Headdress Transfer*, 2012. Antique ledger paper, graphite, colored pencil, ink; 21.2 × 34.7 cm. 26/8908

This drawing shows a ceremony in which an older woman is transferring a sacred headdress to a younger woman to bring her into the War Bonnet Society. The red sash indicates a female headdress. Both men are wearing blankets around their waists out of respect for the sun, as one sings and the other proclaims war stories.

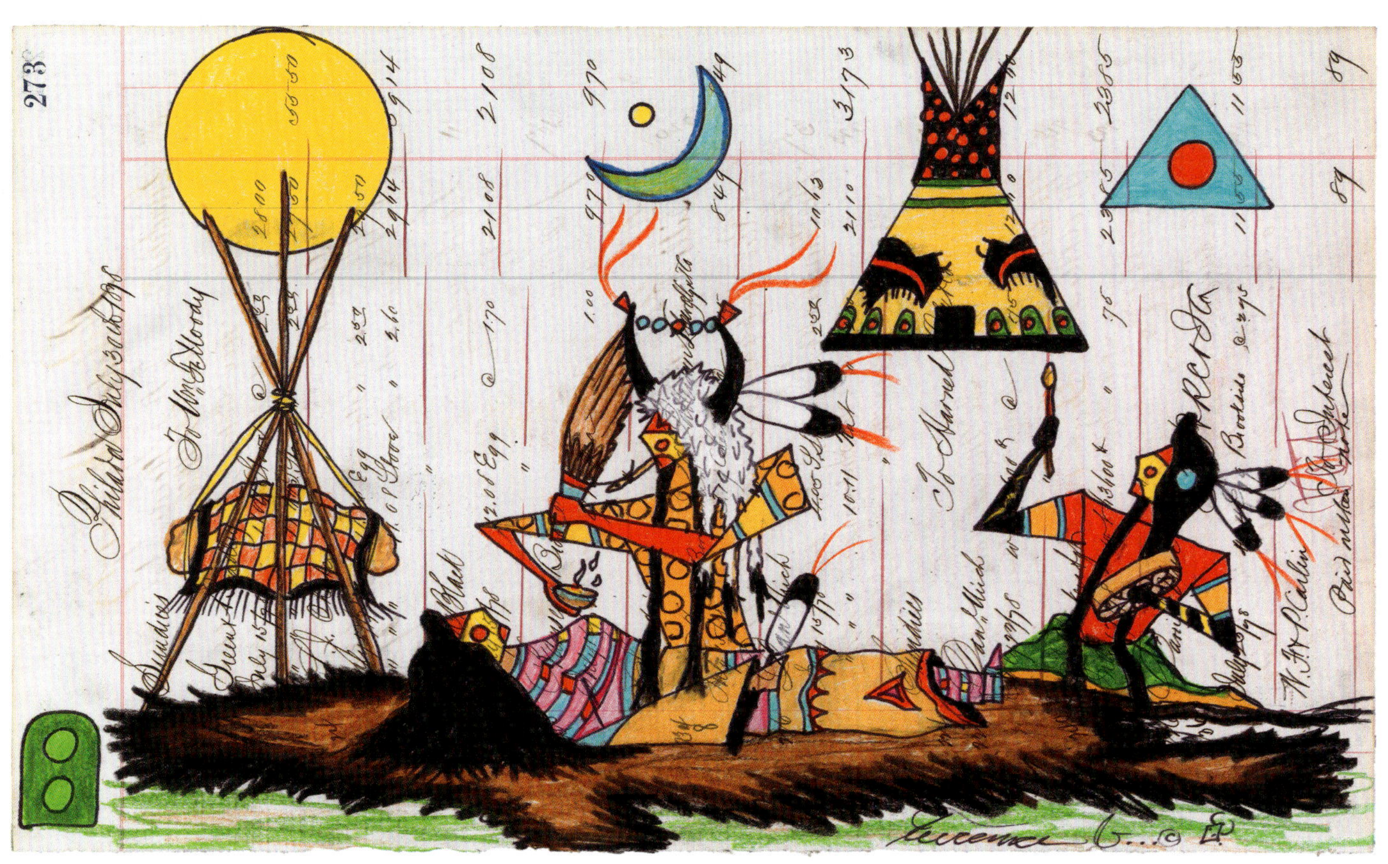

Terrance Guardipee (Blackfeet, b. 1968). *Healing Ceremony*, 2012. Antique ledger paper, colored pencil, graphite, ink; 21.2 × 34.7 cm. 26/8905

A medicine man uses an eagle-feather fan to spread smoke from burning sage over a spiritually ill woman. Another man plays a drum and sings to invoke spirits. A sacred healing bundle hangs from a nearby tripod.

DARRYL GROWING THUNDER (Dakota/Nakoda)

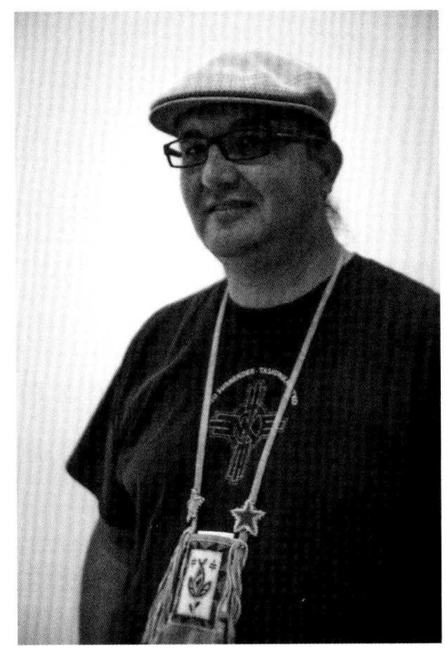

Darryl Growing Thunder, 2015. Photo by NMAI staff

"I get a lot of inspiration from contemporary powwows and celebrations. A simple glimpse of people carrying a flag or eagle staff can give inspiration for my artwork."

Darryl Growing Thunder is an award-winning ledger artist from the Fort Peck Indian Reservation in Montana. He has been surrounded by art since birth. "It was a way of life, whether it was the astounding bead or quillwork created by my mother, Joyce Growing Thunder Fogarty, or the ease with which my father, Jim Fogarty, put paint to canvas in his paintings of Western and American Indian heritage," Growing Thunder says.

This immersion in Dakota and Nakoda art grounds his style. Growing Thunder works in the Plains narrative art tradition to pay tribute to his ancestors and as a means of cultural continuity and identity.

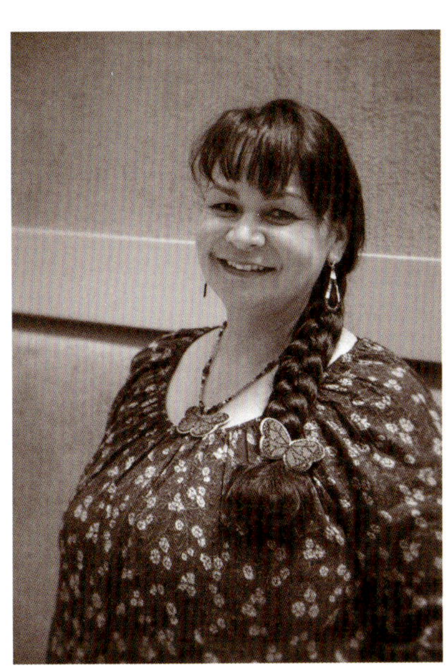

Juanita Growing Thunder Fogarty, 2015.
Photo by NMAI staff

Juanita Growing Thunder Fogarty (Dakota/Nakoda, b. 1969) and Darryl Growing Thunder (Dakota/Nakoda, b. 1967). *Doll with Honor Dress*, 2009. Hide, muslin, porcupine quills, beads, ribbon, brass thimbles, brass spots, paint, horsehair; 52.9 × 27 × 7 cm. 26/7725

This doll is a collaboration between Juanita Growing Thunder Fogarty and her brother Darryl Growing Thunder. He drew the horse-raiding scene on the dress. She made the doll and completed the bead- and quillwork.

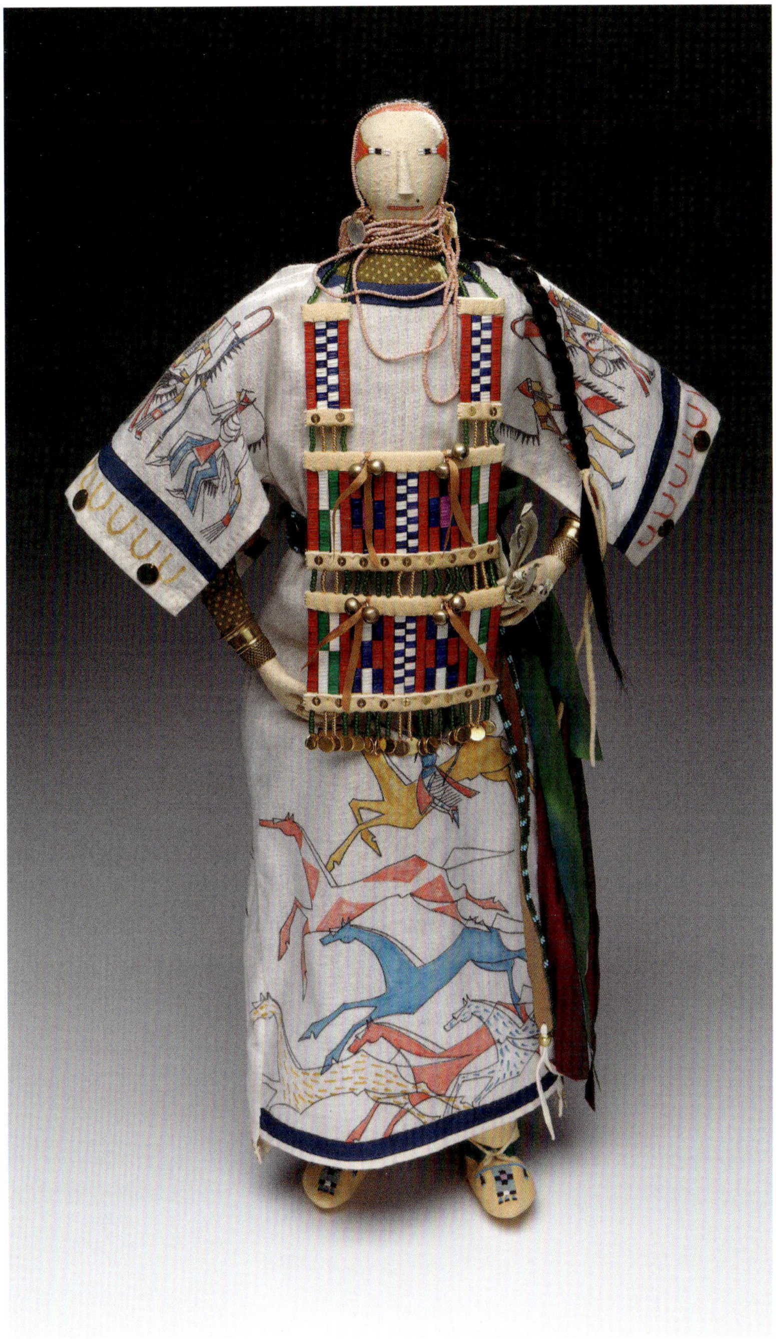

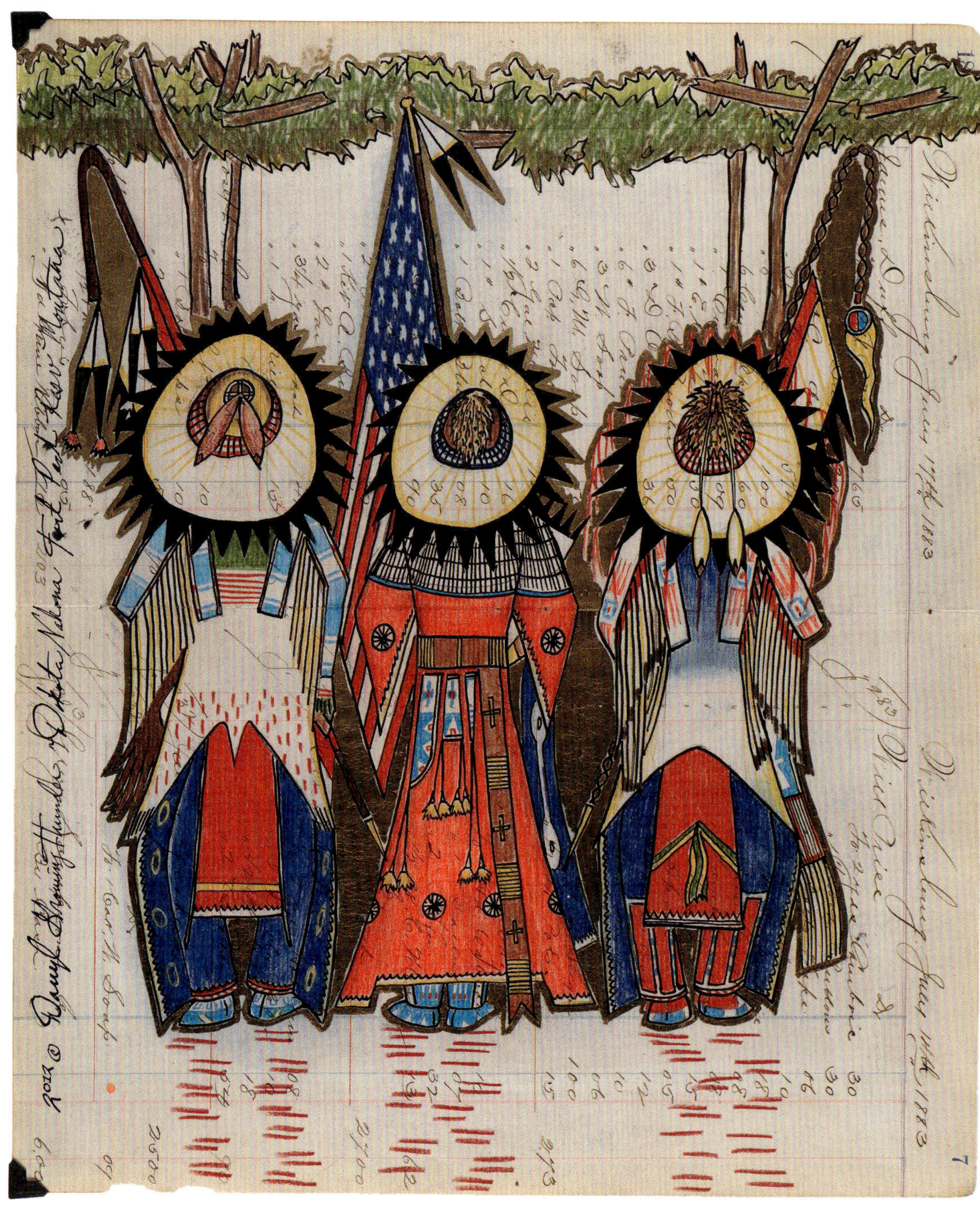

Darryl Growing Thunder (Dakota/Nakoda, b. 1967). *Victory Dance,* 2012. Antique ledger paper, colored pencil, gold marker, graphite, ink; 42.2 × 34.4 cm. 26/8963

Veterans lead a procession of dancers into a powwow. In the center is a woman, in honor of the many female veterans returning from conflicts in the Middle East. The red tracks indicate the direction of movement.

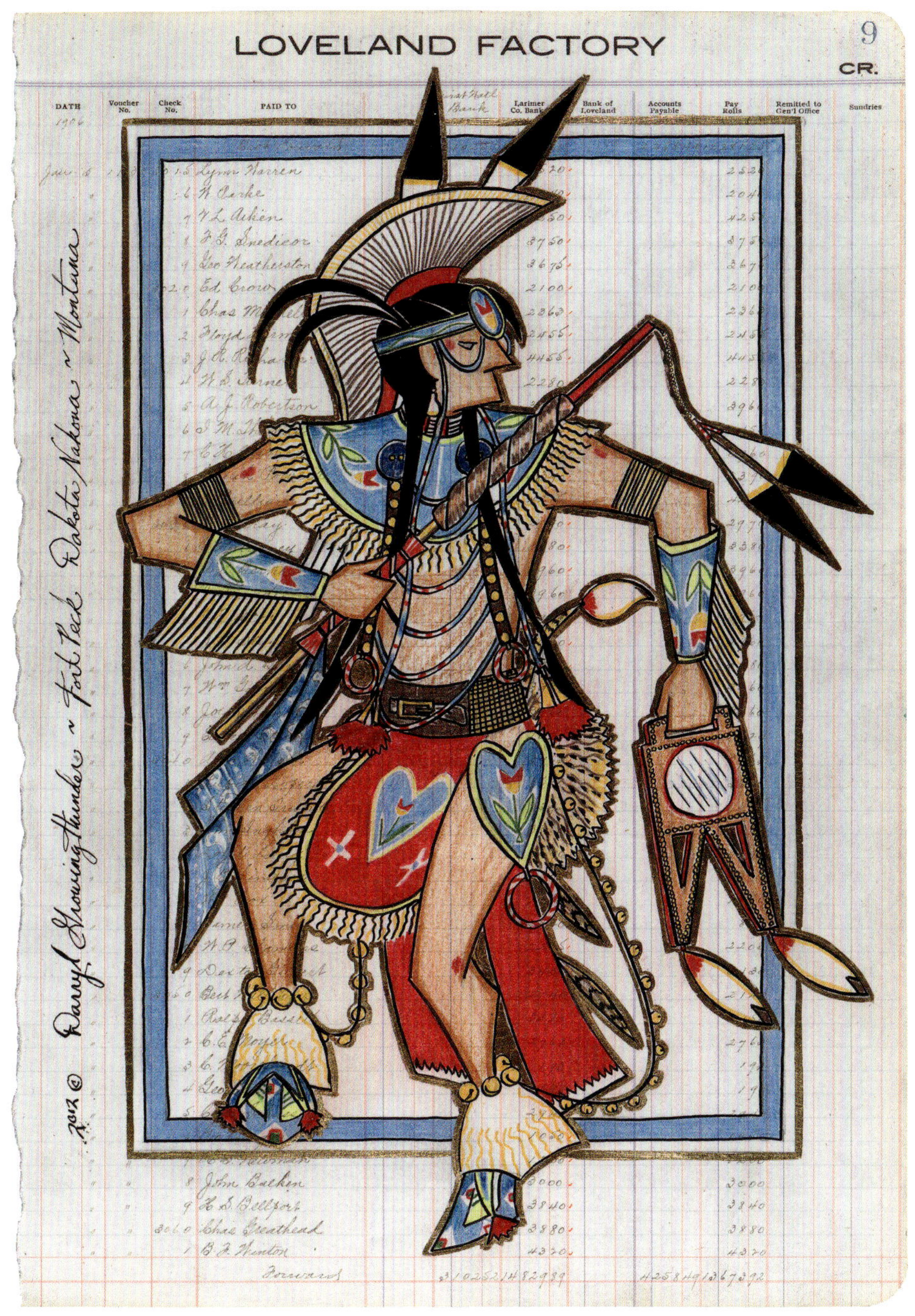

Darryl Growing Thunder (Dakota/Nakoda, b. 1967). *Chicken Dancer*, 2012. Antique ledger paper, colored pencil, gold marker, graphite, ink; 40.5 × 27.5 cm. 26/8959

A dancer holds a dance stick in one hand and a mirror board in the other as he performs a flamboyant Chicken Dance, which is a tradition in many northern Plains tribes. The performer imitates the mating dance of a prairie chicken.

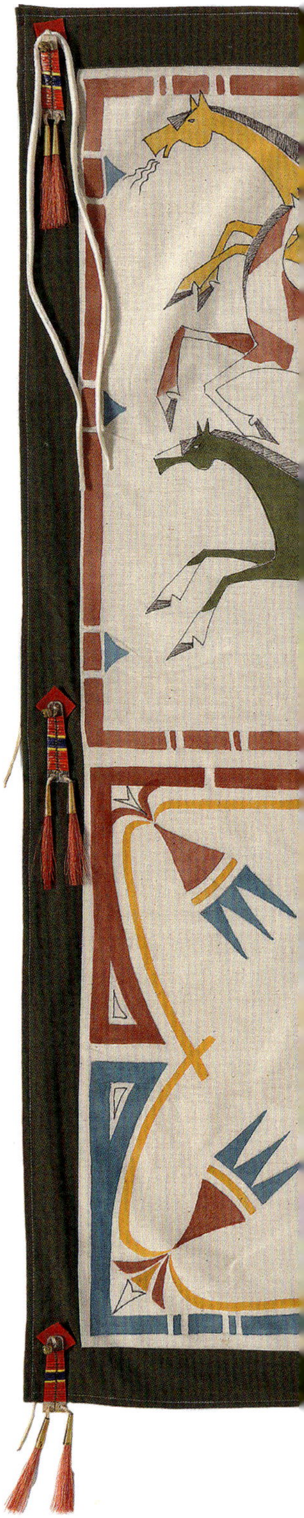

Darryl Growing Thunder (Dakota/Nakoda, b. 1967). *Horse Raid Muslin,* 2012. Canvas, cotton cloth, paint, ink, hide, felt, porcupine quills, horsehair, brass cones, brass bells, dye; 107.3 × 99 × 2.5 cm. 26/8991

"This piece reflects back on those days when men were able to accomplish deeds that may not be so acceptable by today's standards," Growing Thunder says of this depiction of a horse raid. The geometric designs on the lower portion represent eagle tail feathers.

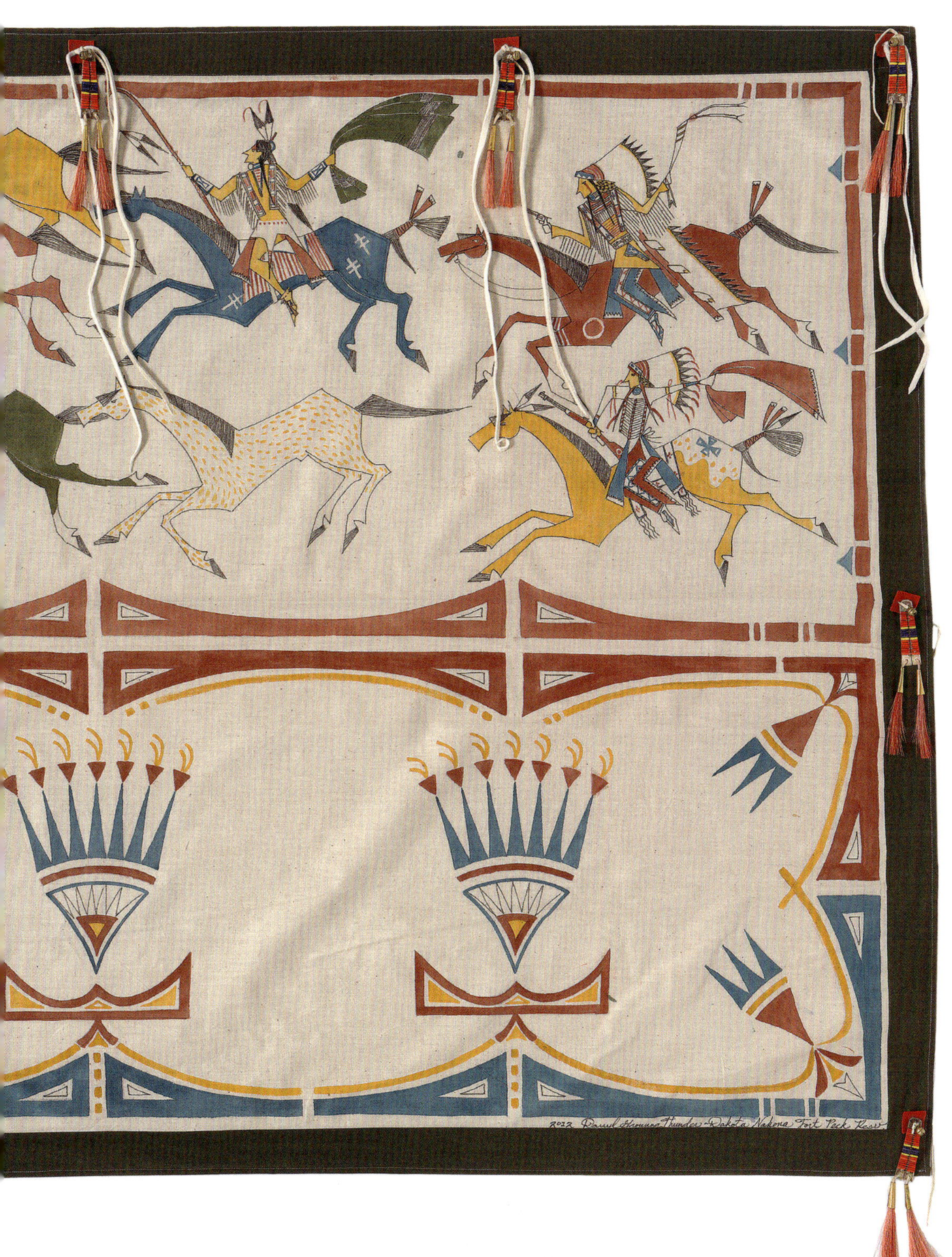
2022
Growing Thunder ~ Dakota Nakona Fort Peck Resv.

CHRIS PAPPAN (Osage/Kaw/Cheyenne River Lakota)

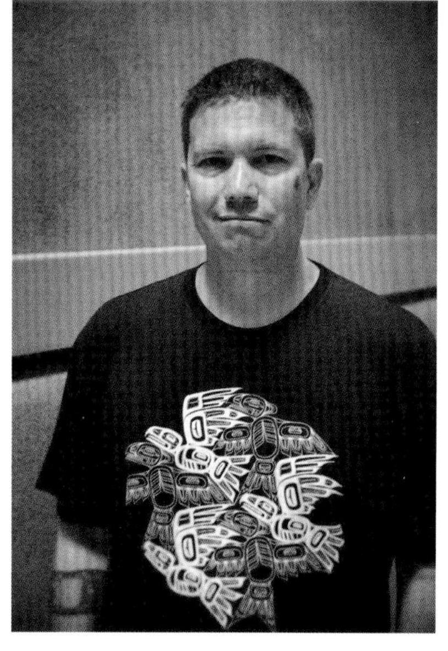

Chris Pappan, 2015. Photo by NMAI staff

"I intentionally distort portraits because people have a distorted idea of Native people. As artists and keepers of culture, we have a responsibility to promote the truth."

Happening on a brand-new ledger book in the supply room at his day job led Chris Pappan to create a series of twenty-first-century ledger drawings. In his work he often uses antique ledger paper to layer additional meaning onto stories he tells through portraiture. Pappan purposely breaks with the pictographic style seen in much of Plains narrative art. "Traditions have to evolve and change in order to survive," he says. "This is my way of keeping the tradition of ledger art fresh, new, and exciting."

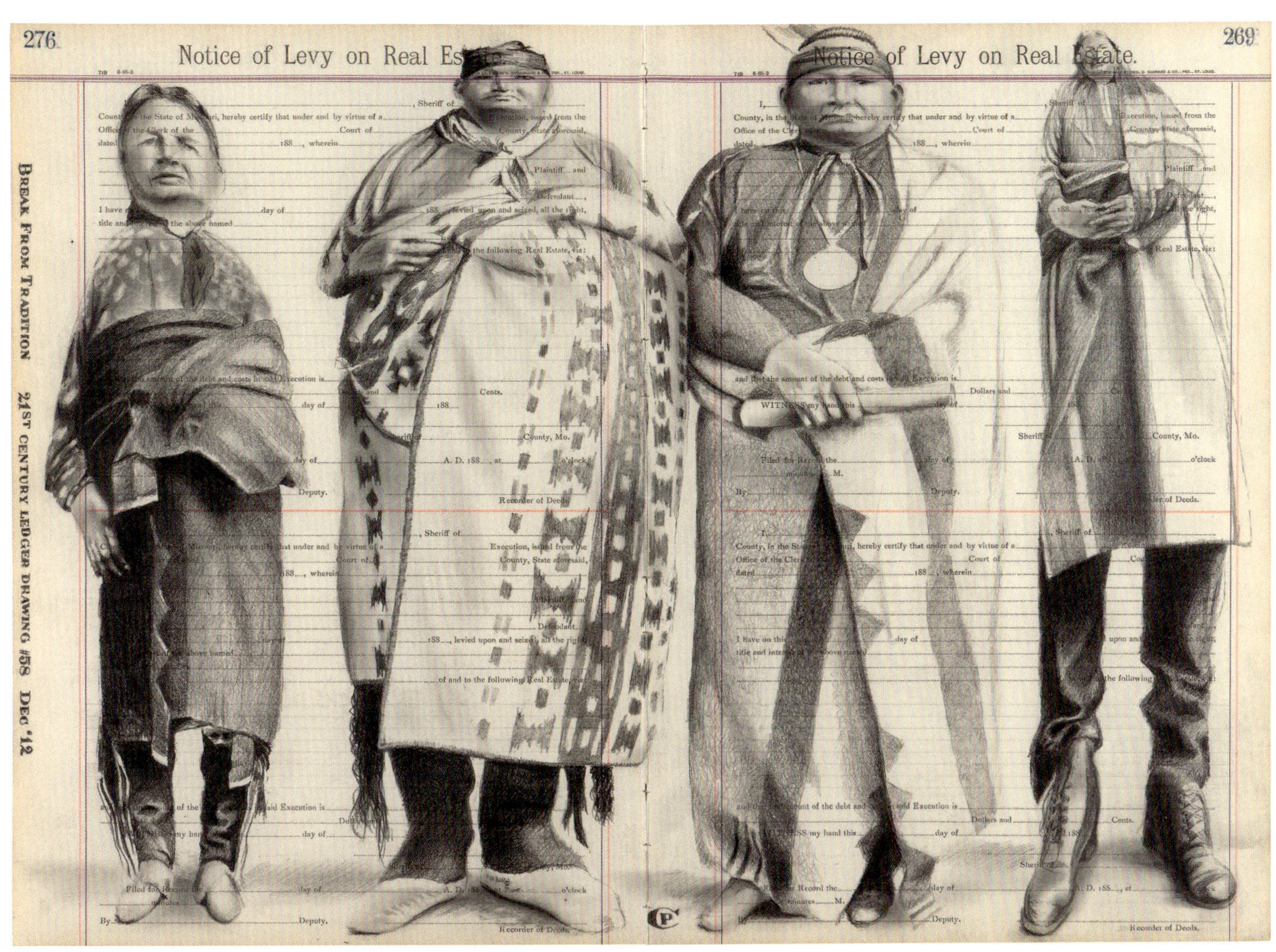

Chris Pappan (Osage/Kaw/Cheyenne River Lakota, b. 1971). *Break from Tradition, 21st-Century Ledger Drawing No. 58*, 2012. Antique ledger paper, graphite; 31.9 × 52.5 cm. 26/8977

This drawing portrays members of a nineteenth-century Osage delegation that traveled to Washington, DC. Most such tribal delegations were pressing the federal government to uphold their land and treaty rights. Poignantly, Pappan drew this image on paper used to record a real estate transaction.

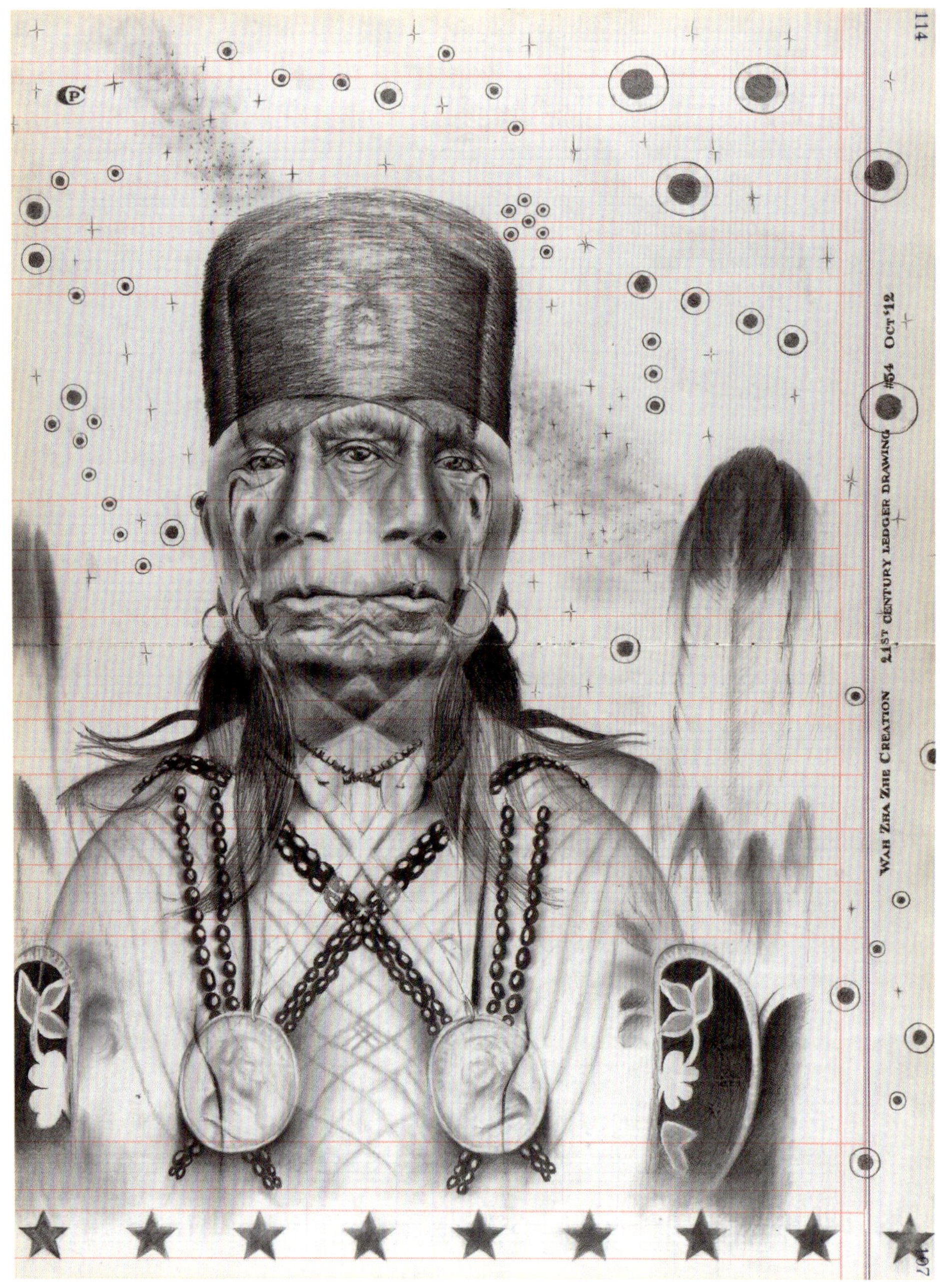

Chris Pappan (Osage/Kaw/Cheyenne River Lakota, b. 1971). *Wah Zha Zhe Creation, 21st-Century Ledger Drawing No. 54*, 2012. Antique ledger paper, graphite; 57.5 × 41.4 cm. 26/8975

Drawn as solid dots inside circles, stars form the background of this portrait of Chief Bacon Rind, one of the last of the Osage chiefs. The stars reference the Wah Zha Zhe, or Osage, creation story about people stepping down from the stars.

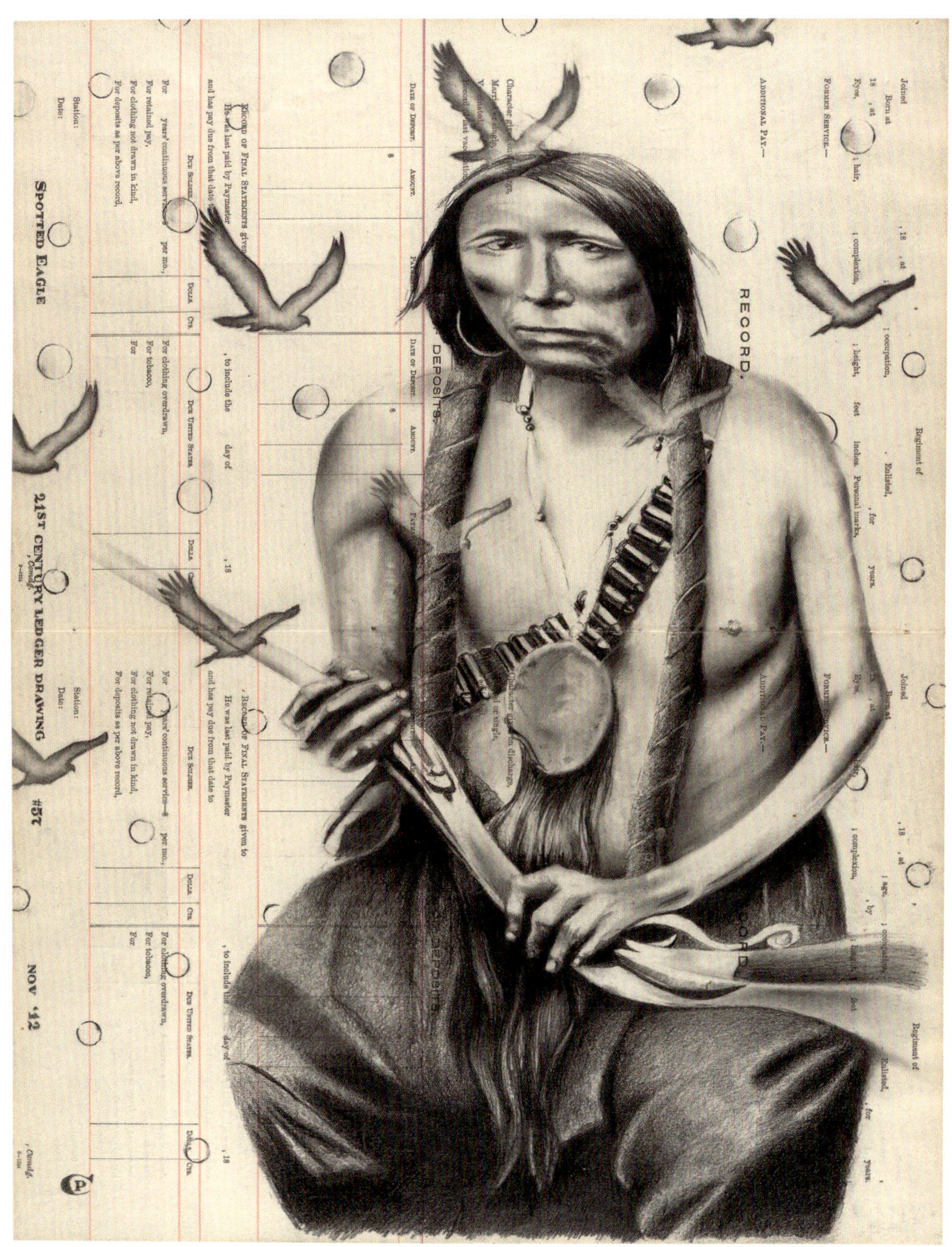

Chris Pappan (Osage/Kaw/Cheyenne River Lakota, b. 1971).
Spotted Eagle, 21st-Century Ledger Drawing No. 57, 2012.
Antique ledger paper, graphite; 52.2 × 39.5 cm. 26/8976

Pappan drew this portrait on a page from a nineteenth-century U.S. Army ledger book. "Knowing the history between our people and the U.S. Army, I see creating artwork on this paper as my form of counting coup," Pappan says.

CHESTER MEDICINE CROW (Apsáalooke [Crow])

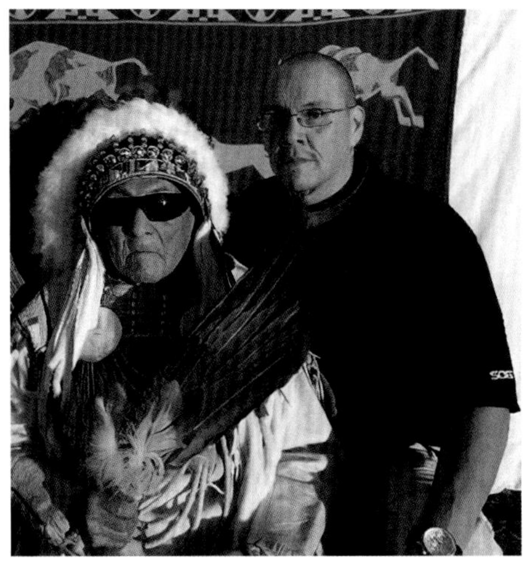

Chester Medicine Crow (right) with his grandfather Highbird, or Joe Medicine Crow, 2014. Photo by Ramona Medicine Crow (Apsáalooke [Crow])

Chester Medicine Crow's traditional name, Sacred Raven, is linked to his ancestry and to the subject matter of his work shown here. Sacred Raven was the name of his great-great-grandfather, who became known as Medicine Crow due to a mistranslation that stuck. Both the deeds of Medicine Crow and the drawings he completed following a delegation trip to Washington, DC, have influenced Chester's work.

Chester began drawing in the Plains narrative art tradition in high school and focused on the style in college. He works in a contemporary style to depict events from the past and present.

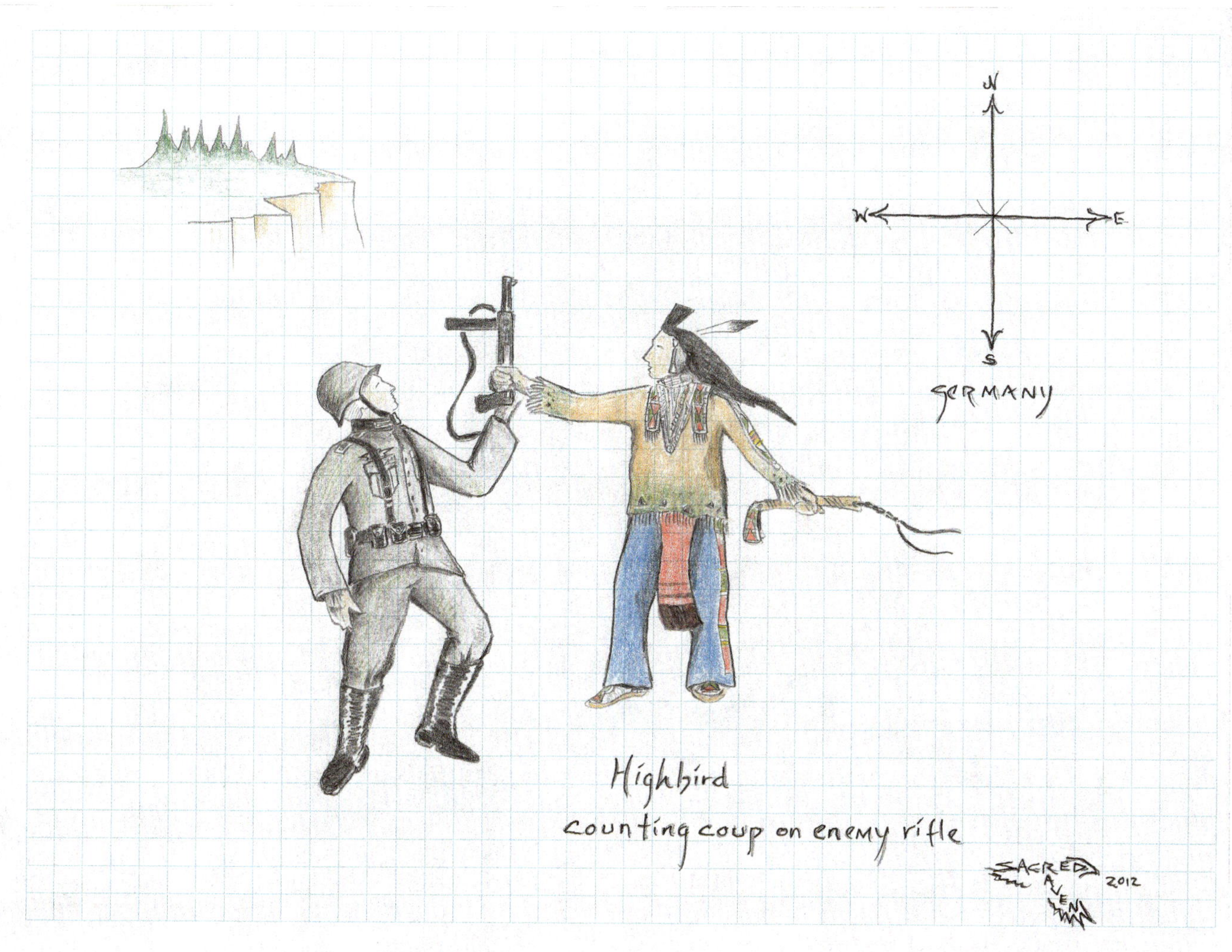

Chester Medicine Crow (Apsáalooke [Crow], b. 1973). *Highbird Counting Coup on Enemy Rifle*, 2012. Graph paper, graphite, colored pencil, ink; 21.6 × 27.8 cm. 26/8973

Plains people have long viewed getting close to an enemy as an act of bravery. In this drawing, Highbird (Joe Medicine Crow) gets close enough to take a German enemy's rifle during World War II. In his left hand Highbird holds a riding quirt, or coup stick.

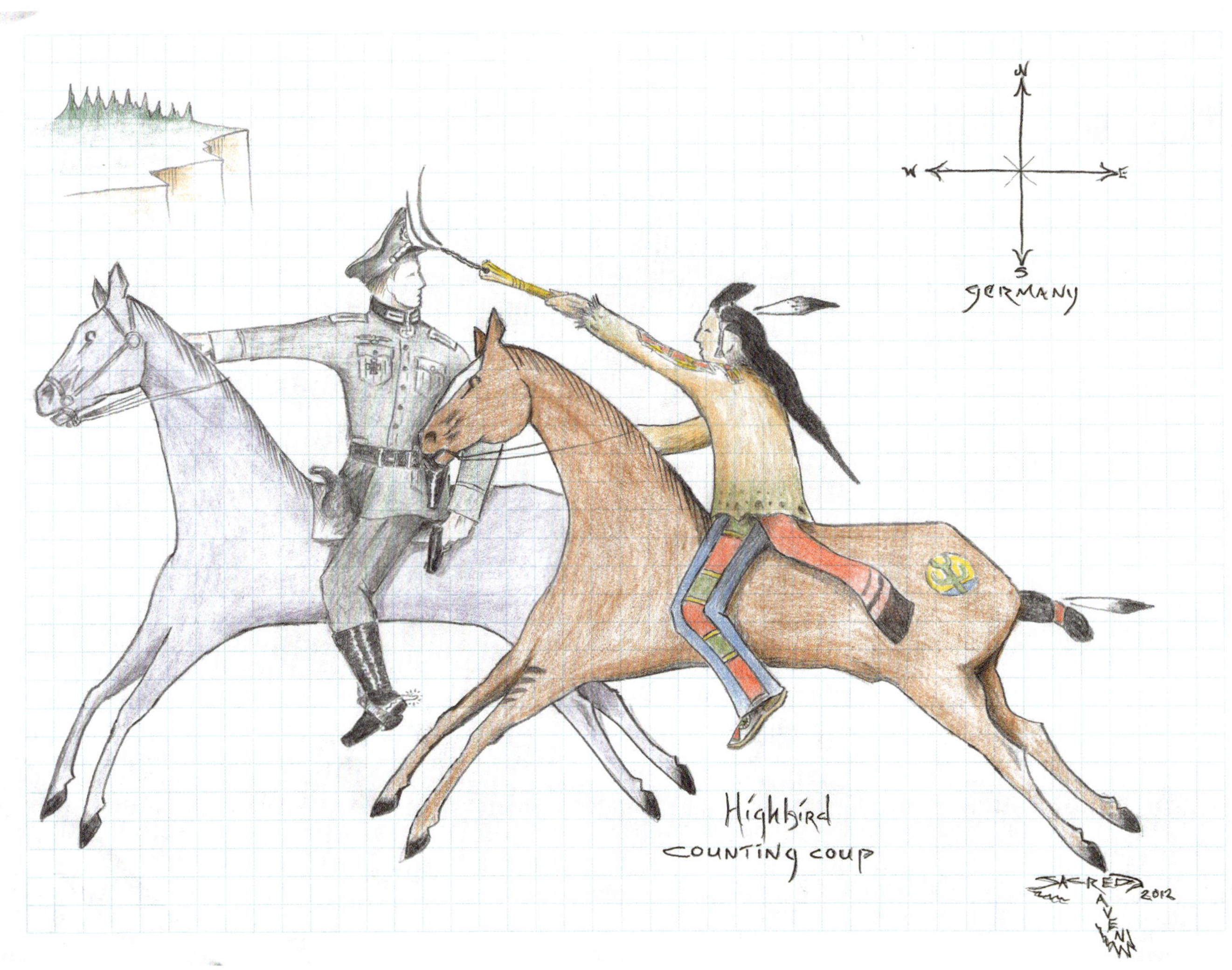

Chester Medicine Crow (Apsáalooke [Crow], b. 1973). *Highbird Counting Coup*, 2012. Graph paper, graphite, colored pencil, ink; 21.6 × 27.8 cm. 26/8974

Highbird (Joe Medicine Crow) rides close to an enemy and hits him on the head with a riding quirt. Getting close to an enemy was considered a coup, or achievement.

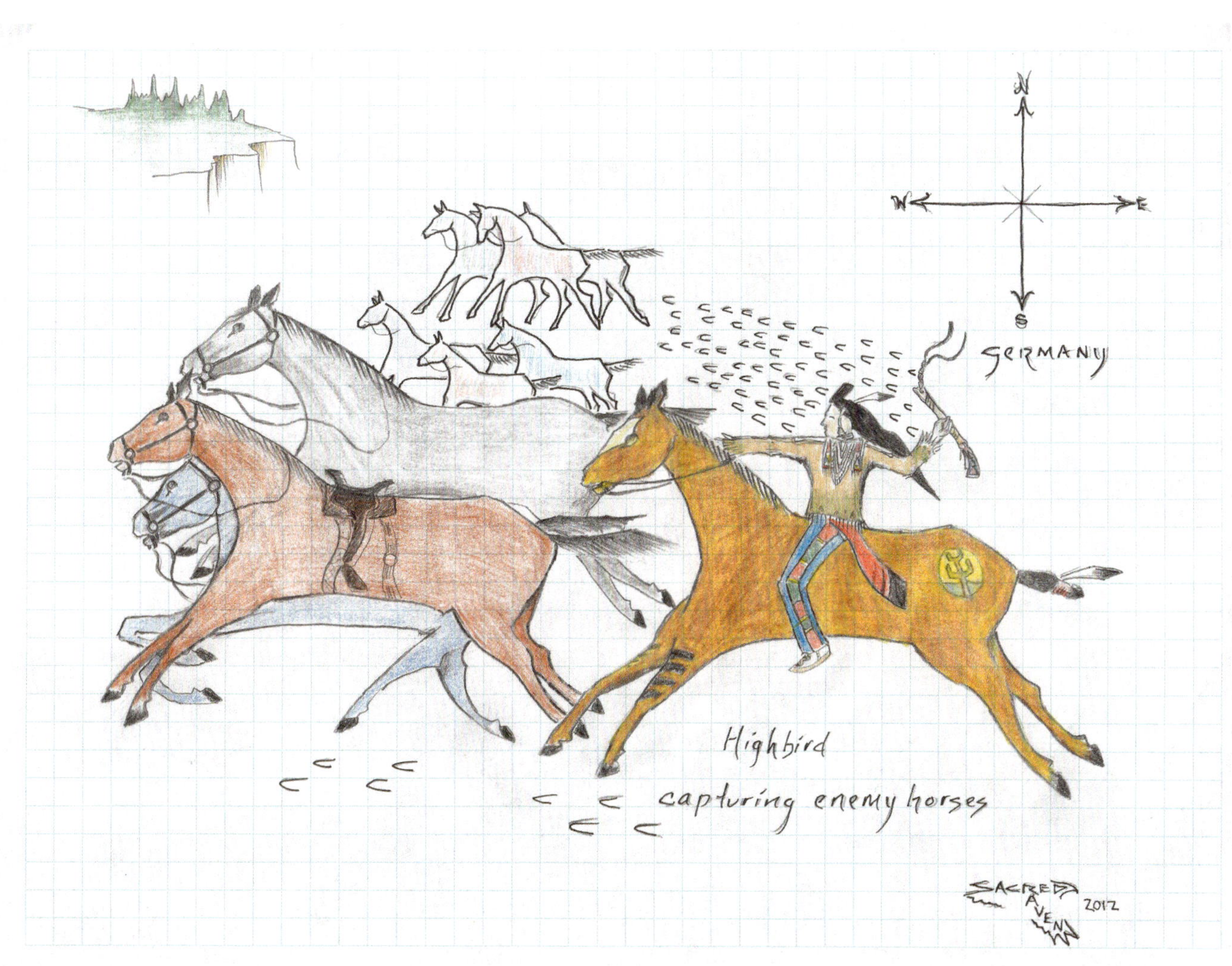

Chester Medicine Crow (Apsáalooke [Crow], b. 1973). *Highbird Capturing Enemy Horses*, 2012. Graph paper, colored pencil, graphite, ink; 21.1 × 27.8 cm. 26/8971

Raiding an enemy's horses is a tradition that survived even into twentieth-century warfare. As a group of German officers was retreating near the end of World War II, Highbird (Joe Medicine Crow) and his platoon followed them. When the officers camped for the night, Highbird captured fifty of their horses.

RONALD L. BURGESS (Comanche)

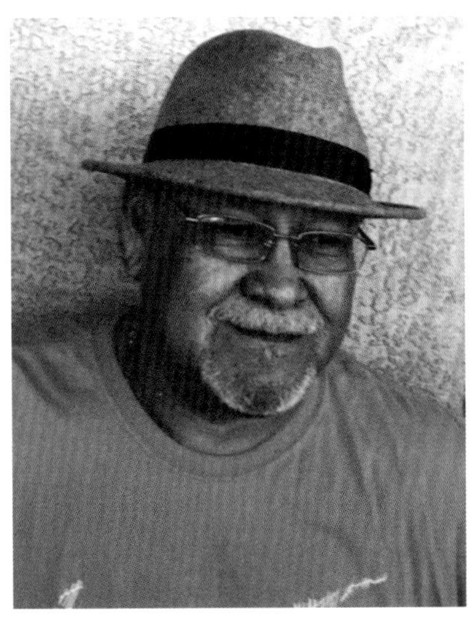

Ronald L. Burgess, 2016. Photo by LaNora Burgess

The simplicity of the narrative art form appeals to Ronald L. Burgess, who describes himself as a minimalist. He was inspired by the artwork of the warriors imprisoned at Fort Marion in Florida in the 1870s, and by the artists known as the Kiowa Five.

Growing up, Burgess got into trouble as a teenager and was sent to two boarding schools. At Fort Sill Indian School, there was no art program, but Burgess, influenced by the artist Doc Tate Nevaquaya, often practiced on his own. He went on to earn his bachelor's degree in art education and a doctorate in education to further his career as a teacher and administrator. Today he is retired, and often attends art shows with his sons, who are also practicing artists.

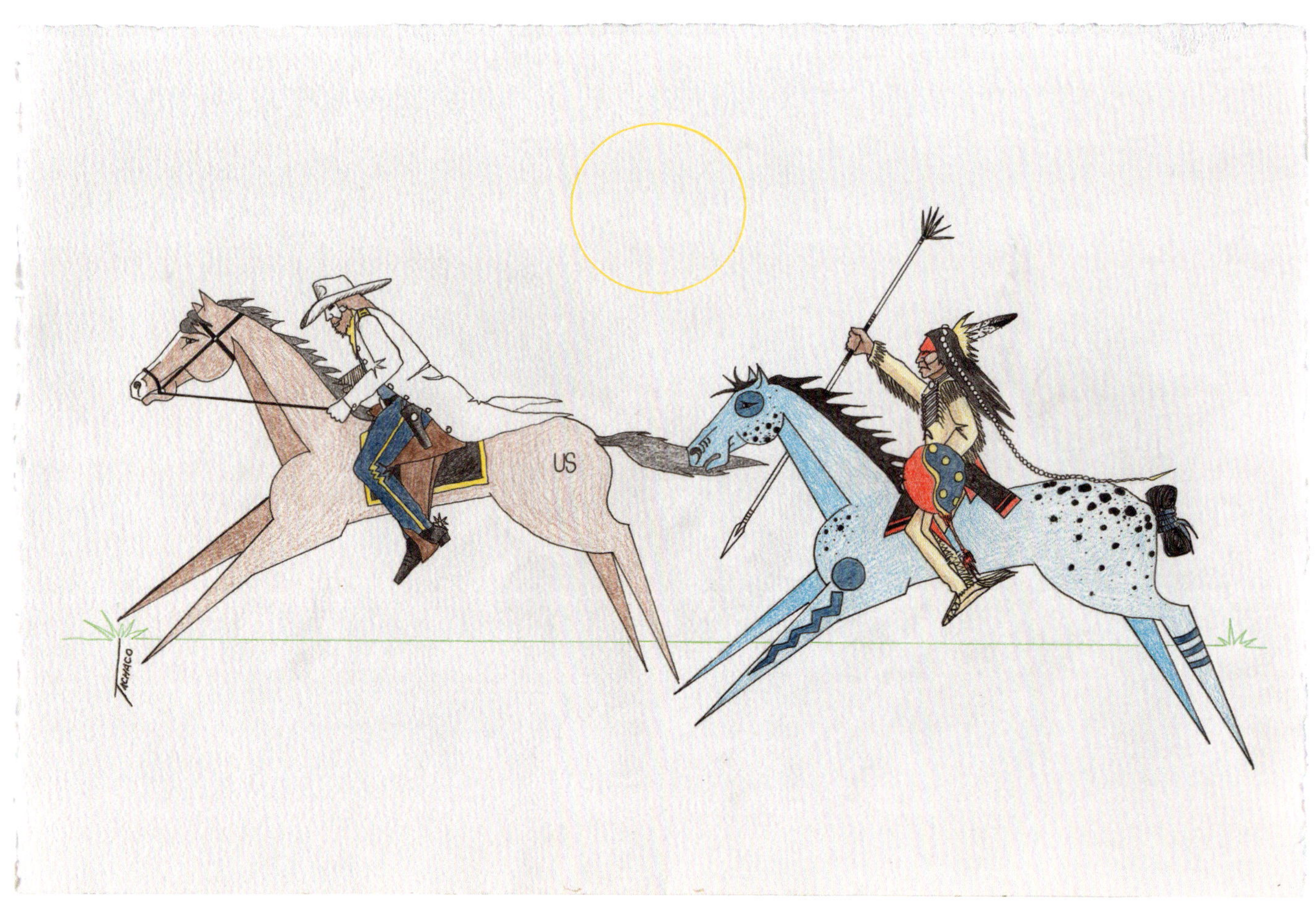

Ronald L. Burgess (Comanche, b. 1950). *Tha Tsi Koa*, 2012. Paper, graphite, colored pencil, ink; 38.5 × 56.5 cm. 26/8933

Burgess titled this image with his family name, which means "Pull up on your enemy and cut them off." Here a warrior approaches a U.S. Army foe and prepares to take him down.

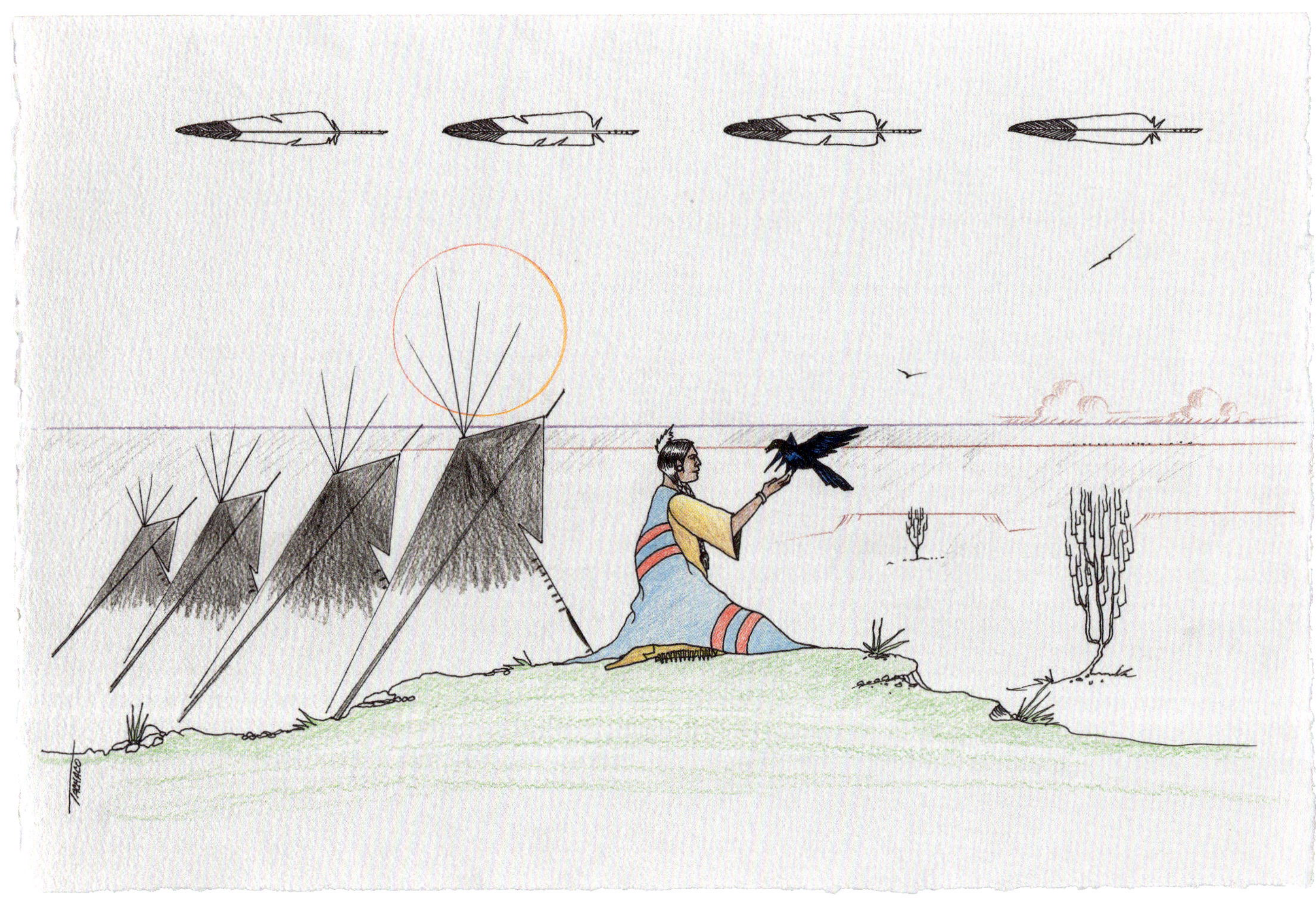

Ronald L. Burgess (Comanche, b. 1950). *How the Wichita Mountains Came to Be (Part 1)*, 2012. Paper, graphite, colored pencil, ink; 38.5 × 56.5 cm. 26/8931

These two drawings illustrate a Comanche story about the origin of the Wichita Mountains.

Back when the Comanche spoke with the Thu We Kaw, or crows, the birds would often warn the people of danger. One day the Thu We Kaw told Saana Pia, or Medicine Woman, that the enemy was coming from the north. The men had gone south to hunt, and only the elders, women, and children were at the camp. Saana Pia sent some older children to get the men. To buy some time, she grabbed a handful of rocks and threw them in the direction of the enemy, asking the Creator to erect a barrier to slow them down. Mountains rose out of the plains and saved the people. They are now called the Wichita Mountains.

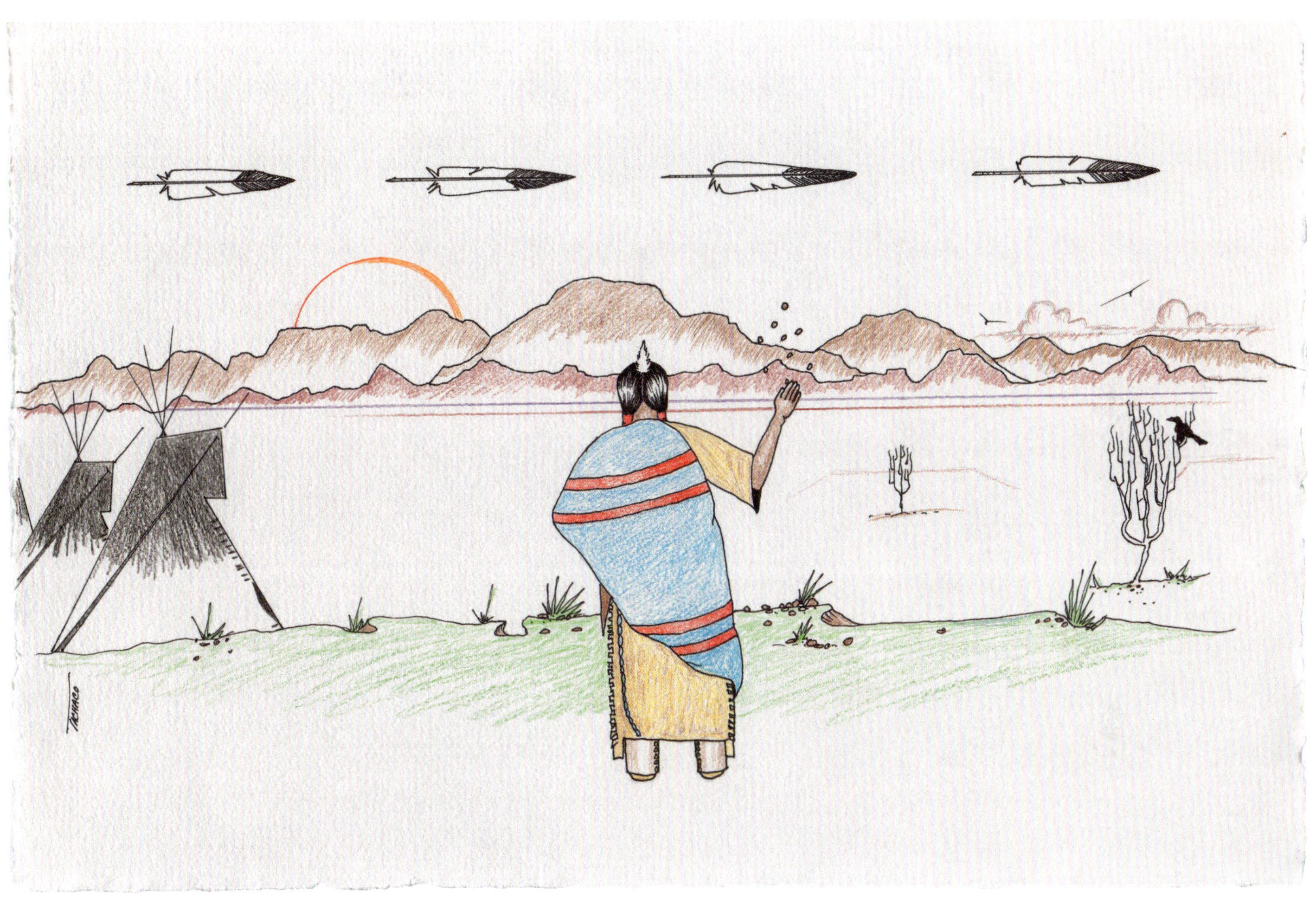

Ronald L. Burgess (Comanche, b. 1950). *How the Wichita Mountains Came to Be (Part 2),* 2012. Paper, graphite, colored pencil, ink; 38.5 × 56.5 cm. 26/8932

DALLIN MAYBEE (Northern Arapaho/Seneca)

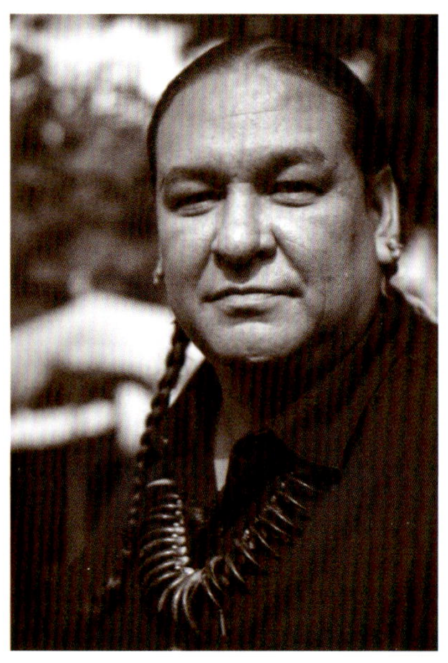

Dallin Maybee, 2015. Photo by NMAI staff

Dallin Maybee is a contemporary ledger artist who explores identity and the interplay between traditional and contemporary Indian life. His work addresses how these forces have allowed Indigenous cultures to evolve, survive, and flourish. In addition to antique ledger pages, his media have included pages from the 1583 Geneva Bible, sixteenth-century rice paper, rawhide, and buffalo robes.

A lawyer, Maybee is the assistant director of development for the Native American Rights Fund and tours occasionally with the American Indian Dance Theater and other performing arts groups. His Arapaho name in English loosely translates as Thunder Sound Comes Down, or A Thunder Being Is Coming This Way.

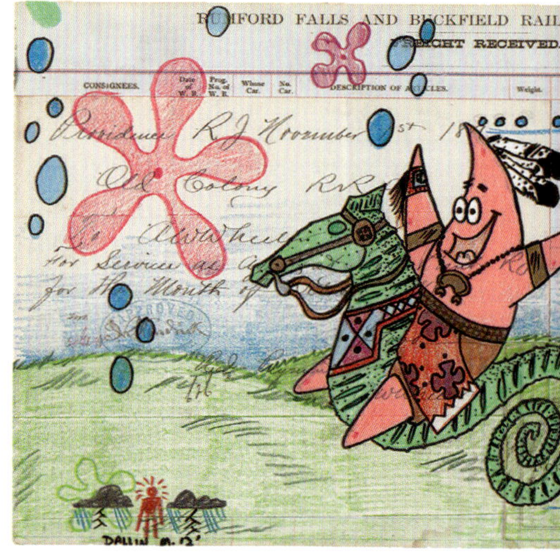

Dallin Maybee (Northern Arapaho/ Seneca, b. 1974). *A Cruise through Bikini Bottom,* 2012. Antique ledger paper, graphite, colored pencil, ink, glue; 21 × 81.3 cm. 26/8966

Here Maybee takes an image from popular culture—Spongebob Squarepants—and gives it a Native twist.

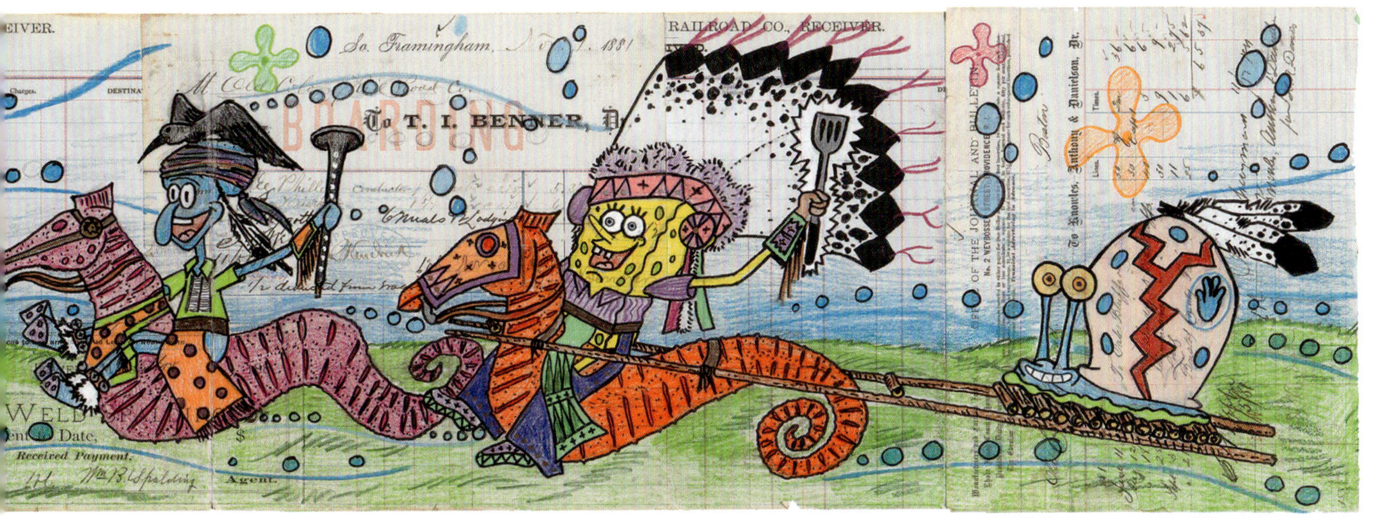
EIVER.
So. Framingham,
1881
RAILROAD CO., RECEIVER.
BOARDING
To T. I. BENNER, Dr.
To Knowles, Anthony & Danielson, Dr.
WELD
Received Payment.
Agent.

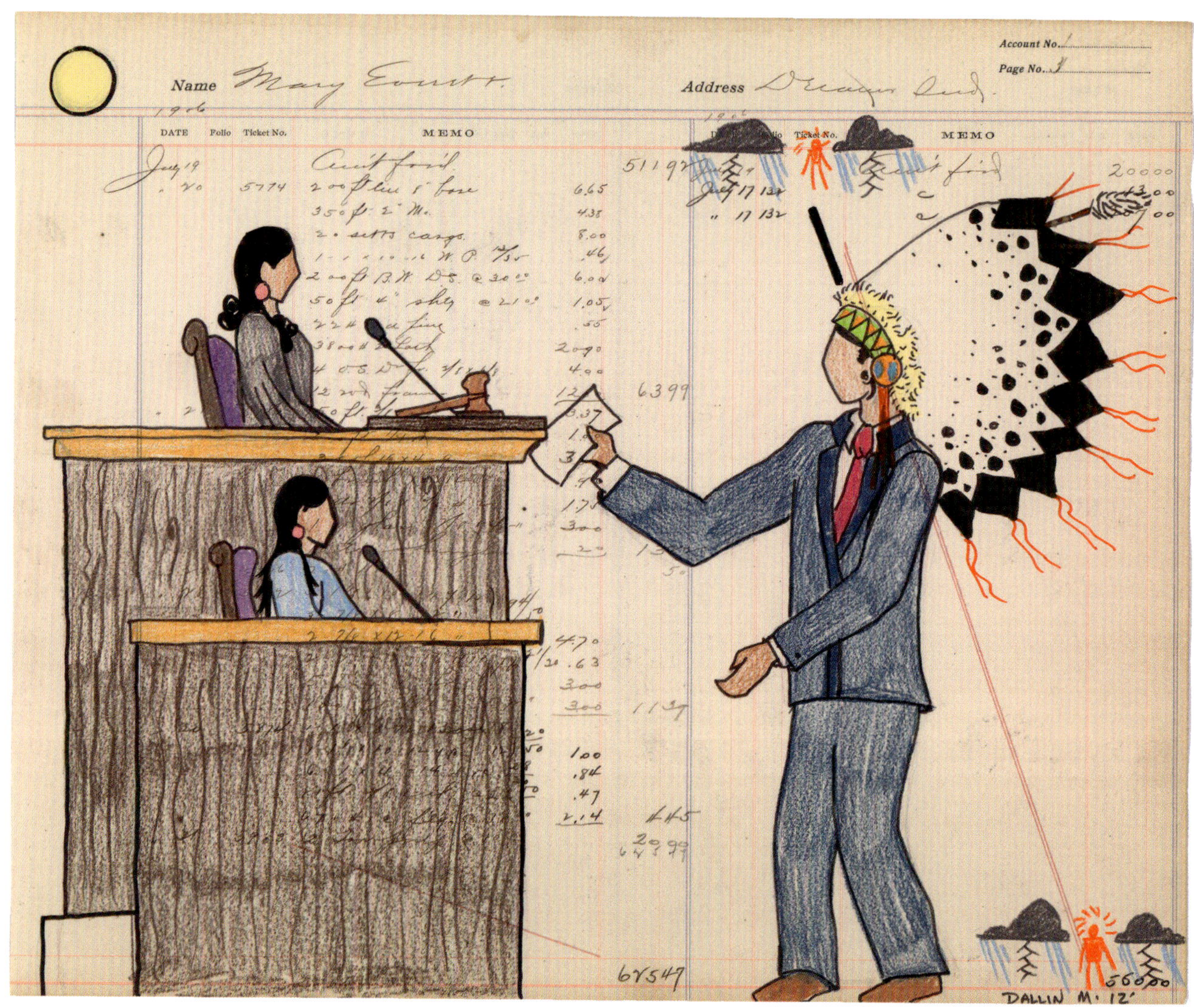

Dallin Maybee (Northern Arapaho/Seneca, b. 1974). *Indian Prosecutor*, 2012. Antique ledger paper, graphite, colored pencil, ink; 28 × 33 cm. 26/8964

This drawing illustrates the period in Maybee's life when he worked as a prosecutor for the Gila River Indian Community near Phoenix. The name glyph signifying Maybee is visible twice—it points to the male figure and appears in the lower right as the artist's signature.

"This bison robe reflects my personal perception of the evolution of Native traditional and contemporary art forms."

—Dallin Maybee

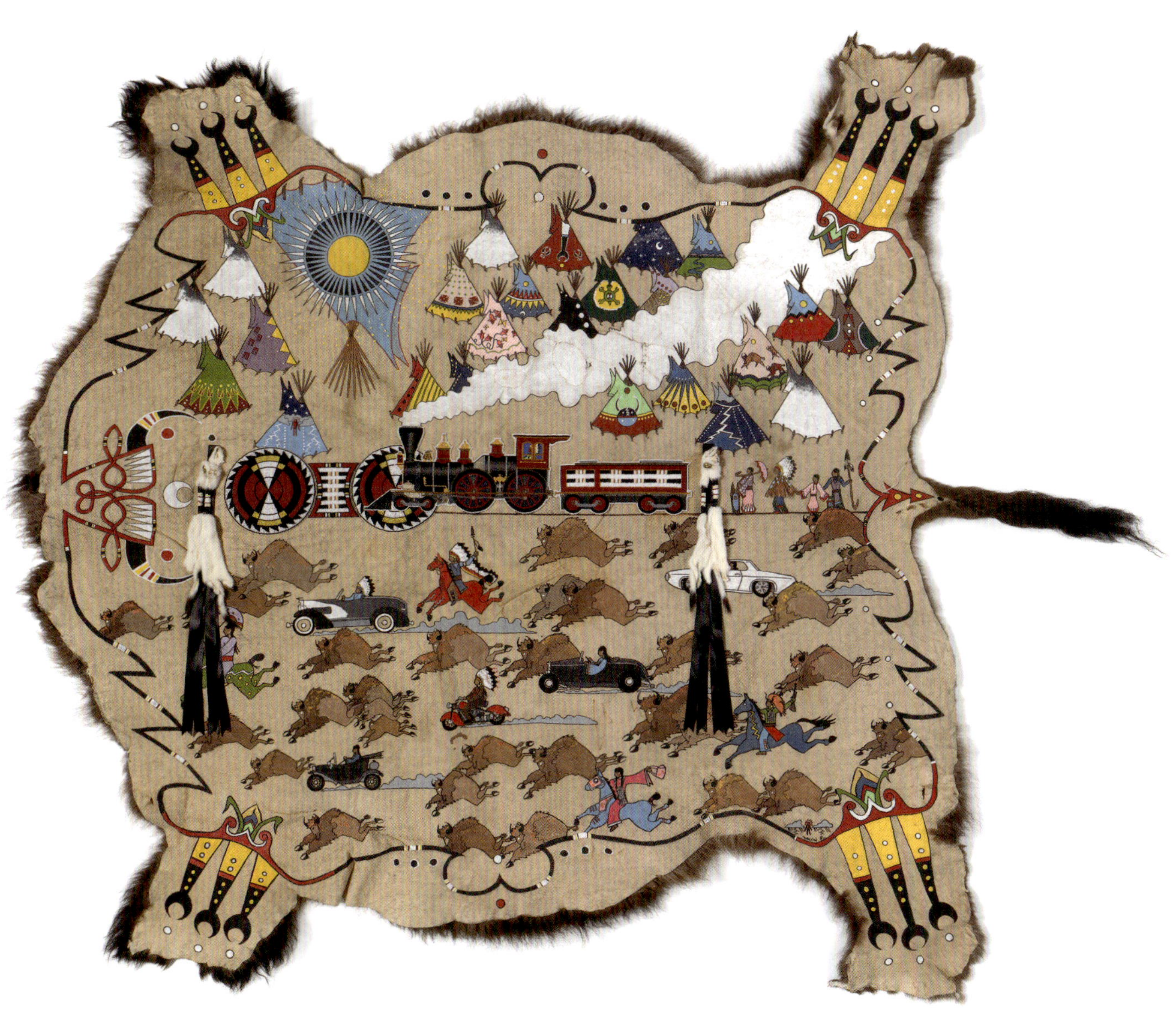

Dallin Maybee (Northern Arapaho/Seneca, b. 1974). *Conductors of Our Own Destiny*, 2013. Commercial tanned bison hide, cut-glass beads, glass seed beads, gold beads, steel beads, copper beads, ermines, satin ribbon, Swarovski crystals, acrylic paint, ink, brass bells; 204.3 × 245.5 × 7 cm. 26/9328

GENERATIONS OF ART

Lauren Good Day

I grew up steeped in culture—creating was just something we always did. There were always star quilts in progress, moccasins in the works, featherwork in process, and dresses to be finished in time for the next celebration. My grandmothers and mother were always busy with their projects, and my grandfather made traditional war bonnets for the community's veterans and their warrior society doings.

Outstanding role models, they passed to me a love for our cultural practices, expressed by dressing our family in finery and providing items for dances and ceremonies. They brought me into the world of art. Seeing the process and progress of their special skills instilled in me a strong interest in our material culture of beadwork, quillwork, regalia making, contemporary fashion, and, importantly, narrative art.

When I was five, my mother sat me down, got out her beads and buckskin, and said she was going to teach me to bead. That day I finished a small bracelet for myself. It was beginner work, but it was mine, and from there I fell in love with creating. Later, at the age of thirteen, I learned to sew powwow regalia by watching my family. My mother and sister were often sewing and working on outfits for the summer powwows. My grandma was the family moccasin maker. We often timed it just right to finish a matching set of beadwork and a fancy shawl outfit for one of our community's powwow celebrations. One summer, I desperately wished for a new shawl and dress for an upcoming powwow. Unfortunately, my mom had to travel for work and couldn't make them for me. But I felt confident enough to try

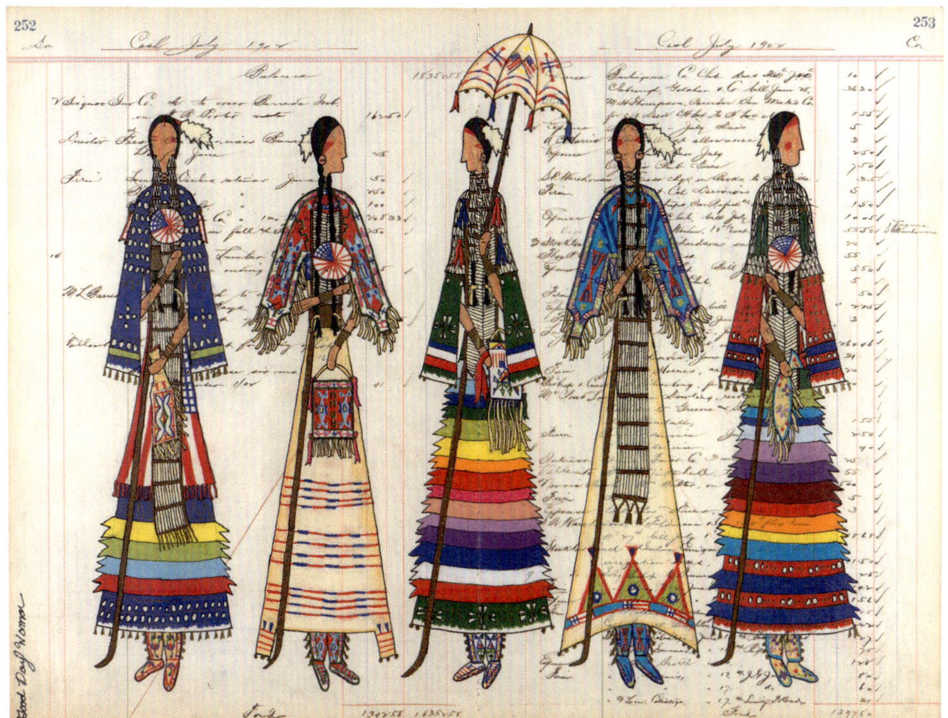

Lauren Good Day (Arikara/Hidatsa/Blackfeet/Plains Cree, b. 1987). *Independence Day Celebration*, 2012. Antique ledger paper, colored pencil, graphite, ink, felt-tipped marker; 57.6 × 44.9 cm. 26/9025

it out, just with the knowledge I had picked up by watching for years. With some technical assistance from my older sister, I completed new regalia for the weekend. The outfit was shiny and bright, with fabrics in the latest powwow trend. My mom and grandma were more old-school, but I was young and into the all the glitz and glamour the contemporary powwow world had to offer. This eventually led me to create wearable art, contemporary fashion, and, ultimately, wearable pictorial art that tells a story.

Looking back, I'm utterly grateful for my upbringing. Being surrounded by makers and creators instilled in me the values and teachings of our culture. Like a second nature, making was in my blood. For years as a teenager, I took orders for powwow regalia. Later my mother encouraged me to pick up and carry on a family tradition of ledger drawing. Within my Arikara lineage, we descend from the ledger artist Bloody Knife, a scout whose drawings are now in the National Museum of the American Indian's collections. Carrying on this tradition was important. My

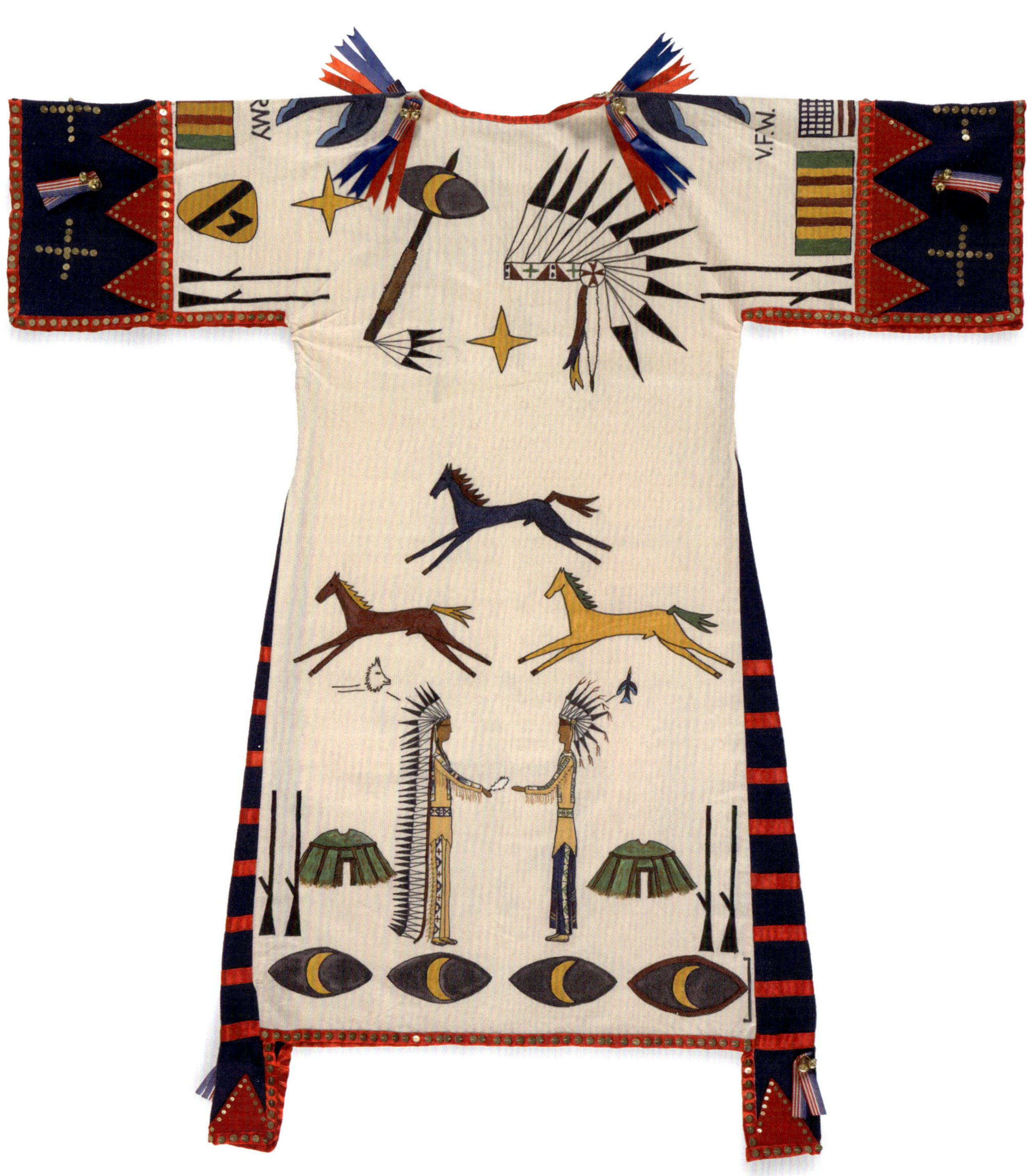
V.F.W.

mother gave me an antique ledger book and colored pencils, and from there I told my stories. Coming full circle in some years' time, my work would be acquired by the museum for the *Unbound* exhibition.

Pictorial drawing was predominantly and historically a male art form. A woman creating art in the ledger style was not common. I knew that I needed to stick with the basics of the form and depict my stories and lifeways as a woman. My work is often filled with stories of womanhood, raising children, creating, courtship, and my perspective on our ceremonies. My ledger pages and other creations are infused with values that have been passed down and details of the cultural doings we continue to this day.

The work the museum has acquired embodies my life as an Arikara and Hidatsa woman. A piece close to my heart honors my late grandfather Blue Bird, or Emery Good Bird Sr. It is a warriors' honoring dress meant to pay tribute to my grandfather's personal medicine story, to his significance as a member of the Stone Hammer warrior society, and to his accomplishments as a respected Hidatsa war veteran. Inspired by the old-time dresses honoring male relatives' war deeds, I wanted to honor my grandfather for his accomplishments, his great significance in the community, and the sacrifices he made for the people by serving in the U.S. Armed Forces. The dress combines my passion for pictorial art with my upbringing of regalia making and dressmaking.

Lauren Good Day (Arikara/Hidatsa/Blackfeet/Plains Cree, b. 1987). *A Warrior's Story, Honoring Grandpa Blue Bird*, 2012. Muslin, dyed wool fabric, pigments, brass sequins, brass bells, satin ribbon, cotton thread, acrylic sinew; 151 × 141.6 × 2.5 cm. Purchase supported by the R. Devon Hutchins Memorial Contemporary Art Fund 26/8817

The reverse side of the dress is pictured on page 53.

Making art that depicts my personal stories coordinates with the narrative drawings created in the past. *We Learn from Our Grandmothers* shows my history of learning and making alongside my female relatives. It honors the women who came before, those who passed on knowledge and continued the arts of our people. My grandmother and mother represent the elder generation, while my sister and I, both of us artists, represent the present. My niece, to whom we continue to pass on the knowledge of our arts, represents the future. Without past generations modeling and prioritizing our lifeways, we would no longer be. In our ancestors' honor, we continue their traditions and storytelling.

Our ceremonial lifeways also are a common theme within my work. My imagery tells stories of the feminine. Preparing for ceremonies is a significant part of my

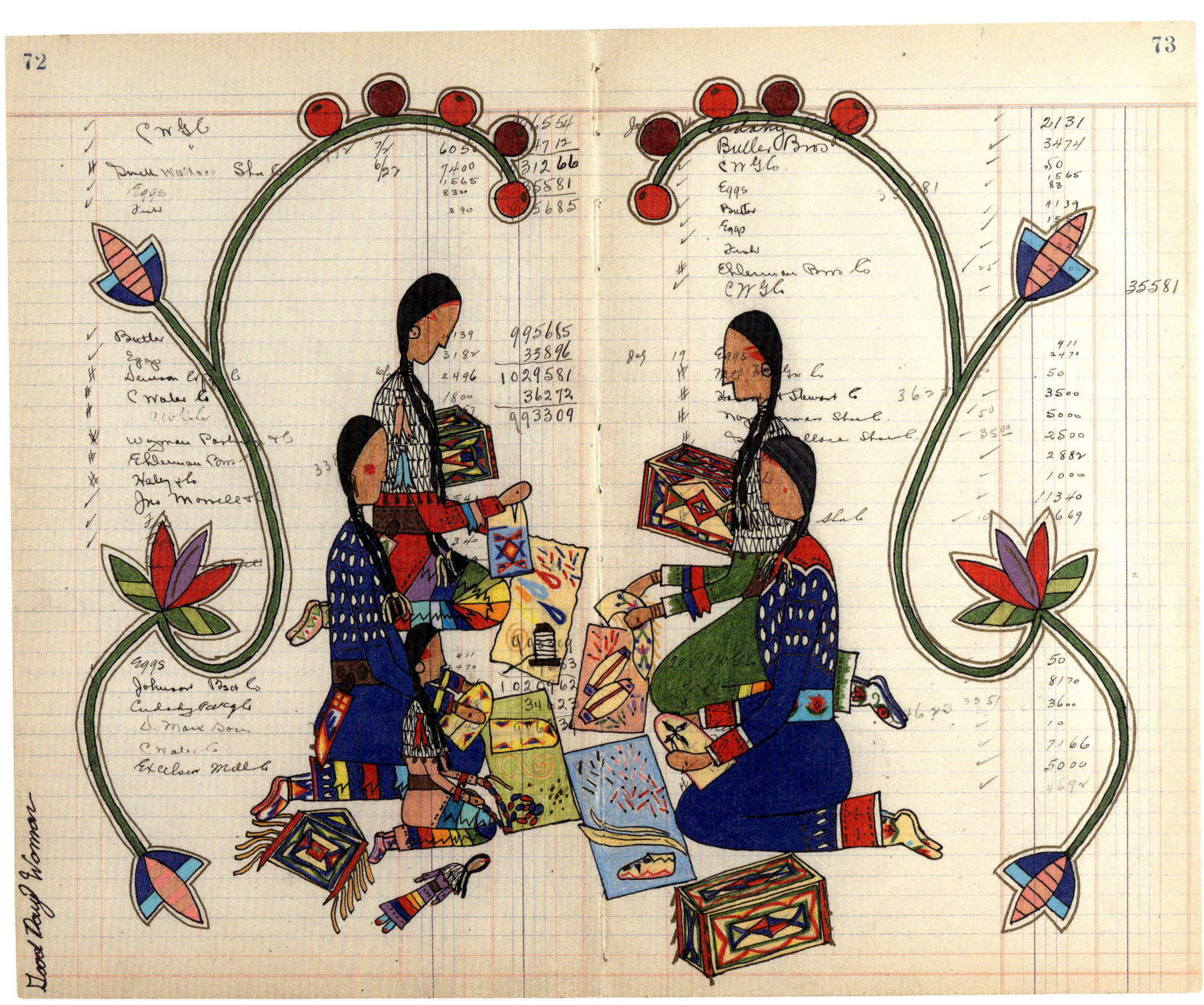

Lauren Good Day (Arikara/Hidatsa/Blackfeet/Plains Cree, b. 1987). *We Learn from Our Grandmothers*, 2012. Antique ledger paper, colored pencil, graphite, ink, felt-tipped marker; 34.9 × 42.3 cm. 26/9021

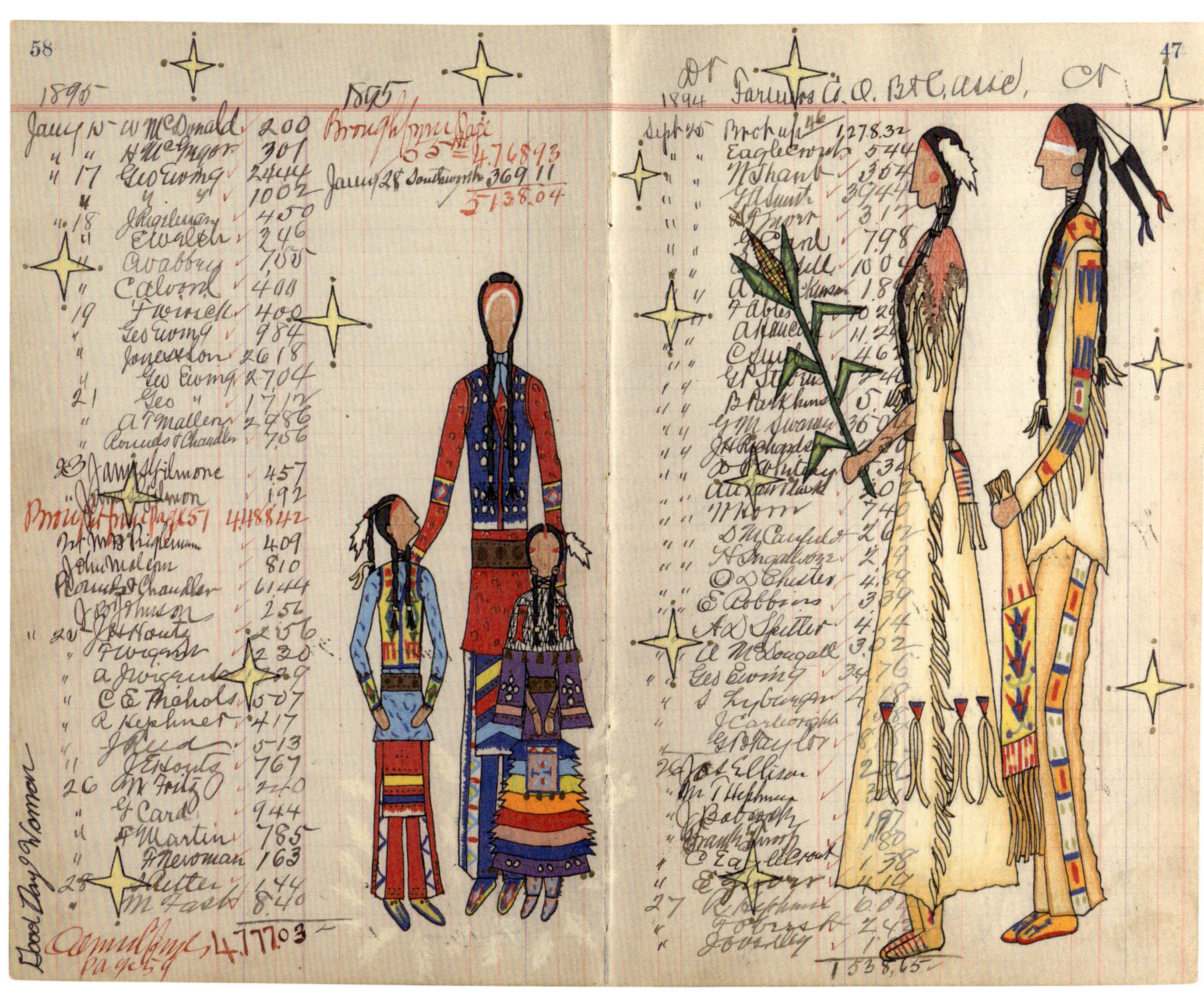

Lauren Good Day (Arikara/Hidatsa/Blackfeet/Plains Cree, b. 1987). *Blessed by the Mother and Father*, 2012. Antique ledger paper, colored pencil, graphite, ink, felt-tipped marker; 34.6 × 42.5 cm. 26/9022

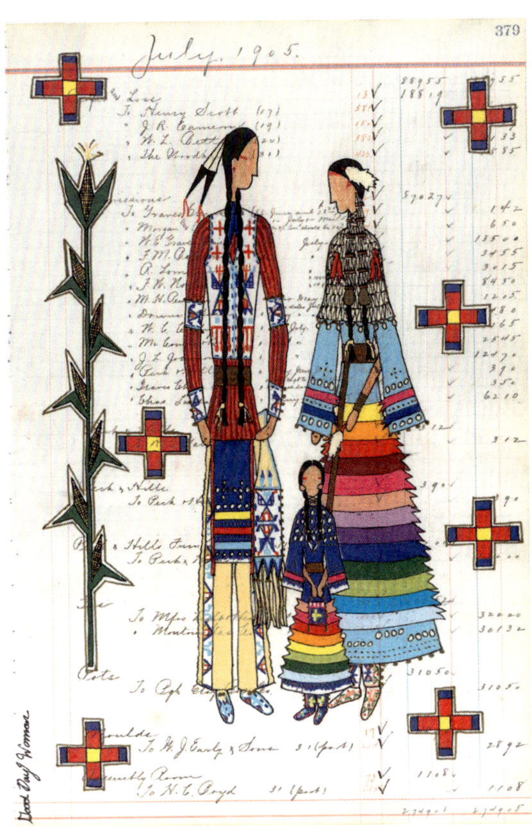

Lauren Good Day (Arikara/Hidatsa/Blackfeet/Plains Cree, b. 1987). *Making of Relatives*, 2012. Antique ledger paper, colored pencil, graphite, ink, felt-tipped marker; 45.1 × 28.8 cm. 26/9023

life and, as a woman, I take on ceremonial responsibilities for the children around me. The drawings *Blessed by the Mother and Father* and *The Making of Relatives* tell stories into which I have put much good thought, prayer, and intention. The drawings document what has made a monumental impact on my role as a mother and woman.

Other pieces such as *War Bonnet Dance* and *Independence Day Celebration* pay respect to our dances at the Fort Berthold Reservation, home to the Mandan, Hidatsa, and Arikara nations. During the reservation era our ceremonial lifeways were forcibly banned by the U.S. government. One of the only times our people were allowed to gather was during the Fourth of July celebrations. Clothing was made for this specific occasion, and we came together as a people to dance. Historical photos of these dances on old Fort Berthold led me to create the *Independence Day* piece. I'm grateful for our ancestors who held on to and passed on our aesthetic

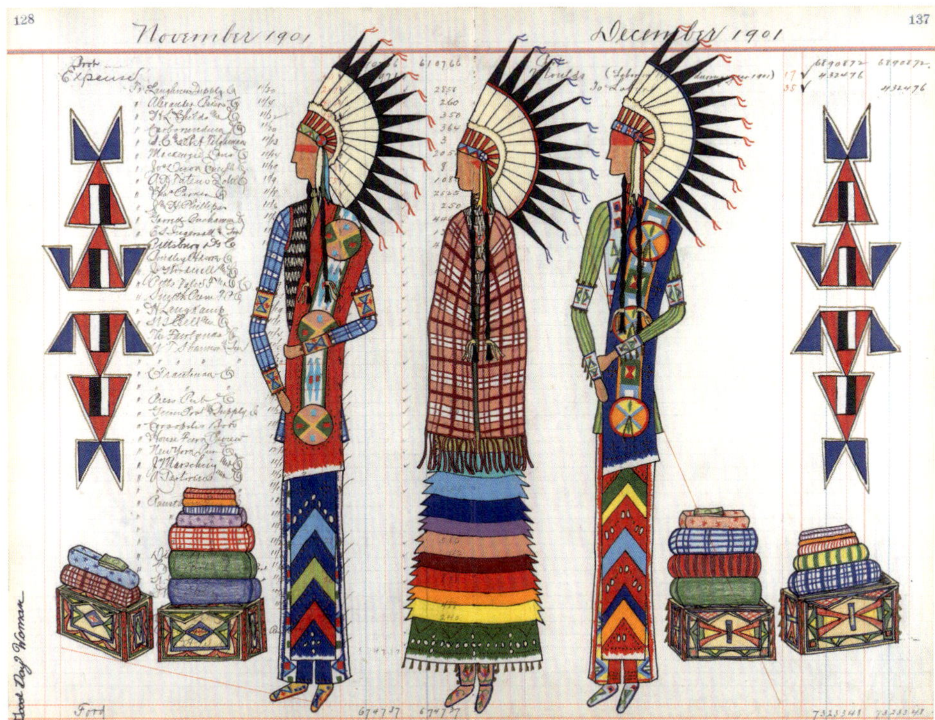

Lauren Good Day (Arikara/Hidatsa/Blackfeet/Plains Cree, b. 1987). *War Bonnet Dance*, 2012. Antique ledger paper, colored pencil, graphite, ink, felt-tipped marker; 45.1 × 57.6 cm. 26/9024

culture and love for our dances, as these have become my life's passion. Going hand in hand with our celebrations are our Warbonnet Dances. The dances are still held yearly in each of my reservation's communities. During these dances, we honor our relatives by giving away material goods such as blankets, shawls, and war bonnets. The Warbonnet Dances prepare our communities for the big summer celebrations. Since I was raised within the dance circle, this lifeway is deeply significant to my life and art.

The ways and perspectives of women were not often expressed in Plains pictorial art. Creating narrative works has allowed me to share the stories of women, honor my male relatives, and express my passion for aesthetic culture while continuing my family's legacy of ledger art. Being a part of the *Unbound* exhibition has brought my pictorial art full circle. It has been a complete honor to see my work among the great artists of the past and present. As a woman raising children, I pray that the values, skills, and stories of narrative art are passed to the future generations.

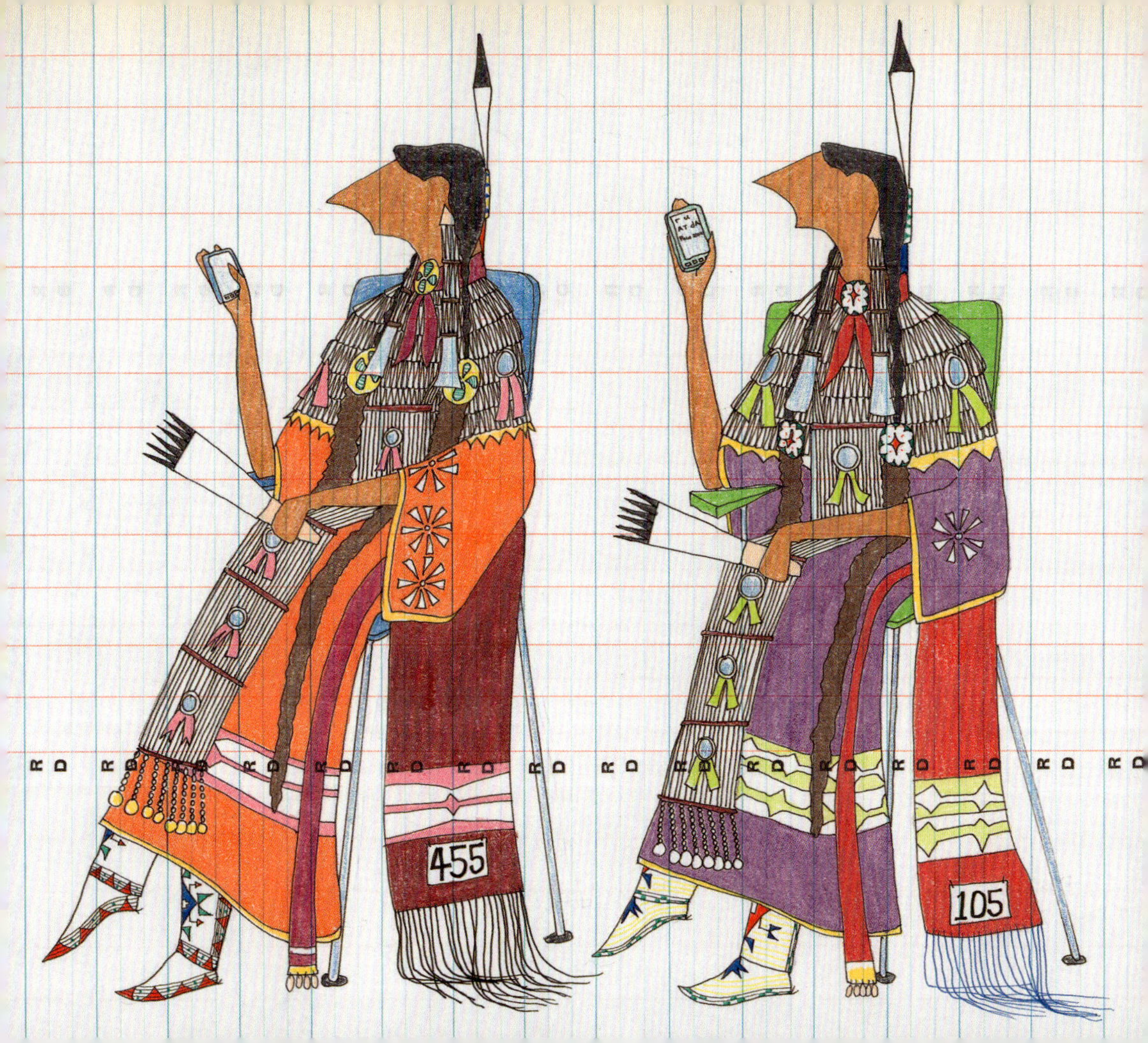
455
105

NOTES

DAVID W. PENNEY [PP. 20–35]

1. Ella Deloria, *Speaking of Indians* (Lincoln: University of Nebraska Press, 1998 [1944]), 56–57.
2. James R. Walker, *Lakota Belief and Ritual*, eds. R. J. DeMallie and E. A. Jahner (Lincoln: University of Nebraska Press, 1980), quoting Short Bull, 188.
3. Walker, quoting Bad Heart Bull, 183.
4. Walker, quoting Short Bull, 190.
5. Frances Densmore, *Teton Sioux Music and Culture* (Lincoln: University of Nebraska Press, 1992 [1918]), 132.
6. Densmore, 134.
7. Walker, *Lakota Belief and Ritual*, 181–82.
8. Royal B. Hassrick, *The Sioux: Life and Customs of a Warrior Society* (Norman: University of Oklahoma Press, 1964), 292.
9. David C. Posthumus, "Transmitting Sacred Knowledge: Aspects of Historical and Contemporary Oglala Lakota Belief and Ritual" (PhD diss., University of Indiana, 2015), 354, https://scholarworks.iu.edu/dspace/handle/2022/19811.
10. Mary Rippey Heistand, "The Way of the 'Medicine Man,'" Scraps from an Army Woman's Diary, *Army and Navy Life* 12, no. 2 (January–June 1908): 206, https://books.google.com/books?id=fyowAQAAMAAJ&dq=Mary+Rippey+Heistand+Army+and+Navy+Life&source=gbs_navlinks_s.
11. Stewart Culin, "A Summer Trip among the Western Indians." *Bulletin of the Free Museum of Science and Art of the University of Pennsylvania* 3 (January 1901): 171.
12. Densmore, *Teton Sioux Music*, 204.
13. Walker, *Lakota Belief and Ritual*, quoting George Sword, 91.
14. These ideas are developed in David W. Penney, "Siyosapa: At the Edge of Art," *Arts* 8, no. 4 (2019): 148, https://doi.org/10.3390/arts8040148.
15. Walker, *Lakota Belief and Ritual*, 82; Posthumus, "Transmitting Sacred Knowledge," 383.
16. Walker, *Lakota Belief and Ritual*, 88–89.
17. James R. Walker, "The Sun Dance and Other Ceremonies of the Oglala Division of the Teton Dakota," *Anthropological Papers of the American Museum of Natural History* 16, Part 2 (1917): 158, quoted in Posthumus, *Transmitting Sacred Knowledge*, 272.
18. See Penney, "Siyosapa: At the Edge of Art."
19. Acc. no. 1923.88.a–b, Collections Records, Chicago Historical Society.
20. Culin, "A Summer Trip among the Western Indians," 171–72.
21. Catalogue cards, Records of the Wannamaker Expedition, Penn Museum Archives, Philadelphia.
22. Eleanor M. King and Bryce P. Little, "George Byron Gordon and the Early Development of the University Museum," in *Raven's Journey: The World of Alaska's Native People*, eds. Susan A. Kaplan, Adria Holmes Katz, and Kristin J. Barsness (Philadelphia: University Museum, University of Pennsylvania, 1986), 32, 44.
23. Christian Feest and C. Ronald Corum, *Frederick Weygold: Artist and Ethnographer of North American Indians* (Knoxville, TN: Speed Art Museum, 2017), 37.
24. Frederick Weygold to Karl von den Steinen, 15 February 1909, Archiv Frederick Weygold, Ethnologisches Museum Berlin (excerpt translated and provided by Christian Feest).
25. Weygold to von den Steinen, 15 February 1909.
26. William Wildschut to F. D. Utley, 6 October 1926, Archives, National Museum of the American Indian.
27. John C. Ewers, "Black Chicken's Sun Dance," in *Creation's Journey: Native American Identity and Belief*, eds. Tom Hill and Richard W. Hill Sr. (Washington, DC: Smithsonian Institution Press, 1994), 139. Note that the

Dwayne Wilcox (Oglala Lakota, b. 1954). *4G Better than One-G* (detail), 2012.
Antique ledger paper, graphite, colored pencil, ink; 28.8 x 45 cm. 26/8952

photograph of Black Chicken and One Bull accompanying the text does not show Siyosapa, or Black Chicken, of Fort Peck. There are at least two other individuals who shared that name during the turn-of-the-last-century era.

28. Arthur Amiotte, Louis S. Warren, and Janet Catherine Berlo, *Transformation and Continuity in Lakota Culture: The Collages of Arthur Amiotte, 1988–2014* (Pierre: South Dakota State Historical Society Press, 2014), 14, 23.

MICHAEL PAUL JORDAN [PP. 54–73]

1. James W. Abert, *Expedition to the Southwest: An 1845 Reconnaissance of Colorado, New Mexico, Texas, and Oklahoma* (Lincoln: University of Nebraska Press, 1999), 14, 16; John C. Ewers, *Murals in the Round: Painted Tipis of the Kiowa and Kiowa-Apache Indians* (Washington, DC: Smithsonian Institution Press, 1978), 15–16; Candace S. Greene, "Southern Plains Graphic Art before the Reservation," *American Indian Art* 22, no. 3 (1997): 44–53; Karen D. Petersen, *Plains Indian Art from Fort Marion* (Norman: University of Oklahoma Press, 1971), 17–18.
2. Candace S. Greene, "From Bison Robes to Ledgers: Changing Contexts in Plains Drawings," *European Review of Native American Studies* 18, no. 1 (2004): 21–29.
3. Brad D. Lookingbill, *War Dance at Fort Marion: Plains Indian War Prisoners* (Norman: University of Oklahoma Press, 2006), 6, 61–62, 107.
4. Lookingbill, *War Dance*, 69; Richard Henry Pratt, *Battlefield and Classroom: Four Decades with the American Indian, 1867–1904*, ed. Robert M. Utley (New Haven, CT: Yale University Press, 1964; Norman: University of Oklahoma Press, 2003), 118. Citations refer to the University of Oklahoma Press edition.
5. Petersen, *Plains Indian Art from Fort Marion*, 175; Joyce M. Szabo, *Art from Fort Marion: The Silberman Collection* (Norman: University of Oklahoma Press, 2007), 65.
6. Lookingbill, *War Dance*, 69; Pratt, *Battlefield and Classroom*, 118.
7. Szabo, *Art from Fort Marion*, 67, 108, figures 45, 83, 123; Herman J. Viola, *Warrior Artists: Historic Cheyenne and Kiowa Indian Ledger Art Drawn by Making Medicine and Zotom* (Washington, DC: National Geographic Society, 1998), 106, 109.
8. Lookingbill, *War Dance*, 109.
9. Lookingbill, *War Dance*, 108–11.
10. Moira F. Harris, *Between Two Cultures: Kiowa Art from Fort Marion* (St. Paul, MN: Pogo Press, 1989), 116, figure 45; Joyce M. Szabo, *Imprisoned Art, Complex Patronage: Plains Drawings by Howling Wolf and Zotom at the Autry National Center* (Santa Fe, NM: School for Advanced Research Press, 2011), plate 31; Viola, *Warrior Artists*, 110–11.
11. Pratt, *Battlefield and Classroom*, 126–27.
12. Pratt, *Battlefield and Classroom*, 126.
13. Lookingbill, *War Dance*, 74–75.
14. Viola, *Warrior Artists*, 104.
15. Lookingbill, *War Dance*, 85, 95.
16. Janet C. Berlo, "Wo-Haw's Notebooks: 19th-Century Kiowa Indian Drawings in the Collections of the Missouri Historical Society," *Gateway Heritage* 3, no. 2 (1982): 11; Joyce M. Szabo, "Howling Wolf: Plains Artist in Transition," *Art Journal* 44 (1984): 370; Joyce M. Szabo, *Howling Wolf and the History of Ledger Art* (Albuquerque: University of New Mexico Press, 1994), 72–73; Szabo, *Art from Fort Marion*, 41–42; Szabo, *Imprisoned Art*, 31.
17. Szabo, *Imprisoned Art*, 109, plates 26, 50, 51.
18. Szabo, *Imprisoned Art*, 52.
19. Janet C. Berlo, ed., *Plains Indian Drawings 1865–1935: Pages from a Visual History* (New York: Harry N. Abrams, 1996), catalog number 69; Ronald McCoy, *Kiowa Memories: Images from Indian Territory, 1880* (Santa Fe, NM: Morning Star Gallery, 1987), plates 4, 12.
20. Berlo, *Plains Indian Drawings*, 146; James Mooney, *Calendar History of the Kiowa Indians* (Washington, DC: Bureau of American Ethnology, Smithsonian Institution, 1898; Washington, DC: Smithsonian Institution Press, 1979), 301, 320–23. Citations refer to the Smithsonian Institution Press edition.
21. McCoy, *Kiowa Memories*, 59.
22. Mooney, *Calendar History*, 336.
23. Daniel C. Swan and Jim Cooley, *Wedding Clothes in the Osage Community: A Giving Heritage* (Bloomington: University of Indiana Press, 2019), 138–41; Jenny Tone-Pah-Hote, "Illustrating Encounter: Trade, Travel, and Warfare in Southern Plains Ledger Drawing, 1875–1880," in *Ledger Narratives: The Plains Indian Drawings of the Lansburgh Collection at Dartmouth College*, ed. Colin G. Calloway (Norman: University of Oklahoma Press, 2012), 34, figure 3.1.
24. Mooney, *Calendar History*, 336.
25. Szabo, *Imprisoned Art*, 105–6, plate 24; Viola, *Warrior Artists*, 56–57.
26. Sherman T. Chaddlesone, recorded interview with the author, Anadarko, Oklahoma, 9 April 2010.
27. Candace S. Greene, *Silver Horn: Master Illustrator of the Kiowa* (Norman: University of Oklahoma Press, 2001), 163.
28. Chaddlesone, recorded interview, 2010; Hugh Corwin,

"The A-nan-thy Odle-paugh Calendar," *Prairie Lore*, October 1967, 66–83; Greene, *Silver Horn*, 164–65.

29. Candace S. Greene, "Exploring the Three 'Little Bluffs' of the Kiowa," *Plains Anthropologist* 41, no. 157 (1996): 228, 230–31; Greene, *Silver Horn*, 165.
30. William L. Merrill, Marian K. Hansson, Candace S. Greene, and Frederick J. Reuss, *A Guide to the Kiowa Collections at the Smithsonian Institution*, Smithsonian Contributions to Anthropology 40 (Washington, DC: Smithsonian Institution Press, 1997), 27, figures 6, 48.
31. Benjamin R. Kracht, *Kiowa Belief and Ritual* (Lincoln: University of Nebraska Press, 2017), 230–32; Hugh L. Scott, "Notes on the Kado, or Sun Dance of the Kiowa," *American Anthropologist* 13, no. 3 (1911): 362.
32. Harris, *Between Two Cultures*, 80–81; Merrill et al., *A Guide to the Kiowa Collections*, figure 65.
33. Maurice Boyd, *Kiowa Voices, Vol. 1: Ceremonial Dance, Ritual, and Song* (Fort Worth: Texas Christian University Press, 1981), 62; Weston LaBarre, Typescript of students' notes (combined notes of William Bascom, Donald Collier, Weston LaBarre, Bernard Mishkin, and Jane Richardson of the 1935 Laboratory of Anthropology Field School, led by Alexander Lesser), Papers of Weston LaBarre, National Anthropological Archives, Smithsonian Institution, Washington, DC, 1935, 607.
34. Michael P. Jordan, "Depictions of Women and Warfare in Kiowa Drawings from Fort Marion: Reassessing Nineteenth-Century Kiowa Gender Roles," in *Material Vernaculars: Objects, Images, and Their Social Worlds*, ed. Jason Baird Jackson (Bloomington: University of Indiana Press, 2016), 117, figure 3.4; McCoy, *Kiowa Memories*, 62, plate 25.
35. Jordan, "Depictions of Women and Warfare," figures 3.5–3.7.
36. Janet C. Berlo, "Creativity and Cosmopolitanism: Women's Enduring Traditions," in *Identity by Design: Tradition, Change, and Celebration in Native Women's Dresses*, ed. Emil Her Many Horses (New York: HarperCollins, 2007), 137–40; William C. Meadows, *Kiowa, Apache, and Comanche Military Societies: Enduring Veterans, 1800 to the Present* (Austin: University of Texas Press, 1999), 161–62.
37. Michael Paul Jordan and Daniel C. Swan, "Painting a New Battle Tipi: Public Art, Intellectual Property, and Heritage Construction in a Contemporary Native American Community," *Plains Anthropologist* 56, no. 219 (2011): 202, figures 3, 5–6.
38. Emil Her Many Horses, personal communication.
39. Meadows, *Kiowa, Apache, and Comanche Military Societies*, 168–69.

SELECTED BIBLIOGRAPHY AND FURTHER READING

Abert, James W. *Expedition to the Southwest: An 1845 Reconnaissance of Colorado, New Mexico, Texas, and Oklahoma.* Lincoln: University of Nebraska Press, 1999.

Berlo, Janet C. "Creativity and Cosmopolitanism: Women's Enduring Traditions." In *Identity by Design: Tradition, Change, and Celebration in Native Women's Dresses*, edited by Emil Her Many Horses, 97–148. New York: HarperCollins, 2007.

———, ed. *Plains Indian Drawings 1865–1935: Pages from a Visual History.* New York: Harry N. Abrams, 1996.

———. "Wo-Haw's Notebooks: 19th Century Kiowa Indian Drawings in the Collections of the Missouri Historical Society." *Gateway Heritage* 3, no. 2 (1982): 2–13.

Blish, Helen H. *A Pictographic History of the Oglala Sioux: 50th Anniversary Edition.* Lincoln: University of Nebraska Press, 2017.

Boyd, Maurice. *Kiowa Voices, Vol. 1: Ceremonial Dance, Ritual, and Song.* Fort Worth: Texas Christian University Press, 1981.

Calloway, Colin G., ed. *Ledger Narratives: The Plains Indian Drawings in the Mark Lansburgh Collection at Dartmouth College.* New Directions in Native American Studies, Volume 8. Norman: University of Oklahoma Press, 2012.

Corwin, Hugh. "The A-nan-thy Odle-paugh Calendar." *Prairie Lore* (October 1967): 66–83.

Deloria, Ella. *Speaking of Indians.* New York: Friendship Press, 1944. Reprint, Lincoln: University of Nebraska Press, 1998.

Densmore, Frances. *Teton Sioux Music and Culture.* Washington, DC: Bureau of American Ethnology, Smithsonian Institution, 1918. Reprint, Lincoln: University of Nebraska Press, 1992.

Earenfight, Phillip, ed. *A Kiowa's Odyssey: A Sketchbook from Fort Marion.* Seattle: University of Washington Press, 2007.

Ewers, John C. *Murals in the Round: Painted Tipis of the Kiowa and Kiowa-Apache Indians.* Washington, DC: Smithsonian Institution Press, 1978.

Greene, Candace S. "Artists in Blue." *American Indian Art Magazine* 18, no. 1 (1992): 50–57.

———. "Being Indian at Fort Marion: Revisiting Three Drawings." *American Indian Quarterly* 37, no. 4 (2013): 289–316.

———. "Exploring the Three 'Little Bluffs' of the Kiowa." *Plains Anthropologist* 41, no. 157 (1996): 221–42.

———. "From Bison Robes to Ledgers: Changing Contexts in Plains Drawings." *European Review of Native American Studies* 18, no. 1 (2004): 21–29.

———. *Silver Horn: Master Illustrator of the Kiowa.* Norman: University of Oklahoma Press, 2001.

———. "Southern Plains Graphic Art before the Reservation." *American Indian Art Magazine* 22, no. 3 (1997): 44–53.

Greene, Candace S., and Russell Thornton, eds. *The Year the Stars Fell: Lakota Winter Counts at the Smithsonian.* Lincoln: University of Nebraska Press, 2007.

Harris, Moira F. *Between Two Cultures: Kiowa Art from Fort Marion.* St. Paul, MN: Pogo Press, 1989.

Jordan, Michael Paul. "Depictions of Women and Warfare in Kiowa Drawings from Fort Marion: Reassessing Nineteenth-Century Kiowa Gender Roles." In *Material Vernaculars: Objects, Images, and Their Social Worlds*, edited by Jason Baird Jackson, 105–42. Bloomington: University of Indiana Press, 2016.

Jordan, Michael Paul, and Daniel C. Swan. "Painting a New Battle Tipi: Public Art, Intellectual Property, and Heritage Construction in a Contemporary Native

American Community." *Plains Anthropologist* 56, no. 219 (2011): 195–213.

Kracht, Benjamin R. *Kiowa Belief and Ritual*. Lincoln: University of Nebraska Press, 2017.

LaBarre, Weston. Papers. Typescript of students' notes (combined notes of William Bascom, Donald Collier, Weston LaBarre, Bernard Mishkin, and Jane Richardson of the Laboratory of Anthropology Field School, led by Alexander Lesser), 1935. National Anthropological Archives, Smithsonian Institution, Washington, DC.

Lookingbill, Brad D. *War Dance at Fort Marion: Plains Indian War Prisoners*. Norman: University of Oklahoma Press, 2006.

McCoy, Ronald. *Kiowa Memories: Images from Indian Territory, 1880*. Santa Fe, NM: Morning Star Gallery, 1987.

Meadows, William C. *Kiowa, Apache, and Comanche Military Societies: Enduring Veterans, 1800 to the Present*. Austin: University of Texas Press, 1999.

Merrill, William L., Marian K. Hansson, Candace S. Greene, and Frederick J. Reuss. *A Guide to the Kiowa Collections at the Smithsonian Institution*. Smithsonian Contributions to Anthropology 40. Washington, DC: Smithsonian Institution Press, 1997.

Mooney, James. *Calendar History of the Kiowa Indians*. Washington, DC: Bureau of American Ethnology, Smithsonian Institution, 1898. Reprint, Washington, DC: Smithsonian Institution Press, 1979.

Nearburg, Karen Miller, ed. *Visual/Language: The Ledger Drawings of Dwayne Wilcox*. Staunton, VA: George F. Thompson Publishing, 2021.

Penney, David W. "Siyosapa: At the Edge of Art." *Arts* 8, no. 4 (2019): 148, https://doi.org/10.3390/arts8040148.

Pratt, Richard Henry. *Battlefield and Classroom: Four Decades with the American Indian, 1867–1904*. Edited by Robert M. Utley. New Haven, CT: Yale University Press, 1964. Reprint, Norman: University of Oklahoma Press, 2003.

Pearce, Richard. *Women and Ledger Art: Four Contemporary Native American Artists*. Tucson: University of Arizona Press, 2013.

Petersen, Karen D. *Plains Indian Art from Fort Marion*. Norman: University of Oklahoma Press, 1971.

Scott, Hugh L. "Notes on the Kado, or Sun Dance of the Kiowa." *American Anthropologist* 13, no. 3 (1911): 345–79.

Szabo, Joyce M. *Art from Fort Marion: The Silberman Collection*. Norman: University of Oklahoma Press, 2007.

———. "From General Souvenir to Personal Memento: Fort Marion Drawings and the Significance of Books." In *Painters, Patrons, and Identity: Essays in Native American Art to Honor J. J. Brody*, edited by Joyce M. Szabo, 49–70. Albuquerque: University of New Mexico Press, 2001.

———. "Howling Wolf: A Plains Artist in Transition." *Art Journal* 44 (1984): 367–373.

———. *Howling Wolf and the History of Ledger Art*. Albuquerque: University of New Mexico Press, 1994.

———. *Imprisoned Art, Complex Patronage: Plains Drawings by Howling Wolf and Zotom at the Autry National Center*. Santa Fe, NM: School for Advanced Research Press, 2011.

Tone-Pah-Hote, Jenny. "Illustrating Encounter: Trade, Travel, and Warfare in Southern Plains Ledger Drawing, 1875–1880." In *Ledger Narratives: The Plains Indian Drawings of the Lansburgh Collection at Dartmouth College*, edited by Colin G. Calloway, 34–42. Norman: University of Oklahoma Press, 2012.

Viola, Herman J. *Warrior Artists: Historic Cheyenne and Kiowa Indian Ledger Art Drawn by Making Medicine and Zotom*. Washington DC: National Geographic Society, 1998.

Walker, James R. *Lakota Belief and Ritual*, edited by R. J. DeMallie and E. A. Jahner. Lincoln: University of Nebraska Press, 1980.

CONTRIBUTORS

LAUREN GOOD DAY is an award-winning artist and fashion designer. She is an enrolled member of the Three Affiliated Tribes (Mandan, Hidatsa, Arikara Nation) of the Ft. Berthold Reservation in North Dakota and a registered Treaty Indian with the Sweet Grass Cree First Nation in Saskatchewan, Canada. She has shown her art at prestigious Native American juried shows such as the Santa Fe Indian Market, the Heard Museum Guild Indian Fair and Market, and the Autry American Indian Arts Marketplace. Her work, which includes beadwork, quillwork, and regalia making in addition to narrative art, has been featured in numerous exhibitions at galleries and museums across the United States.

A curator at the National Museum of the American Indian (NMAI) and the curator of the exhibition *Unbound: Narrative Art of the Plains*, **EMIL HER MANY HORSES** (Oglala Lakota) specializes in the Native cultures of North America's central plains. He was the lead curator of the museum's 2004 inaugural exhibition *Our Universes: Traditional Knowledge Shapes Our World*, a co-curator of *Identity by Design: Tradition, Change, and Celebration in Native Women's Dresses* (2007), and the curator of *A Song for the Horse Nation: Horses in Native American Cultures* (2009). Her Many Horses also co-curated, with Anthony Chavarria of the Museum of Indian Arts and Culture in Santa Fe, the exhibition *Creating Tradition: Innovation and Change in American Indian Art*, which opened in 2018 at Walt Disney World's Epcot Center in Orlando, Florida. Most recently, he served as NMAI's in-house curator for the traveling exhibition *Preston Singletary: Raven and the Box of Daylight* (2022). Her Many Horses is also an award-winning artist who creates contemporary beadwork and dolls.

MICHAEL PAUL JORDAN is an associate professor of anthropology at Texas Tech University and a research associate at the National Museum of Natural History and the Denver Museum of Nature and Science. In 2016, he received the Chancellor's Council Distinguished Research Award in recognition of his collaborative work with members of the Kiowa and Cheyenne and Arapaho nations. Dr. Jordan's research focuses on the ethnohistory and expressive culture of the Southern Plains. He has contributed essays on nineteenth-century Kiowa and Cheyenne drawings to several edited volumes, including *Ledger Narratives: The Plains Indian Drawings of the Lansburgh Collection at Dartmouth College* (2012) and *Material Vernaculars: Objects, Images and Their Social Worlds* (2016). His current research focuses on the relationship between federally recognized tribes and lands administered by the National Park Service, and it includes ethnographic studies of Alibates Flint Quarries National Monument and Washita Battlefield National Historic Site.

DAVID W. PENNEY is the associate director of Museum Research, Scholarship, and Public Engagement at the National Museum of the American Indian and an internationally recognized scholar of American Indian art history. Penney arrived at the Smithsonian in 2011 after a thirty-one-year career at the Detroit Institute of Arts, where he last served as vice president of Exhibitions and Collections Strategies. The author of numerous publications, Penney's most recent work includes essays for the exhibition catalogues *Robert Houle: Red is Beautiful* (2022) and *Shelley Niro: 500 Year Itch* (2023). He produced "Native North American Art: Pre-Contact" for the acclaimed online Oxford Bibliographies in Art History and authored the art history textbook *Native North American Art*, published by Thames & Hudson in 2004. His essay "Siyosapa: At the Edge of Art" for the online publication *Arts* earned a Secretary's Research Award from the Smithsonian Institution's Congress of Scholars in 2020.

INDEX

Page numbers in *italics* refer to the illustrations